11th Linguistic Annotation Workshop (LAW XI 2017)

Valencia, Spain
3 April 2017

ISBN: 978-1-5108-3865-9

Preface

The Linguistic Annotation Workshop (The LAW) is organized annually by the Association for Computational Linguistics Special Interest Group for Annotation (ACL SIGANN). It provides a forum to facilitate the exchange and propagation of research results concerned with the annotation, manipulation, and exploitation of corpora; work towards harmonization and interoperability from the perspective of the increasingly large number of tools and frameworks for annotated language resources; and work towards a consensus on all issues crucial to the advancement of the field of corpus annotation.

Last fall, when workshop proposals were solicited, we were asked for a tagline that would telegraph the essence of LAW. Naturally, this prompted a healthy dose of wordsmithing on the part of the organizing committee. The initial suggestions (including "Annotation schemers unite!" and "Don't just annoTATE—annoGREAT!") were deemed too corny. Then, playing on the abbreviation "LAW", various legal puns emerged: "the fine print of linguistic annotation"; "the letter and spirit of linguistic annotation"; "LAW, the authority on linguistic annotation"; "LAW, where language is made to behave"; and so forth. "Annotation schemers on parole" took the punning to the extreme (as students of Saussure will recognize).

In the end, we settled on "LAW: Due process for linguistic annotation". The concept of "due process" underscores the care required not just to annotate, but to annotate *well*. To produce a high-quality linguistic resource, diligence is required in all phases: assembling the source data; designing and refining the annotation scheme and guidelines; choosing or developing appropriate annotation software and data formats; applying automatic tools for preprocessing and provisional annotation; selecting and training human annotators; implementing quality control procedures; and documenting and distributing the completed resource.

The 14 papers in this year's workshop study methods for annotation in the domains of emotion and attitude; conversations and discourse structure; events and causality; semantic roles; and translation (among others). Compared to previous years, syntax plays a much smaller role: indeed, this may be the first ever LAW where no paper has the word "treebank" in the title. (We leave it to the reader to speculate whether this reflects broader trends in the field or has an innocuous explanation.) Also groundbreaking in this year's LAW will be a best paper award, to be announced at the workshop.

LAW XI would not have been possible without the fine contributions of the authors; the remarkably thorough and thoughtful reviews from the program committee; and the sage guidance of the organizing committee. Two invited talks will add multilingual perspective to the program, Deniz Zeyrek and Johan Bos having generously agreed to share their wisdom. We thank our publicity chair, Marc Verhagen, as well as those who have worked to coordinate the various aspects of EACL workshops, including logistics and publications.

We hope that after reading the collected wisdom in this volume, you will be empowered to give the linguistic annotation process its due.

Nathan Schneider and Nianwen Xue, program co-chairs

Program Co-chairs:

Nathan Schneider	Georgetown University
Nianwen Xue	Brandeis University

Publicity Chair:

Marc Verhagen	Brandeis University

Program Committee:

Adam Meyers	New York University
Alexis Palmer	University of North Texas
Amália Mendes	University of Lisbon
Amir Zeldes	Georgetown University
Andrew Gargett	University of Birmingham
Annemarie Friedrich	Saarland University
Antonio Pareja-Lora	Universidad Complutense de Madrid / ATLAS, UNED
Archna Bhatia	IHMC
Benoît Sagot	Université Paris Diderot
Bonnie Webber	University of Edinburgh
Collin Baker	ICSI Berkeley
Dirk Hovy	University of Copenhagen
Djamé Seddah	Paris-Sorbonne University
Els Lefever	Ghent University
Heike Zinsmeister	University of Hamburg
Ines Rehbein	Leibniz Science Campus, Institute for German Language and Heidelberg University
Joel Tetreault	Grammarly
John S. Y. Lee	City University of Hong Kong
Josef Ruppenhofer	Leibniz Science Campus, Institute for German Language and Heidelberg University
Katrin Tomanek	OpenTable
Kemal Oflazer	Carnegie Mellon University—Qatar
Kilian Evang	University of Groningen
Kim Gerdes	Sorbonne Nouvelle
Kiril Simov	Bulgarian Academy of Sciences
Lori Levin	Carnegie Mellon University
Manfred Stede	University of Potsdam
Marie Candito	Université Paris Diderot
Markus Dickinson	Indiana University
Martha Palmer	University of Colorado at Boulder
Massimo Poesio	University of Essex
Nancy Ide	Vassar College
Nicoletta Calzolari	CNR-ILC
Nizar Habash	New York University Abu Dhabi
Özlem Çetinoğlu	University of Stuttgart
Pablo Faria	State University of Campinas
Ron Artstein	Institute for Creative Technologies, USC
Sandra Kübler	Indiana University
Stefanie Dipper	Ruhr University Bochum
Tomaž Erjavec	Jožef Stefan Institute

| Udo Hahn | Jena University |
| Valia Kordoni | Humboldt University of Berlin |

SIGANN Organizing Commitee:

Stefanie Dipper	Ruhr University Bochum
Annemarie Friedrich	Saarland University
Chu-Ren Huang	The Hong Kong Polytechnic University
Nancy Ide	Vassar College
Lori Levin	Carnegie Mellon University
Adam Meyers	New York University
Antonio Pareja-Lora	Universidad Complutense de Madrid / ATLAS, UNED
Massimo Poesio	University of Essex
Sameer Pradhan	Boulder Learning, Inc.
Ines Rehbein	Leibniz Science Campus, Institute for German Language and Heidelberg University
Manfred Stede	University of Potsdam
Katrin Tomanek	OpenTable
Fei Xia	University of Washington
Heike Zinsmeister	University of Hamburg

Table of Contents

Workshop Program

Monday, April 3, 2017

9:30–9:40	*Welcome*

9:40–10:40   *Invited Talk I: The TED-Multilingual Discourse Bank*
Deniz Zeyrek

10:40–11:00   **Emotion**

10:40–11:00   *Readers vs. Writers vs. Texts: Coping with Different Perspectives of Text Understanding in Emotion Annotation*
Sven Buechel and Udo Hahn

11:00–11:30   *Coffee Break*

11:30–12:10   **Conversations & Discourse**

11:30–11:50   *Finding Good Conversations Online: The Yahoo News Annotated Comments Corpus*
Courtney Napoles, Joel Tetreault, Aasish Pappu, Enrica Rosato and Brian Provenzale

11:50–12:10   *Crowdsourcing discourse interpretations: On the influence of context and the reliability of a connective insertion task*
Merel Scholman and Vera Demberg

12:10–13:00   Posters

A Code-Switching Corpus of Turkish-German Conversations
Özlem Çetinoğlu

Annotating omission in statement pairs
Héctor Martínez Alonso, Amaury Delamaire and Benoît Sagot

Annotating Speech, Attitude and Perception Reports
Corien Bary, Leopold Hess, Kees Thijs, Peter Berck and Iris Hendrickx

Consistent Classification of Translation Revisions: A Case Study of English-Japanese Student Translations
Atsushi Fujita, Kikuko Tanabe, Chiho Toyoshima, Mayuka Yamamoto, Kyo Kageura and Anthony Hartley

Representation and Interchange of Linguistic Annotation: An In-Depth, Side-by-Side Comparison of Three Designs
Richard Eckart de Castilho, Nancy Ide, Emanuele Lapponi, Stephan Oepen, Keith Suderman, Erik Velldal and Marc Verhagen

TDB 1.1: Extensions on Turkish Discourse Bank
Deniz Zeyrek and Murathan Kurfalı

Two Layers of Annotation for Representing Event Mentions in News Stories
Maria Pia di Buono, Martin Tutek, Jan Šnajder, Goran Glavaš, Bojana Dalbelo Bašić and Natasa Milic-Frayling

Word Similarity Datasets for Indian Languages: Annotation and Baseline Systems
Syed Sarfaraz Akhtar, Arihant Gupta, Avijit Vajpayee, Arjit Srivastava and Manish Shrivastava

13:00–14:30   *Lunch*

Readers *vs.* Writers *vs.* Texts:
Coping with Different Perspectives of Text Understanding in Emotion Annotation

Sven Buechel and **Udo Hahn**

Jena University Language & Information Engineering (JULIE) Lab
Friedrich-Schiller-Universität Jena, Jena, Germany
`{sven.buechel,udo.hahn}@uni-jena.de`
`http://www.julielab.de`

Abstract

We here examine how different perspectives of understanding written discourse, like the reader's, the writer's or the text's point of view, affect the quality of emotion annotations. We conducted a series of annotation experiments on two corpora, a popular movie review corpus and a genre- and domain-balanced corpus of standard English. We found statistical evidence that the writer's perspective yields superior annotation quality overall. However, the quality one perspective yields compared to the other(s) seems to depend on the domain the utterance originates from. Our data further suggest that the popular movie review data set suffers from an atypical bimodal distribution which may decrease model performance when used as a training resource.

1 Introduction

In the past years, the analysis of subjective language has become one of the most popular areas in computational linguistics. In the early days, a simple classification according to the semantic polarity (positiveness, negativeness or neutralness) of a document was predominant, whereas in the meantime, research activities have shifted towards a more sophisticated modeling of sentiments. This includes the extension from only few basic to more varied emotional classes sometimes even assigning real-valued scores (Strapparava and Mihalcea, 2007), the aggregation of multiple aspects of an opinion item into a composite opinion statement for the whole item (Schouten and Frasincar, 2016), and sentiment compositionality on sentence level (Socher et al., 2013).

There is also an increasing awareness of different perspectives one may take to interpret written discourse in the process of text comprehension. A typical distinction which mirrors different points of view is the one between the writer and the reader(s) of a document as exemplified by utterance (1) below (taken from Katz et al. (2007)):

(1)   Italy defeats France in World Cup Final

The emotion of the writer, presumably a professional journalist, can be expected to be more or less neutral, but French or Italian readers may show rather strong (and most likely opposing) emotional reactions when reading this news headline. Consequently, such finer-grained emotional distinctions must also be considered when formulating instructions for an annotation task.

NLP researchers are aware of this multi-perspectival understanding of emotion as contributions often target either one or the other form of emotion expression or mention it as a subject of future work (Mukherjee and Joshi, 2014; Lin and Chen, 2008; Calvo and Mac Kim, 2013). However, contributions aiming at quantifying the effect of altering perspectives are rare (see Section 2). This is especially true for work examining differences in annotation results relative to these perspectives. Although this is obviously a crucial design decision for gold standards for emotion analytics, we know of only one such contribution (Mohammad and Turney, 2013).

In this paper, we systematically examine differences in the quality of emotion annotation regarding different understanding perspectives. Apart from inter-annotator agreement (IAA), we will also look at other quality criteria such as how well the resulting annotations cover the space of possible ratings and check for the representativeness of the rating distribution. We performed a series of annotation experiments with varying instruc-

1

Proceedings of the 11th Linguistic Annotation Workshop, pages 1–12,
Valencia, Spain, April 3, 2017. ©2017 Association for Computational Linguistics

tions and domains of raw text, making this the first study ever to address the impact of text understanding perspective on sentence-level emotion annotation. The results we achieved directly influenced the design and creation of EMOBANK, a novel large-scale gold standard for emotion analysis employing the VAD model for affect representation (Buechel and Hahn, 2017).

2   Related Work

Representation Schemes for Emotion. Due to the multi-disciplinary nature of research on emotions, different representation schemes and models have emerged hampering comparison across different approaches (Buechel and Hahn, 2016).

In NLP-oriented sentiment and emotion analysis, the most popular representation scheme is based on *semantic polarity*, the positiveness or negativeness of a word or a sentence, while slightly more sophisticated schemes include a neutral class or even rely on a multi-point polarity scale (Pang and Lee, 2008).

Despite their popularity, these bi- or tri-polar schemes have only loose connections to emotion models currently prevailing in psychology (Sander and Scherer, 2009). From an NLP point of view, those can be broadly subdivided into *categorical* and *dimensional* models (Calvo and Mac Kim, 2013). Categorical models assume a small number of distinct emotional classes (such as *Anger*, *Fear* or *Joy*) that all human beings are supposed to share. In NLP, the most popular of those models are the six *Basic Emotions* by Ekman (1992) or the 8-category scheme of the *Wheel of Emotion* by Plutchik (1980).

Dimensional models, on the other hand, are centered around the notion of compositionality. They assume that emotional states can be best described as a combination of several fundamental factors, i.e., emotional *dimensions*. One of the most popular dimensional models is the Valence-Arousal-Dominance (VAD; Bradley and Lang (1994)) model which postulates three orthogonal dimensions, namely *Valence* (corresponding to the concept of polarity), *Arousal* (a calm-excited scale) and *Dominance* (perceived degree of control in a (social) situation); see Figure 1 for an illustration. An even more wide-spread version of this model uses only the Valence and Arousal dimension, the VA model (Russell, 1980).

For a long time, categorical models were pre-

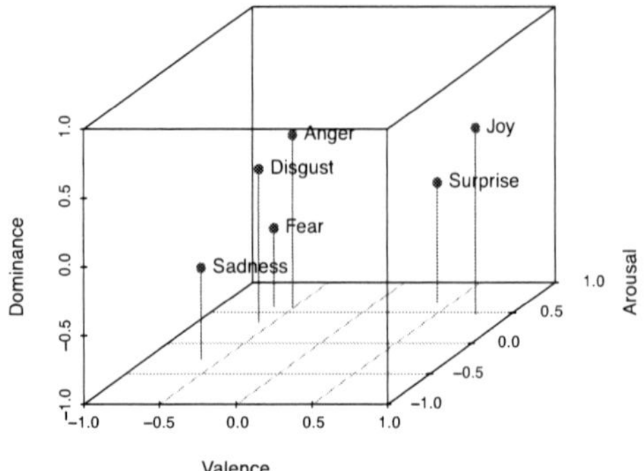

Figure 1: The emotional space spanned by the Valence-Arousal-Dominance model. For illustration, the position of Ekman's six *Basic Emotions* are included (as determined by Russell and Mehrabian (1977)).

dominant in emotion analysis (Ovesdotter Alm et al., 2005; Strapparava and Mihalcea, 2007; Balahur et al., 2012). Only recently, the VA(D) model found increasing recognition (Paltoglou et al., 2013; Yu et al., 2015; Buechel and Hahn, 2016; Wang et al., 2016). When one of these dimensional models is selected, the task of emotion analysis is most often interpreted as a regression problem (predicting real-valued scores for each of the dimension) so that another set of metrics must be taken into account than those typically applied in NLP (see Section 3).

Despite its growing popularity, the first large-scale gold standard for dimensional models has only very recently been developed as a follow-up to this contribution (EMOBANK; Buechel and Hahn (2017)). The results we obtained here were crucial for the design of EMOBANK regarding the choice of annotation perspective and the domain the raw data were taken from. However, our results are not only applicable to VA(D) but also to semantic polarity (as Valence is equivalent to this representation format) and may probably generalize over other models of emotion, as well.

Resources and Annotation Methods. For the VAD model, the Self-Assessment Manikin (SAM; Bradley and Lang (1994)) is the most important and to our knowledge only standardized instrument for acquiring emotion ratings based on human self-perception in behavioral psychology (Sander and Scherer, 2009). SAM iconically displays differences in Valence, Arousal and Dominance by a set of anthropomorphic cartoons on

2

a multi-point scale (see Figure 2). Subjects refer to one of these figures per VAD dimension to rate their feelings as a response to a stimulus.

SAM and derivatives therefrom have been used for annotating a wide range of resources for word-emotion associations in psychology (such as Warriner et al. (2013), Stadthagen-Gonzalez et al. (2016), Yao et al. (2016) and Schmidtke et al. (2014)), as well as VAD-annotated corpora in NLP; Preoţiuc-Pietro et al. (2016) developed a corpus of 2,895 English Facebook posts (but they rely on only two annotators). Yu et al. (2016) generated a corpus of 2,009 Chinese sentences from different genres of online text.

A possible alternative to SAM is Best-Worst Scaling (BSW; Louviere et al. (2015)), a method only recently introduced into NLP by Kiritchenko and Mohammad (2016). This annotation method exploits the fact that humans are typically more consistent when *comparing* two items relative to each other with respect to a given scale rather than *attributing numerical ratings* to the items directly. For example, deciding whether one sentence is more positive than the other is easier than scoring them (say) as 8 and 6 on a 9-point scale.

Although BWS provided promising results for polarity (Kiritchenko and Mohammad, 2016), in this paper, we will use SAM scales. First, with this decision, there are way more studies to compare our results with and, second, the adequacy of BWS for emotional dimensions other than Valence (polarity) remains to be shown.

Perspectival Understanding of Emotions. As stated above, research on the linkage of different annotation perspectives (typically reader *vs.* writer) is really rare. Tang and Chen (2012) examine the relation between the sentiment of microblog posts and the sentiment of their comments (as a proxy for reader emotion) using a positive-negative scheme. They examine which linguistic features are predictive for certain emotion transitions (combinations of an initial *writer* and a responsive *reader* emotion). Liu et al. (2013) model the emotion of a news reader jointly with the emotion of a comment writer using a co-training approach. This contribution was followed up by Li et al. (2016) who criticized that important assumptions underlying co-training, *viz.* sufficiency and independence of the two views, had actually been violated in that work. Instead, they propose a two-view label propagation approach.

Various (knowledge) representation formalisms have been suggested for inferring sentiment or opinions by either readers, writers or both from a piece of text. Reschke and Anand (2011) propose the concept of predicate-specific *evaluativity functors* which allow for inferring the writers' evaluation of a proposition based on the evaluation of the arguments of the predicate. Using description logics as modeling language Klenner (2016) advocates the concept of *polarity frames* to capture polarity constraints verbs impose on their complements as well as polarity implications they project on them. Deng and Wiebe (2015) employ probabilistic soft logic for entity and event-based opinion inference from the viewpoint of the author or intra-textual entities. Rashkin et al. (2016) introduce *connotation frames* of (verb) predicates as a comprehensive formalism for modeling various evaluative relationships (being positive, negative or neutral) between the arguments of the predicate as well as the reader's and author's view on them. However, up until know, the power of this formalism is still restricted by assuming that author and reader evaluate the arguments in the same way.

In summary, different from our contribution, this line of work tends to focus less on the reader's perspective and also addresses cognitive evaluations (*opinions*) rather than instantaneous affective reactions. Although these two concepts are closely related, they are yet different and in fact their relationship has been the subject of a long lasting and still unresolved debate in psychology (Davidson et al., 2003) (e.g., are we afraid of something because we evaluate it as dangerous, or do we evaluate something as dangerous because we are afraid?).

To the best of our knowledge, only Mohammad and Turney (2013) investigated the effects of different perspectives on annotation quality. They conducted an experiment on how to formulate the emotion annotation question and found that asking whether a term is *associated* with an emotion actually resulted in higher IAA than asking whether a term *evokes* a certain emotion. Arguably, the former phrasing is rather unrelated to either writer or reader emotion, while the latter clearly targets the emotion of the reader. Their work renders evidence for the importance of the *perspective* of text comprehension for annotation quality. Note that they focused on word emotion rather than sentence emotion.

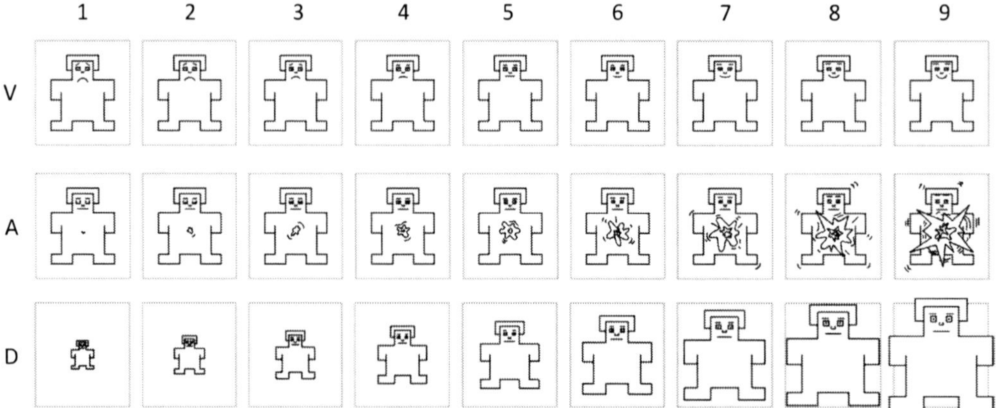

Figure 2: The icons of the 9-point Self-Assessment Manikin (SAM). Dimensions (Valence, Arousal and Dominance; VAD) in rows, rating scores (1-9) in columns. Comprised in PXLab, an open source toolkit for psychological experiments (http://irtel.uni-mannheim.de/pxlab/index.html).

3 Methods

Inter-Annotator Agreement. Annotating emotion on numerical scales demands for another statistical tool set than the one that is common in NLP. Well-known metrics such as the κ-coefficient should not be applied for measuring IAA because these are designed for nominal-scaled variables, i.e., ones whose possible values do not have any intrinsic order (such as part-of-speech tags as compared to (say) a multi-point sentiment scale).

In the literature, there is no consensus on what metrics for IAA should be used instead. However, there is a set of repetitively used approaches which are typically only described verbally. In the following, we offer comprehensive formal definitions and a discussion of them.

First, we describe a leave-one-out framework for IAA where the ratings of an individual annotator are compared against the average of the remaining ratings. As one of the first papers, it was used and verbally described by Strapparava and Mihalcea (2007) and was later taken on by Yu et al. (2016) and Preoţiuc-Pietro et al. (2016).

Let $X := (x_{ij}) \in \mathbb{R}^{m \times n}$ be a matrix where m corresponds to the number of items and n corresponds to the number of annotators. X stores all the individual ratings of the m items (organized in rows) and n annotators (organized in columns) so that x_{ij} represents the rating of the i-th item by the j-th annotator. Since we use the three-dimensional VAD model, in practice, we will have one such matrix for each VAD dimension.

Let b_j denote $(x_{1j}, x_{2j}, .., x_{mj})$, the vector composed out of the j-th column of the matrix and let $f : \mathbb{R}^m \times \mathbb{R}^m \to \mathbb{R}$ be an arbitrary metric for comparing two data series, then $L1O_f(X)$, the leave-one-out IAA for the rating matrix X relative to the metric f, is defined as

$$L1O_f(X) := \frac{1}{n} \sum_{j=1}^{n} f(b_j, b_j^{\varnothing}) \qquad (1)$$

where $b_j^{\varnothing}$ is the average annotation vector of the remaining raters:

$$b_j^{\varnothing} := \frac{1}{n-1} \sum_{k \in \{1,...,n\} \setminus \{j\}} b_k \qquad (2)$$

For our experiments, we will use three different metrics specifying the function f, namely r, MAE and RMSE.

In general, the Pearson correlation coefficient r captures the linear dependence between two data series, $\mathbf{x} = \mathbf{x}_1, \mathbf{x}_2, ..., \mathbf{x}_m$ and $\mathbf{y} = \mathbf{y}_1, \mathbf{y}_2, ..., \mathbf{y}_m$. In our case $\mathbf{x}, \mathbf{y}$ correspond to the rating vector of an individual annotator and the aggregated rating vector of the remaining annotators, respectively.

$$r(\mathbf{x}, \mathbf{y}) := \frac{\sum_{i=1}^{m} (\mathbf{x}_i - \bar{\mathbf{x}})(\mathbf{y}_i - \bar{\mathbf{y}})}{\sqrt{\sum_{i=1}^{m} (\mathbf{x}_i - \bar{\mathbf{x}})^2} \sqrt{\sum_{i=1}^{m} (\mathbf{y}_i - \bar{\mathbf{y}})^2}} \qquad (3)$$

where $\bar{\mathbf{x}}, \bar{\mathbf{y}}$ denote the mean value of $\mathbf{x}, \mathbf{y}$, respectively.

When comparing a model's prediction to the actual data, it can be very important not only to take correlation-based metrics like r into account, but also error-based metrics (Buechel and Hahn, 2016). This is so because a model may produce very accurate predictions in terms of correlation, while at the same time it may perform poorly when taking errors into account (for instance, when the predicted values range in a much smaller interval than the actual values).

To be able to compare a system's performance more directly to the human ceiling, we also apply error-based metrics within this leave-one-out framework. The most popular ones for emotion analysis are Mean Absolute Error (MAE) and Root Mean Square Error (RMSE) (Paltoglou et al., 2013; Yu et al., 2016; Wang et al., 2016):

$$\text{MAE}(\mathbf{x}, \mathbf{y}) := \frac{1}{m} \sum_{i=1}^{m} |(\mathbf{x}_i - \mathbf{y}_i)| \qquad (4)$$

$$\text{RMSE}(\mathbf{x}, \mathbf{y}) := \sqrt{\frac{1}{m} \sum_{i=1}^{m} (\mathbf{x}_i - \mathbf{y}_i)^2} \qquad (5)$$

One of the drawbacks of this framework is that each x_{ij} from matrix X has to be known in order to calculate the IAA. An alternative method was verbally described by Buechel and Hahn (2016) which can be computed out of mean and SD values for each item alone (a format often available from psychological papers). Let X be defined as above and let $\overline{a_i}$ denote the mean value for the i-th item. Then, the Average Annotation Standard Deviation (AASD) is defined as

$$\text{AASD}(X) := \frac{1}{m} \sum_{i=1}^{m} \sqrt{\frac{1}{n} \sum_{j=1}^{n} (x_{ij} - \overline{a_i})^2} \qquad (6)$$

Emotionality. While IAA is indubitably the most important quality criterion for emotion annotation, we argue that there is at least one additional criterion that is not covered by prior research: When using numerical scales (especially ones with a large number of rating points, e.g., the 9-point scales we will use in our experiments) annotations where only neutral ratings are used will be unfavorable for future applications (e.g., training models). Therefore, it is important that the annotations are properly distributed over the full range of the scale. This issue is especially relevant in our setting as different perspectives may very well differ in the extremity of their reactions,

as evident from Example (1). We call this desirable property the *emotionality* (EMO) of the annotations.

For the EMO metric, we first derive aggregated ratings from the individual rating decisions of the annotators, i.e., the ratings that would later form the final ratings of a corpus. For that, we aggregate the rating matrix X from Equation 1 into the vector y consisting of the respective row means $\overline{y_i}$.

$$\overline{y_i} := \frac{1}{n} \sum_{j=1}^{n} x_{ij} \qquad (7)$$

$$y := (\overline{y_1}, ..., \overline{y_i}, ..., \overline{y_m}) \qquad (8)$$

Since we use the VAD model, we will have one such aggregated vector per VAD dimension. We denote them y^1, y^2 and y^3. Let the matrix $Y = (y_i^j) \in \mathbb{R}^{m \times 3}$ hold the aggregated ratings of item i for dimension j, and let $\mathcal{N}$ denote the neutral rating (e.g., 5 on a 9-point scale). Then,

$$\text{EMO}(Y) := \frac{1}{3 \times m} \sum_{j=1}^{3} \sum_{i=1}^{m} |y_i^j - \mathcal{N}| \qquad (9)$$

Representative Distribution. A closely related quality indicator relates to the representativeness of the resulting rating distribution. For large sets of stimuli (words as well as sentences), numerous studies consistently report that when using SAM-like scales, typically the emotion ratings closely resemble a normal distribution, i.e., the density plot displays a Gaussian, "bell-shaped" curve (see Figure 3b) (Preoţiuc-Pietro et al., 2016; Warriner et al., 2013; Stadthagen-Gonzalez et al., 2016; Montefinese et al., 2014).

Intuitively, it makes sense that most of the sentences under annotation should be rather neutral, while only few of them carry extreme emotions. Therefore, we argue that ideally the resulting aggregated ratings for an emotion annotation task should be normally distributed. Otherwise, it must be seriously called into question in how far the respective data set can be considered representative, possibly reducing the performance of models trained thereon. Consequently, we will also take the density plot of the ratings into account when comparing different set-ups.

4 Experiments

Perspectives to Distinguish. Considering Example (1) and our literature review from Section

2, it is obvious that at least the perspective of the *writer* and the *reader* of an utterance must be distinguished. Accordingly, writer emotion refers to how someone feels while producing an utterance, whereas reader emotion relates to how someone feels right after reading or hearing this utterance.

Also taking into account the finding by Mohammad and Turney (2013) that agreement among annotators is higher when asking whether a word is *associated* with an emotion rather than asking whether it *evokes* this emotion, we propose to extend the common writer-reader framework by a third category, the *text* perspective, where no actual person is specified as perceiving an emotion. Rather, we assume for this perspective that emotion is an intrinsic property of a sentence (or an alternative linguistic unit like a phrase or the entire text). In the following, we will use the terms WRITER, TEXT and READER to concisely refer to the respective perspectives.

Data Sets. We collected two data sets, a movie review data set highly popular in sentiment analysis and a balanced corpus of general English. In this way, we can estimate the annotation quality resulting from different perspectives, also covering interactions regarding different domains.

The first data set builds upon the corpus originally introduced by Pang and Lee (2005). It consists of about 10k snippets from movie reviews by professional critics collected from the website `rottentomatoes.com`. The data was further enriched by Socher et al. (2013) who annotated individual nodes in the constituency parse trees according to a 5-point polarity scale, forming the Stanford Sentiment Treebank (SST) which contains 11,855 sentences.

Upon closer inspection, we noticed that the SST data have some encoding issues (e.g., *Absorbing character study by AndrÃ© Turpin .*) that are not present in the original Rotten Tomatoes data set. So we decided to replicate the creation of the SST data from the original snippets. Furthermore, we filtered out fragmentary sentences automatically (e.g., beginning with comma, dashes, lower case, etc.) as well as manually excluded grammatically incomplete and therefore incomprehensible sentences, e.g., "Or a profit" or "Over age 15?". Subsequently, a total of 10,987 sentences could be mapped back to SST IDs forming the basis for our experiments (the SST* collection).

To complement our review language data set, a domain heavily focused on in sentiment analysis (Liu, 2015), for our second data set, we decided to rely on a genre-balanced corpus. We chose the Manually Annotated Sub-Corpus (MASC) of the American National Corpus which is already annotated for various linguistic levels (Ide et al., 2008; Ide et al., 2010). We excluded registers containing spoken, mainly dialogic or non-standard language, e.g., telephone conversations, movie scripts and tweets. To further enrich this collection of raw data for potential emotion analysis applications, we additionally included the corpus of the SEM-EVAL-2007 Task 14 focusing on *Affective Text* (SE07; Strapparava and Mihalcea (2007)), one of the most important data sets in emotion analysis. This data set already bears annotations according to Ekman's six Basic Emotions (see Section 2) so that the gold standard we ultimately supply already contains a bi-representational part (being annotated according to a dimensional *and* a categorical model of emotion). Such a double encoding will easily allow for research on automatically mapping between different emotion formats (Buechel and Hahn, 2017).

In order to identify individual sentence in MASC, we relied on the already available annotations. We noticed, however, that a considerable portion of the sentence boundary annotations were duplicates which we consequently removed (about 5% of the preselected data). This left us with a total of 18,290 sentences from MASC and 1,250 headlines from SE07. Together, they form our second data set, MASC*.

Study Design. We pulled a 40 sentences random sample from MASC* and SST*, respectively. For each of the three perspectives WRITER, READER and TEXT, we prepared a separate set of instructions. Those instructions are identical, except for the exact phrasing of what a participant should annotate: For WRITER, it was consistently asked "what emotion is expressed by the author", while TEXT and READER queried "what emotion is conveyed" by and "how do you [the participant of the survey] feel after reading" an individual sentence, respectively.

After reviewing numerous studies from NLP and psychology that had created emotion annotations (e.g., Katz et al. (2007), Strapparava and Mihalcea (2007), Mohammad and Turney (2013), Pinheiro et al. (2016), Warriner et al. (2013)), we largely relied on the instructions used by Bradley and Lang (1999) as this is one of the first and probably the most influential resource from psychology which also greatly influenced work in NLP (Yu et al., 2016; Preoţiuc-Pietro et al., 2016).

The instructions were structured as follows. After a general description of the study, the individual scales of SAM were explained to the participants. After that, they performed three trial ratings to familiarize themselves with the usage of the SAM scales before proceeding to judge the actual 40 sentences of interest. The study was implemented as a web survey using Google Forms.[1] The sentences were presented in randomized order, i.e., they were shuffled for each participant individually.

For each of the six resulting surveys (one for each combination of perspective and data set), we recruited 80 participants via the crowdsourcing platform `crowdflower.com` (CF). The number was chosen so that the differences in IAA may reach statistical significance (according to the leave-one-out evaluation (see Section 3), the number of cases is equal to the number of raters). The surveys went online one after the other, so that as few participants as possible would do more than one of the surveys. The task was available from within the UK, the US, Ireland, Canada, Australia and New Zealand.

We preferred using an external survey over running the task directly via the CF platform because this set-up offers more design options, such as randomization, which is impossible via CF; there, the data is only shuffled once and will then be presented in the same order to each participant. The drawback of this approach is that we cannot rely on CF's quality control mechanisms.

In order to still be able to exclude malicious raters, we introduced an algorithmic filtering process where we summed up the absolute error the participants made on the trial questions—those were asking them to indicate the VAD values for a verbally described emotion so that the correct answers were evident from the instructions. Raters whose absolute error was above a certain threshold were excluded.

We set this parameter to 20 (removing about a third of the responses) because this was approximately the ratio of raters which struck us as unreliable when manually inspecting the data while, at the same time, leaving us with a reasonable

	Perspective	r	MAE	RMSE	AASD
	WRITER	.53	1.41	1.70	1.73
SST*	TEXT	.41	1.73	2.03	2.10
	READER	.40	1.66	1.96	2.02
	WRITER	.43	1.56	1.88	1.95
MASC*	TEXT	.43	1.49	1.81	1.89
	READER	.36	1.58	1.89	1.98

Table 1: IAA values obtained on the SST* and the MASC* data set. r, MAE and RMSE refer to the respective leave-one-out metric (see Section 3).

number of cases to perform statistical analysis. The results of this analysis is presented in the following section. Our two small sized yet multi-perspectival data sets are publicly available for further analysis.[2]

5 Results

In this section, we compare the three annotation perspectives (WRITER, READER and TEXT) on two different data sets (SST* and MASC*; see Section 4), according to three criteria for annotation quality: IAA, emotionality and distribution (see Section 3).

Inter-Annotator Agreement. Since there is no consensus on a fixed set of metrics for numerical emotion values, we compare IAA according to a range of measures. We use r, MAE and RMSE in the leave-one-out framework, as well as AASD (see Section 3). Table 1 displays our results for the SST* and MASC* data set. We calculated IAA individually for Valence, Arousal and Dominance. However, to keep the number of comparisons feasible, we restrict ourselves to presenting the respective mean values (average over VAD), only. The relative ordering between the VAD dimensions is overall consistent with prior work so that Valence shows better IAA than Arousal or Dominance (in line with findings from Warriner et al. (2013) and Schmidtke et al. (2014)).

We find that on the review-style SST* data, WRITER displays the best IAA according to all of the four metrics ($p < 0.05$ using a two-tailed t-test, respectively). Note that MAE, RMSE and AASD are error-based so that the smaller the value the better the agreement. Concerning the ordering of the remaining perspectives, TEXT is marginally better regarding r, while the results from the three error-based metrics are clearly in favor of READER. Consequently, for IAA on the

---

	Perspective	EMO
	WRITER	1.09
SST*	TEXT	1.04
	READER	0.91
	WRITER	0.75
MASC*	TEXT	0.70
	READER	0.63

Table 2: Emotionality results for the SST* and the MASC* data set.

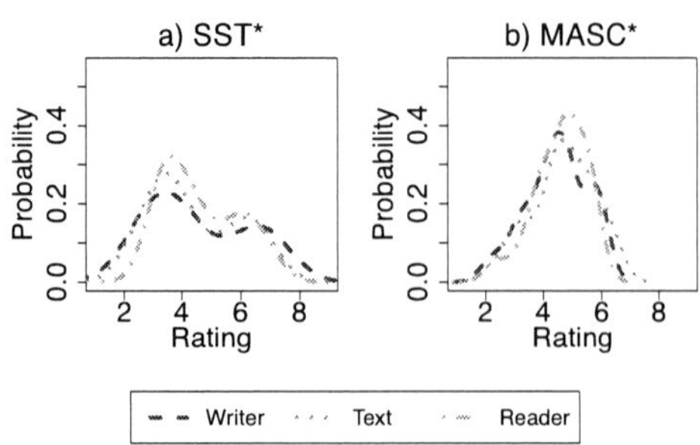

Figure 3: Density plots of the aggregated Valence ratings for the two data sets and three perspectives.

SST* data set, WRITER yields the best performance, while the order of the other perspectives is not so clear.

Surprisingly, the results look markedly different on the MASC* data. Here, regarding r, WRITER and TEXT are on par with each other. This contrasts with the results from the error-based metrics. There, TEXT shows the best value, while WRITER, in turn, improves upon READER only by a small margin. Most importantly, for neither of the four metrics we obtain statistical significance between the best and the second best perspective ($p \geq 0.05$ using a two-tailed t-test, respectively). Thus, concerning IAA on the MASC* sample, the results remain rather opaque.

The fact that, contrary to that, on SST* the results are conclusive and statistically significant, strongly suggests that the resulting annotation quality is not only dependent on the annotation perspective. Instead, there seem to be considerable dependencies and interactions concerning the domain of the raw data, as well.

Interestingly, on both corpora correlation- and error-based sets of metrics behave inconsistently which we interpret as a piece of evidence for using both types of metrics, in parallel (Buechel and Hahn, 2016; Wang et al., 2016).

Emotionality. For emotionality, we rely on the EMO metric which we defined in Section 3 (see Table 2 for our results). For both corpora, the ordering of the perspectives according to the EMO score is consistent: WRITER yields the most emotional ratings followed by TEXT and READER. ($p < 0.05$ for each of the pairs using a two-tailed t-test). These unanimous and statistically significant results further underpin the advantage of the TEXT and especially the WRITER perspective as already suggested by our findings for IAA.

Distribution. We also looked at the distribution of the resulting aggregated annotations relative to the chosen data sets and the three perspectives by examining the respective density plots. In Figure 3, we give six examples of these plots, displaying the Valence density curve for both corpora, SST* and MASC*, as well as the three perspectives. For Arousal and Dominance, the plots show the same characteristics although slightly less pronounced.

The left density plots, for the SST*, display a bimodal distribution (having two local maxima), whereas the MASC* plots are much closer to a normal distribution. This second shape has been consistently reported by many contributions (see Section 3), whereas we know of no other study reporting a bimodal emotion distribution. This highly atypical finding for SST* might be an artifact of the website from which the original movie review snippets were collected—there, movies are classified into either *fresh* (positive) or *rotten* (negative). Consequently, this binary classification scheme might have influenced the selection of snippets from full-scale reviews (as performed by the website) so that these snippets are either clearly positive or negative.

Thus, our findings seriously call into question in how far the movie review corpus by Pang and Lee (2005)—one of the most popular data sets in sentiment analysis—can be considered representative for review language or general English. Ultimately, this may result in a reduced performance of models trained on such skewed data.

6 Discussion

Overall, we interpret our data as suggesting the WRITER perspective to be superior to TEXT and READER: Considering IAA, it is significantly better on one data set (SST*), while it is on par with or only marginally worse than the best perspective on the other data set (MASC*). Regarding emotionality of the aggregated ratings (EMO), the superiority of this perspective is even more obvious.

The relative order of TEXT and WRITER on the other hand, is not so clear. Regarding IAA, TEXT is better on MASC* while for SST* READER seems to be slightly better (almost on par regarding r but markedly better relative to the error measures we propose here). However, regarding the emotionality of the ratings, TEXT clearly surpasses READER.

Our data suggest that the results of Mohammad and Turney (2013) (the only comparable study so far, though considering emotion on the *word* rather than *sentence* level) may be also true for sentences in most of the cases. However, our data indicate that the validity of their findings may depend on the domain the raw data originate from. They found that phrasing the emotion annotation task relative to the TEXT perspective yields higher IAA than relating to the READER perspective. However, more importantly, our data complement their results by presenting evidence that WRITER seems to be even better than any of the two perspectives they took into account.

7 Conclusion

This contribution presented a series of annotation experiments examining which *annotation perspective* (WRITER, TEXT or READER) yields the best IAA, also taking domain differences into account—the first study of this kind for sentence-level emotion annotation. We began by reviewing different popular representation schemes for emotion before (formally) defining various metrics for annotation quality—for the VAD scheme we use, this task was so far neglected in the literature.

Our findings strongly suggest that WRITER is overall the superior perspective. However, the exact ordering of the perspectives strongly depends on the domain the data originate from. Our results are thus mainly consistent with, but substantially go beyond, the only comparable study so far (Mohammad and Turney, 2013). Furthermore, our data provide strong evidence that the movie review corpus by Pang and Lee (2005)—one of the most popular ones for sentiment analysis—may not be representative in terms of its rating distribution potentially casting doubt on the quality of models trained on this data.

For the subsequent creation of EMOBANK, a large-scale VAD gold standard, we took the following decisions in the light of these not fully conclusive outcomes. First, we decided to anno-

tate a 10k sentences subset of the MASC* corpus considering the atypical rating distribution in the SST* data set. Furthermore, we decided to annotate the whole corpus bi-perspectively (according to WRITER *and* READER viewpoint) as we hope that the resulting resource helps clarifying which factors exactly influence emotion annotation quality. This freely available resource is further described in Buechel and Hahn (2017).

References

A. Balahur, J. M. Hermida, and A. Montoyo. 2012. Building and exploiting EmotiNet, a knowledge base for emotion detection based on the appraisal theory model. *IEEE Transactions on Affective Computing*, 3(1):88–101.

Margaret M. Bradley and Peter J. Lang. 1994. Measuring emotion: The self-assessment manikin and the semantic differential. *Journal of Behavior Therapy and Experimental Psychiatry*, 25(1):49–59.

Margaret M. Bradley and Peter J. Lang. 1999. Affective norms for English words (ANEW): Stimuli, instruction manual and affective ratings. Technical Report C-1, The Center for Research in Psychophysiology, University of Florida, Gainesville, FL.

Sven Buechel and Udo Hahn. 2016. Emotion analysis as a regression problem: Dimensional models and their implications on emotion representation and metrical evaluation. In Gal A. Kaminka, Maria Fox, Paolo Bouquet, Eyke Hüllermeier, Virginia Dignum, Frank Dignum, and Frank van Harmelen, editors, *ECAI 2016 — Proceedings of the 22nd European Conference on Artificial Intelligence. The Hague, The Netherlands, August 29 - September 2, 2016*, pages 1114–1122.

Sven Buechel and Udo Hahn. 2017. EMOBANK: Studying the impact of annotation perspective and representation format on dimensional emotion analysis. In *EACL 2017 — Proceedings of the 15th Annual Meeting of the European Chapter of the Association for Computational Linguistics. Valencia, Spain, April 3-7, 2017*.

Rafael A. Calvo and Sunghwan Mac Kim. 2013. Emotions in text: Dimensional and categorical models. *Computational Intelligence*, 29(3):527–543.

Richard J. Davidson, Klaus R. Scherer, and H. Hill Goldsmith. 2003. *Handbook of Affective Sciences*. Oxford University Press, Oxford, New York, NY.

Lingjia Deng and Janyce Wiebe. 2015. Joint prediction for entity/event-level sentiment analysis using probabilistic soft logic models. In Lluís Màrquez, Chris Callison-Burch, and Jian Su, editors, *EMNLP 2015 — Proceedings of the 2015 Conference on Empirical Methods in Natural Language Processing*.

Lisbon, Portugal, September 17–21, 2015, pages 179–189.

Paul Ekman. 1992. An argument for basic emotions. *Cognition & Emotion*, 6(3-4):169–200.

Nancy C. Ide, Collin F. Baker, Christiane Fellbaum, Charles J. Fillmore, and Rebecca J. Passonneau. 2008. MASC: The Manually Annotated Sub-Corpus of American English. In Nicoletta Calzolari, Khalid Choukri, Bente Maegaard, Joseph Mariani, Jan E. J. M. Odijk, Stelios Piperidis, and Daniel Tapias, editors, *LREC 2008 — Proceedings of the 6th International Conference on Language Resources and Evaluation. Marrakech, Morocco, May 26 – June 1, 2008*, pages 2455–2461.

Nancy C. Ide, Collin F. Baker, Christiane Fellbaum, and Rebecca J. Passonneau. 2010. The Manually Annotated Sub-Corpus: A community resource for and by the people. In Jan Hajič, M. Sandra Carberry, and Stephen Clark, editors, *ACL 2010 — Proceedings of the 48th Annual Meeting of the Association for Computational Linguistics. Uppsala, Sweden, July 11–16, 2010*, volume 2: Short Papers, pages 68–73.

Phil Katz, Matthew Singleton, and Richard Wicentowski. 2007. SWAT-MP: The SemEval-2007 systems for Task 5 and Task 14. In Eneko Agirre, Lluís Màrquez, and Richard Wicentowski, editors, *SemEval-2007 — Proceedings of the 4th International Workshop on Semantic Evaluations @ ACL 2007. Prague, Czech Republic, June 23-24, 2007*, pages 308–313.

Svetlana Kiritchenko and Saif M. Mohammad. 2016. Capturing reliable fine-grained sentiment associations by crowdsourcing and best-worst scaling. In Kevin Knight, Ani Nenkova, and Owen Rambow, editors, *NAACL-HLT 2016 — Proceedings of the 2016 Conference of the North American Chapter of the Association for Computational Linguistics: Human Language Technologies. San Diego, California, USA, June 12-17, 2016*, pages 811–817.

Manfred Klenner. 2016. A model for multi-perspective opinion inferences. In Larry Birnbaum, Octavian Popescu, and Carlo Strapparava, editors, *Proceedings of IJCAI 2016 Workshop Natural Language Meets Journalism, New York, USA, July 10, 2016*, pages 6–11.

Shoushan Li, Jian Xu, Dong Zhang, and Guodong Zhou. 2016. Two-view label propagation to semi-supervised reader emotion classification. In Nicoletta Calzolari, Yuji Matsumoto, and Rashmi Prasad, editors, *COLING 2016 — Proceedings of the 26th International Conference on Computational Linguistics. Osaka, Japan, December 11-16, 2016*, volume Technical Papers, pages 2647–2655.

Hsin-Yih Kevin Lin and Hsin-Hsi Chen. 2008. Ranking reader emotions using pairwise loss minimization and emotional distribution regression. In *EMNLP 2008 — Proceedings of the 2008 Conference on Empirical Methods in Natural Language Processing. Honolulu, Hawaii, October 25–27, 2008*, pages 136–144.

Huanhuan Liu, Shoushan Li, Guodong Zhou, Chu-Ren Huang, and Peifeng Li. 2013. Joint modeling of news reader's and comment writer's emotions. In Hinrich Schütze, Pascale Fung, and Massimo Poesio, editors, *ACL 2013 — Proceedings of the 51st Annual Meeting of the Association for Computational Linguistics. Sofia, Bulgaria, August 4-9, 2013*, volume 2: Short Papers, pages 511–515.

Bing Liu. 2015. *Sentiment Analysis: Mining Opinions, Sentiments, and Emotions*. Cambridge University Press, New York.

Jordan J Louviere, Terry N Flynn, and AAJ Marley. 2015. *Best-worst scaling: Theory, methods and applications*. Cambridge University Press, Cambridge.

Saif M. Mohammad and Peter D. Turney. 2013. Crowdsourcing a word-emotion association lexicon. *Computational Intelligence*, 29(3):436–465.

Maria Montefinese, Ettore Ambrosini, Beth Fairfield, and Nicola Mammarella. 2014. The adaptation of the Affective Norms for English Words (ANEW) for Italian. *Behavior Research Methods*, 46(3):887–903.

Subhabrata Mukherjee and Sachindra Joshi. 2014. Author-specific sentiment aggregation for polarity prediction of reviews. In Nicoletta Calzolari, Khalid Choukri, Thierry Declerck, Loftsson Hrafn, Bente Maegaard, Joseph Mariani, Asuncion Moreno, Jan Odijk, and Stelios Piperidis, editors, *LREC 2014 — Proceedings of the 9th International Conference on Language Resources and Evaluation. Reykjavik, Iceland, May 26-31, 2014*, pages 3092—3099.

Cecilia Ovesdotter Alm, Dan Roth, and Richard Sproat. 2005. Emotions from text: Machine learning for text-based emotion prediction. In Raymond J. Mooney, Christopher Brew, Lee-Feng Chien, and Katrin Kirchhoff, editors, *HLT-EMNLP 2005 — Proceedings of the Human Language Technology Conference & 2005 Conference on Empirical Methods in Natural Language Processing. Vancouver, British Columbia, Canada, 6-8 October 2005*, pages 579–586.

G. Paltoglou, M. Theunis, A. Kappas, and M. Thelwall. 2013. Predicting emotional responses to long informal text. *IEEE Transactions on Affective Computing*, 4(1):106–115.

Bo Pang and Lillian Lee. 2005. Seeing stars: Exploiting class relationships for sentiment categorization with respect to rating scales. In Kevin Knight, Tou Hwee Ng, and Kemal Oflazer, editors, *ACL 2005 — Proceedings of the 43rd Annual Meeting of the Association for Computational Linguistics. Ann*

Arbor, Michigan, USA, June 25–30, 2005, pages 115–124.

Bo Pang and Lillian Lee. 2008. Opinion mining and sentiment analysis. *Foundations and Trends in Information Retrieval*, 2(1-2):1–135.

Ana P. Pinheiro, Marcelo Dias, Joo Pedrosa, and Ana P. Soares. 2016. Minho Affective Sentences (MAS): Probing the roles of sex, mood, and empathy in affective ratings of verbal stimuli. *Behavior Research Methods*. Online First Publication.

Robert Plutchik. 1980. A general psychoevolutionary theory of emotion. *Emotion: Theory, Research and Experience*, 1(3):3–33.

Daniel Preoţiuc-Pietro, Hansen Andrew Schwartz, Gregory Park, Johannes C. Eichstaedt, Margaret L. Kern, Lyle H. Ungar, and Elizabeth P. Shulman. 2016. Modelling valence and arousal in Facebook posts. In Alexandra Balahur, Erik van der Goot, Piek Vossen, and Andrés Montoyo, editors, *WASSA 2016 — Proceedings of the 7th Workshop on Computational Approaches to Subjectivity, Sentiment and Social Media Analysis @ NAACL-HLT 2016. San Diego, California, USA, June 16, 2016*, pages 9–15.

Hannah Rashkin, Sameer Singh, and Yejin Choi. 2016. Connotation frames: A data-driven investigation. In Antal van den Bosch, Katrin Erk, and Noah A. Smith, editors, *ACL 2016 — Proceedings of the 54th Annual Meeting of the Association for Computational Linguistics. Berlin, Germany, August 7–12, 2016*, volume 1: Long Papers, pages 311–321.

Kevin Reschke and Pranav Anand. 2011. Extracting contextual evaluativity. In Johan Bos and Stephen Pulman, editors, *IWCS 2011 — Proceedings of the 9th International Conference on Computational Semantics. Oxford, UK, January 12–14, 2011*, pages 370–374.

James A. Russell and Albert Mehrabian. 1977. Evidence for a three-factor theory of emotions. *Journal of Research in Personality*, 11(3):273–294.

James A. Russell. 1980. A circumplex model of affect. *Journal of Personality and Social Psychology*, 39(6):1161–1178.

David Sander and Klaus R. Scherer, editors. 2009. *The Oxford Companion to Emotion and the Affective Sciences*. Oxford University Press, Oxford, New York.

David S. Schmidtke, Tobias Schröder, Arthur M. Jacobs, and Markus Conrad. 2014. ANGST: Affective norms for German sentiment terms, derived from the affective norms for English words. *Behavior Research Methods*, 46(4):1108–1118.

Kim Schouten and Flavius Frasincar. 2016. Survey on aspect-level sentiment analysis. *IEEE Transactions on Knowledge and Data Engineering*, 28(3):813–830.

Richard Socher, Alex Perelygin, Jean Y. Wu, Jason Chuang, Christopher D. Manning, Andrew Y. Ng, and Christopher Potts. 2013. Recursive deep models for semantic compositionality over a sentiment treebank. In Timothy Baldwin and Anna Korhonen, editors, *EMNLP 2013 — Proceedings of the 2013 Conference on Empirical Methods in Natural Language Processing. Seattle, Washington, USA, 18-21 October 2013*, pages 1631–1642.

Hans Stadthagen-Gonzalez, Constance Imbault, Miguel A. Pérez Sánchez, and Marc Brysbaert. 2016. Norms of valence and arousal for 14,031 Spanish words. *Behavior Research Methods*. Online First Publication.

Carlo Strapparava and Rada Mihalcea. 2007. SemEval-2007 Task 14: Affective text. In Eneko Agirre, Lluís Màrquez, and Richard Wicentowski, editors, *SemEval-2007 — Proceedings of the 4th International Workshop on Semantic Evaluations @ ACL 2007. Prague, Czech Republic, June 23-24, 2007*, pages 70–74.

Yi-jie Tang and Hsin-Hsi Chen. 2012. Mining sentiment words from microblogs for predicting writer-reader emotion transition. In Nicoletta Calzolari, Khalid Choukri, Thierry Declerck, Mehmet Uğur Doğan, Bente Maegaard, Joseph Mariani, Asunción Moreno, Jan E. J. M. Odijk, and Stelios Piperidis, editors, *LREC 2012 — Proceedings of the 8th International Conference on Language Resources and Evaluation. Istanbul, Turkey, May 21-27, 2012*, pages 1226–1229.

Jin Wang, Liang-Chih Yu, K. Robert Lai, and Xuejie Zhang. 2016. Dimensional sentiment analysis using a regional CNN-LSTM model. In Antal van den Bosch, Katrin Erk, and Noah A. Smith, editors, *ACL 2016 — Proceedings of the 54th Annual Meeting of the Association for Computational Linguistics. Berlin, Germany, August 7–12, 2016*, volume 2: Short Papers, pages 225–230.

Amy Beth Warriner, Victor Kuperman, and Marc Brysbært. 2013. Norms of valence, arousal, and dominance for 13,915 English lemmas. *Behavior Research Methods*, 45(4):1191–1207.

Zhao Yao, Jia Wu, Yanyan Zhang, and Zhendong Wang. 2016. Norms of valence, arousal, concreteness, familiarity, imageability, and context availability for 1,100 Chinese words. *Behavior Research Methods*. Online First Publication.

Liang-Chih Yu, Jin Wang, K. Robert Lai, and Xuejie Zhang. 2015. Predicting valence-arousal ratings of words using a weighted graph method. In Yuji Matsumoto, Chengqing Zong, and Michael Strube, editors, *ACL-IJCNLP 2015 — Proceedings of the 53rd Annual Meeting of the Association for Computational Linguistics & 7th International Joint Conference on Natural Language Processing of the Asian Federation of Natural Language Processing. Beijing, China, July 26-31, 2015*, volume 2: Short Papers, pages 788–793.

Liang-Chih Yu, Lung-Hao Lee, Shuai Hao, Jin Wang, Yunchao He, Jun Hu, K. Robert Lai, and Xuejie Zhang. 2016. Building Chinese affective resources in valence-arousal dimensions. In Kevin C. Knight, Ani Nenkova, and Owen Rambow, editors, *NAACL-HLT 2016 — Proceedings of the 2016 Conference of the North American Chapter of the Association for Computational Linguistics: Human Language Technologies. San Diego, California, USA, June 12–17, 2016*, pages 540–545.

Finding Good Conversations Online:
The Yahoo News Annotated Comments Corpus

Courtney Napoles,[1] **Joel Tetreault,**[2] **Enrica Rosato,**[3] **Brian Provenzale,**[4] and **Aasish Pappu**[3]
[1] Johns Hopkins University, `napoles@cs.jhu.edu`
[2] Grammarly, `joel.tetreault@grammarly.com`
[3] Yahoo, {`aasishkp|enricar`}`@yahoo-inc.com`
[4] Accellion, `bprovenzale@gmail.com`

Abstract

This work presents a dataset and annotation scheme for the new task of identifying "good" conversations that occur online, which we call ERICs: Engaging, Respectful, and/or Informative Conversations. We develop a taxonomy to reflect features of entire threads and individual comments which we believe contribute to identifying ERICs; code a novel dataset of Yahoo News comment threads ($2.4k$ threads and $10k$ comments) and $1k$ threads from the Internet Argument Corpus; and analyze the features characteristic of ERICs. This is one of the largest annotated corpora of online human dialogues, with the most detailed set of annotations. It will be valuable for identifying ERICs and other aspects of argumentation, dialogue, and discourse.

1 Introduction

Automatically curating online comments has been a large focus in recent NLP and social media work, as popular news outlets can receive millions of comments on their articles each month (Warzel, 2012). Comment threads often range from vacuous to hateful, but good discussions *do* occur online, with people expressing different viewpoints and attempting to inform, convince, or better understand the other side, but they can get lost among the multitude of unconstructive comments. We hypothesize that identifying and promoting these types of conversations (ERICs) will cultivate a more civil and constructive atmosphere in online communities and potentially encourage participation from more users.

ERICs are characterized by:

- A respectful exchange of ideas, opinions, and/or information in response to a given topic(s).
- Opinions expressed as an attempt to elicit a dialogue or persuade.
- Comments that seek to contribute some new information or perspective on the relevant topic.

ERICs have no single identifying attribute: for instance, an exchange where communicants are in total agreement throughout can be an ERIC, as can an exchange with heated disagreement. Figures 1 and 2 contain two threads that are characterized by continual disagreement, but one is an ERIC and the other is not. We have developed a new coding scheme to label ERICs and identify six dimensions of comments and three dimensions of threads that are frequently seen in the comments section. Many of these labels are for characteristics of online conversations not captured by traditional argumentation or dialogue features. Some of the labels we collect have been annotated in previous work (§2), but this is the first time they are aggregated in a single corpus at the dialogue level.

In this paper, we present the Yahoo News Annotated Comments Corpus (YNACC), which contains $2.4k$ threads and $10k$ comments from the comments sections of Yahoo News articles. We additionally collect annotations on $1k$ threads from the Internet Argument Corpus (Abbott et al., 2016), representing another domain of online debates. We contrast annotations of Yahoo and IAC threads, explore ways in which threads perceived to be ERICs differ in this two venues, and identify some unanticipated characteristics of ERICs.

This is the first exploration of how characteristics of individual comments contribute to the dialogue-level classification of an exchange. YNACC will facilitate research to understand ERICS and other aspects of dialogue. The corpus and annotations will be available at `https://github.com/cnap/ynacc`.

Proceedings of the 11th Linguistic Annotation Workshop, pages 13–23,
Valencia, Spain, April 3, 2017. ©2017 Association for Computational Linguistics

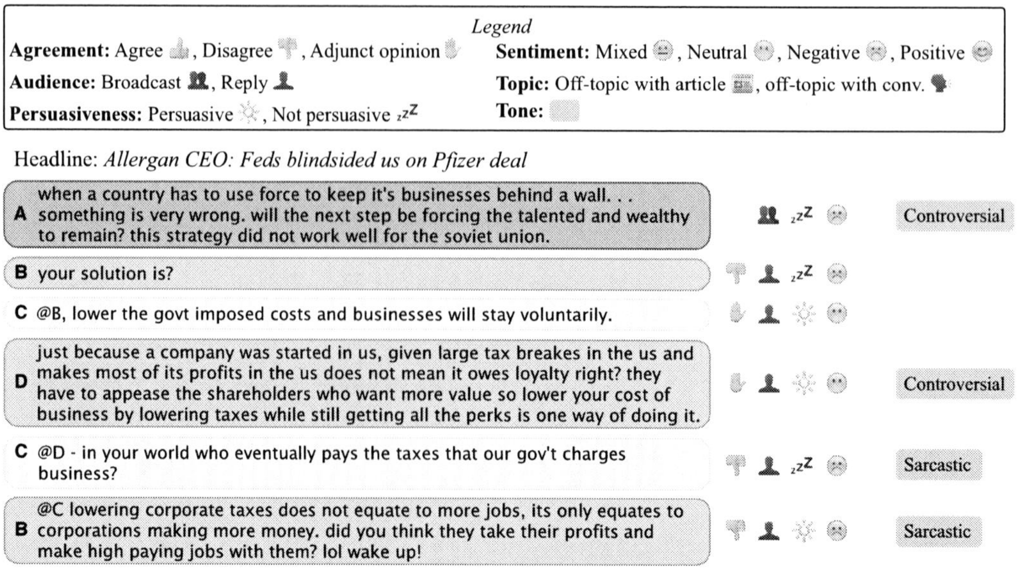

Legend

Agreement: Agree 👍, Disagree 🌱, Adjunct opinion 🖐 **Sentiment:** Mixed 😐, Neutral 🙂, Negative 😖, Positive 😊

Audience: Broadcast 👥, Reply 👤 **Topic:** Off-topic with article 🖼, off-topic with conv. 🐟

Persuasiveness: Persuasive ☀, Not persuasive ᴢᶻ **Tone:**

Headline: *Allergan CEO: Feds blindsided us on Pfizer deal*

Figure 1: An ERIC that is labeled *argumentative*, *positive/respectful*, and having *continual disagreement*.

Headline: *'The Daily Show' Nailed How Islamophobia Hurts the Sikh Community Too*

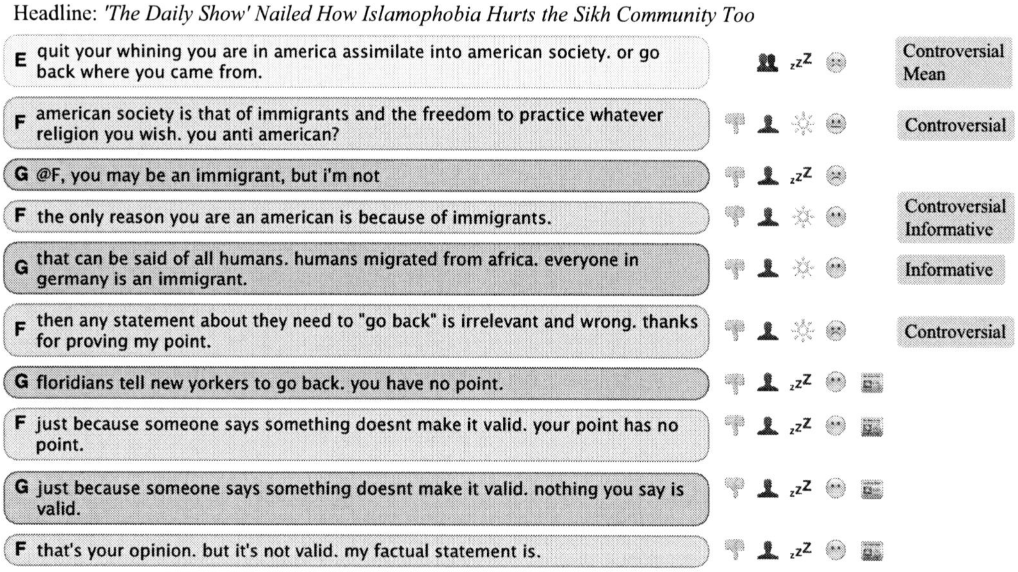

Figure 2: A non-ERIC that is labeled *argumentative* and *off-topic* with *continual disagreement*.

2 Related work

Recent work has focused on the analysis of user-generated text in various online venues, including labeling certain qualities of individual comments, comment pairs, or the roles of individual commenters. The largest and most extensively annotated corpus predating this work is the Internet Argument Corpus (IAC), which contains approximately $480k$ comments in $16.5k$ threads from online forums in which users debate contentious issues. The IAC has been coded for for topic ($3k$ threads), stance ($2k$ authors), and agreement, sarcasm, and hostility ($10k$ comment pairs) (Abbott et al., 2016; Walker et al., 2012). Comments from online news articles are annotated in the SENSEI corpus, which contains human-authored summaries of $1.8k$ comments posted on *Guardian* articles (Barker et al., 2016). Participants described each comment with short, free-form text labels and then wrote a 150–250-word comment summary with these labels. Barker et al. (2016) recognized that comments have diverse qualities, many of which are coded in this work (§3), but did not explicitly collect labels of them.

Previous works present a survey of how editors and readers perceive the quality of comments posted in online news publications (Diakopoulos and Naaman, 2011) and review the criteria professional editors use to curate comments (Diakopoulos, 2015). The latter identifies 15 criteria for curating user-generated responses, from online and radio comments to letters to the editor. Our annotation scheme overlaps with those criteria but also diverges as we wish for the labels to reflect the nature of all comments posted on online articles instead of just the qualities sought in editorially curated comments. ERICs can take many forms and may not reflect the formal tone or intent that editors in traditional news outlets seek.

Our coding scheme intersects with attributes examined in several different areas of research. Some of the most recent and relevant discourse corpora from online sources related to this work include the following: Concepts related to *persuasiveness* have been studied, including annotations for "convincing-ness" in debate forums (Habernal and Gurevych, 2016), influencers in discussions from blogs and Wikipedia (Biran et al., 2012), and user relations as a proxy of *persuasion* in reddit (Tan et al., 2016; Wei et al., 2016). *Politeness* was labeled and identified in Stack Exchange and Wikipedia discussions (Danescu-Niculescu-Mizil et al., 2013). Some previous work focused on detecting agreement has considered blog and Wikipedia discussions (Andreas et al., 2012) and debate forums (Skeppstedt et al., 2016). *Sarcasm* has been identified in a corpus of microblogs identified with the hashtag #sarcasm on Twitter (González-Ibánez et al., 2011; Davidov et al., 2010) and in online forums (Oraby et al., 2016). *Sentiment* has been studied widely, often in the context of reviews (Pang and Lee, 2005), and in the context of user-generated exchanges, positive and negative attitudes have been identified in Usenet discussions (Hassan et al., 2010). Other qualities of user-generated text that are not covered in this work but have been investigated before include metaphor (Jang et al., 2014) and tolerance (Mukherjee et al., 2013) in online discussion

threads, "dogmatism" of reddit users (Fast and Horvitz, 2016), and argumentation units in discussions related to technology (Ghosh et al., 2014).

3 Annotation scheme

This section outlines our coding scheme for identifying ERICs, with labels for comment threads and each comment contained therein.

Starting with the annotation categories from the IAC and the curation criteria of Diakopoulos (2015), we have adapted these schemes and identified new characteristics that have broad coverage over 100 comment threads (§4) that we manually examined.

Annotations are made at the *thread-level* and the *comment-level*. Thread-level annotations capture the qualities of a thread on the whole, while comment-level annotations reflect the characteristics of each comment. The labels for each dimension are described below. Only one label per dimension is allowed unless otherwise specified.

3.1 Thread labels

Agreement The overall agreement present in a thread.
- *Agreement throughout*
- *Continual disagreement*
- *Agreement → disagreement*: Begins with agreement which turns into disagreement.
- *Disagreement → agreement*: Starts with disagreement that converges into agreement.

Constructiveness A binary label indicating when a conversation is an ERIC, or has a clear exchange of ideas, opinions, and/or information done so somewhat respectfully.[1]
- *Constructive*
- *Not constructive*

Type The overall type or tone of the conversation, describing the majority of comments. Two labels can be chosen if conversations exhibit more than one dominant feature.
- *Argumentative*: Contains a lot of "back and forth" between participants that does not necessarily reach a conclusion.
- *Flamewar*: Contains insults, users "yelling" at each other, and no information exchanged.

---

[1]Note that this definition of *constructive* differs from that of Niculae and Danescu-Niculescu-Mizil (2016), who use the term to denote discrete progress made towards identifying a point on a map. Our definition draws from the more traditional meaning when used in the context of conversations as "intended to be useful or helpful" (Macmillan, 2017).

- *Off-Topic/digression*: Comments are completely irrelevant to the article or each other, or the conversation starts on topic but veers off into another direction.
- *Personal stories*: Participants exchange personal anecdotes.
- *Positive/respectful*: Consists primarily of comments expressing opinions in a respectful, potentially empathetic manner.
- *Snarky/humorous*: Participants engage with each other using humor rather than argue or sympathize. May be on- or off-topic.

3.2 Comment labels

Agreement   Agreement expressed with explicit phrasing (e.g., *I disagree...*) or implicitly, such as in Figure 2. Annotating the target of (dis)agreement is left to future work due to the number of other codes the annotators need to attend to. Multiple labels can be chosen per comment, since a comment can express agreement with one statement and disagreement with another.

- *Agreement with another commenter*
- *Disagreement with another commenter*
- *Adjunct opinion*: Contains a perspective that has not yet been articulated in the thread.

Audience   The target audience of a comment.

- *Reply to specific commenter*: Can be explicit (i.e., @HANDLE) or implicit (not directly naming the commenter). The target of a reply is not coded.
- *Broadcast message*: Is not directed to a specific person(s).

Persuasiveness   A binary label indicating whether a comment contains persuasive language or an intent to persuade.

- *Persuasive*
- *Not persuasive*

Sentiment   The overall sentiment of a comment, considering how the user feels with respect to what information they are trying to convey.

- *Negative*
- *Neutral*
- *Positive*
- *Mixed*: Contains both positive and negative sentiments.

Tone   These qualities describe the overall tone of a comment, and more than one can apply.

- *Controversial*: Puts forward a strong opinion that will most likely cause disagreement.
- *Funny*: Expresses or intends to express humor.
- *Informative*: Contributes new information to the discussion.
- *Mean*: The purpose of the comment is to be rude, mean, or hateful.
- *Sarcastic*: Uses sarcasm with either intent to humor (overlaps with *Funny*) or offend.
- *Sympathetic*: A warm, friendly comment that expresses positive emotion or sympathy.

Topic   The topic addressed in a comment, and more than one label can be chosen. Comments are on-topic unless either *Off-topic* label is selected.

- *Off-topic with the article*
- *Off-topic with the conversation*: A digression from the conversation.
- *Personal story*: Describes the user's personal experience with the topic.

4   Corpus collection

With the taxonomy described above, we coded comments from two separate domains: online news articles and debate forums.

Threads from online news articles   YNACC contains threads from the "comments section" of Yahoo News articles from April 2016.[2] Yahoo filters comments containing hate speech (Nobata et al., 2016) and abusive language using a combination of manual review and automatic algorithms, and these comments are not included in our corpus. From the remaining comments, we identified threads, which contain an initial comment and at least one comment posted in reply. Yahoo threads have a single-level of embedding, meaning that users can only post replies under a top-level comment. In total, we collected 521,608 comments in 137,620 threads on 4,714 articles on topics including finance, sports, entertainment, and lifestyle. We also collected the following metadata for each comment: unique user ID, time posted, headline, URL, category, and the number of *thumbs up* and *thumbs down* received. We included comments posted on a thread regardless of how much time had elapsed since the initial comment because the vast majority of comments were posted in close sequence: 48% in the first hour after an initial comment, 67% within the first three hours, and 92% within the first 24 hours.

We randomly selected 2,300 threads to annotate, oversampling longer threads since the aver-

---

[2]Excluding comments labeled *non-English* by LangID, a high-accuracy tool for identifying languages in multiple domains (Lui and Baldwin, 2012)

	IAC	Yahoo
# Threads	1,000	2,400
# Comments	16,555	9,160
Thread length	29 ± 55	4 ± 3
Comment length	568 ± 583	232 ± 538
Trained	0	1,400 threads
		9,160 comments
Untrained	1,000 threads	1,300 threads

Table 1: Description of the threads and comments annotated in this work and and the number coded by trained and untrained annotators. Thread length is in comments, comment length in characters.

age Yahoo thread has only 3.8 comments. The distribution of thread lengths is 20% with 2–4 comments, 60% 5–8, and 20% 9–15. For a held-out test set, we collected an additional 100 threads from Yahoo articles posted in July 2016, with the same length distribution. Those threads are not included in the analysis performed herein.

Threads from web debate forums To test this annotation scheme on a different domain, we also code online debates from the IAC 2.0 (Abbott et al., 2016). IAC threads are categorically different from Yahoo ones in terms of their stated purpose (debate on a particular topic) and length. The mean IAC thread has 29 comments and each comment has 102 tokens, compared to Yahoo threads which have 4 comments with 51 tokens each. Because significant attention is demanded to code the numerous attributes, we only consider IAC threads with 15 comments or fewer for annotation, but do not limit the comment length. In total, we selected 1,000 IAC thread to annotate, specifically: 474 threads from 4forums that were coded in the IAC, all 23 threads from CreateDebate, and 503 randomly selected threads from ConvinceMe.

4.1 Annotation

The corpus was coded by two groups of annotators: professional trained editors and untrained crowdsourced workers. Three separate annotators coded each thread. The trained editors were paid contractors who received two 30–45-minute training sessions, editorial guidelines (2,000-word document), and two sample annotated threads. The training sessions were recorded and available to the annotators during annotation, as were the guidelines. They could communicate their questions to the trainers, who were two authors of this paper, and receive feedback during the training and annotation phases.

Because training is expensive and time consuming, we also collected annotations from untrained coders on Amazon Mechanical Turk (AMT). To simplify the task for AMT, we only solicited thread-level labels, paying $0.75 per thread. For quality assurance, only workers located in the United States or Canada with a minimum HIT acceptance rate of 95% could participate, and the annotations were spot-checked by the authors. Trained annotators coded 1,300 Yahoo threads and the 100-thread test set on the comment- and thread-levels; untrained annotators coded thread-level labels of 1,300 Yahoo threads (300 of which overlapped with the trained annotations) and 1,000 IAC threads (Table 1). In total, 26 trained and 495 untrained annotators worked on this task.

4.2 Confidence

To assess the difficulty of the task, we also collected a rating for each thread from the trained annotators describing how confident they were with their judgments of each thread and the comments it comprises. Ratings were made on a 5-level Likert scale, with 1 being not at all confident and 5 fully confident. The levels of confidence were high (3.9 ± 0.7), indicating that coders were able to distinguish the thread and comment codes with relative ease.

4.3 Agreement levels

We measure inter-annotator agreement with Krippendorff's alpha (Krippendorff, 2004) and find that, over all labels, there are substantial levels of agreement within groups of annotators: $\alpha = 0.79$ for trained annotators and $\alpha = 0.71$ and 72 for untrained annotators on the Yahoo and IAC threads, respectively. However, there is lower agreement on thread labels than comment labels (Table 2). The agreement of *thread type* is 25% higher for the Yahoo threads than the IAC (0.62–0.64 compared to 0.48). The less subjective comment labels (i.e., agreement, audience, and topic) have higher agreement than persuasiveness, sentiment, and tone. While some of the labels have only moderate agreement ($0.5 < \alpha < 0.6$), we find these results satisfactory as the agreement levels are higher than those reported for similarly subjective discourse annotation tasks (e.g., Walker et al. (2012)).

To evaluate the untrained annotators, we compare the thread-level annotations made on 300 Yahoo threads by both trained and untrained coders,

| Thread label | Yahoo | | IAC |
	Trained	Untrained	Untrained
Agreement	0.52	0.50	0.53
Constructive	0.48	0.52	0.63
Type	0.62	0.64	0.48
Comment label			
Agreement	0.80	–	–
Audience	0.74	–	–
Persuasiveness	0.48	–	–
Sentiment	0.50	–	–
Tone	0.63	–	–
Topic	0.82	–	–

Table 2: Agreement levels found for each label category within trained and untrained groups of annotators, measured by Krippendorff's alpha.

Category	Label	Matches
Constructive class	–	0.61
Agreement	–	0.62
Thread type	*Overall*	0.81
	Argumentative	0.72
	Flamewar	0.80
	Off-topic	0.82
	Personal stories	0.94
	Respectful	0.81
	Snarky/humorous	0.85

Table 3: Percentage of threads (out of 300) for which the majority label of the trained annotators matched that of the untrained annotators.

by taking the majority label per item from each group of annotators and calculating the percent of exact matches (Table 3). When classifying the *thread type*, multiple labels are allowed for each thread, so we convert each option into a boolean and analyze them separately. Only 8% of the threads have no majority *constructive* label in the trained and/or untrained annotations, and 20% have no majority *agreement* label. Within both annotation groups, there are majority labels on all of the *thread type* labels. The category with the lowest agreement is *constructive class* with only 61% of the majority labels matching, followed closely by *agreement* (only 62% matching). A very high percent of the thread type labels (81%). The strong agreement levels between trained and untrained annotators suggest that crowdsourcing is reliable for coding thread-level characteristics.

5 Annotation analysis

To understand what makes a thread constructive, we explore the following research questions:

1. How does the overall thread categorization differ between ERICs and non-ERICs? (§5.1)
2. What types of comments make up ERICs compared to non-ERICs? (§5.2)
3. Are social signals related to whether a thread is an ERIC? (§5.3)

5.1 Thread-level annotations

Before examining what types of threads are ERICs, we first compare the threads coded by different sets of annotators (trained or untrained) and from different sources (IAC or Yahoo). We measure the significance of annotation group for each label with a test of equal proportions for binary categories (*constructiveness* and each *thread type*) and a chi-squared test of independence for the *agreement* label. Overall, annotations by the trained and untrained annotators on Yahoo threads are very similar, with significant differences only between some of the *thread type* labels (Figure 3). We posit that the discrepancies between the trained and untrained annotators is due to the former's training sessions and ability to communicate with the authors, which could have swayed annotators to make inferences into the coding scheme that were not overtly stated in the instructions.

The differences between Yahoo and IAC threads are more pronounced. The only label for which there is no significant difference is *personal stories* ($p = 0.41$, between the IAC and trained Yahoo labels). All other IAC labels are significantly different from both trained and untrained Yahoo labels ($p < 0.001$). ERICs are more prevalent in the IAC, with 70% of threads labeled *constructive*, compared to roughly half of Yahoo threads. On the whole, threads from the IAC are more concordant and positive than from Yahoo: they have more agreement and less disagreement, more than twice as many positive/respectful threads, and fewer than half the flamewars.

For Yahoo threads, there is no significant difference between trained and untrained coders for *constructiveness* ($p = 0.11$) and the *argumentative* thread type ($p = 0.07$; all other thread types are significant with $p < 10^{-5}$). There is no significant difference between the *agreement* labels, either ($p = 1.00$). Untrained coders are more likely than trained to classify threads using emotional labels like *snarky*, *flamewar*, and *positive/respectful*, while trained annotators more frequently recognize *off-topic* threads. These differences should be taken into consideration for evaluating the IAC codes, and for future efforts collecting subjective annotations through crowdsourcing.

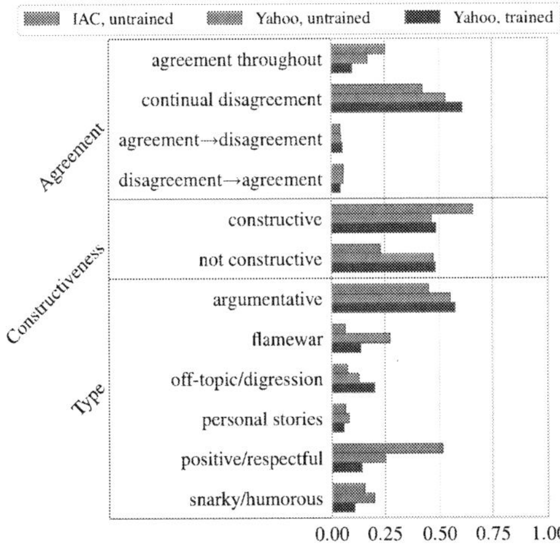

Figure 3: % threads assigned labels by annotator type (trained, untrained) and source (Yahoo, IAC).

We measure the strength of relationships between labels with the phi coefficient (Figure 4). There is a positive association between ERICs and all *agreement* labels in both Yahoo (trained) and IAC threads, which indicates that concord is not necessary for threads to be constructive. The example in Figure 1 is a *constructive* thread that is *argumentative* and contains *disagreement*. Thread types associated with non-ERICs are *flamewars*, *off-topic digressions*, and *snarky/humorous* exchanges, which is consistent across data sources. The labels from untrained annotators show a stronger correlation between *flamewars* and *not constructive* compared to the trained annotators, but the former also identified more *flamewars*. Some correlations are expected: across all annotating groups, there is a positive correlation between threads labeled with *agreement throughout* and *positive/respectful*, and *disagreement throughout* is correlated with *argumentative* (Figures 1 and 2) and, to a lesser degree, *flamewar*.

The greatest difference between the IAC and Yahoo are the *thread types* associated with ERICs. In the IAC, the *positive/respectful* label has a much stronger positive relationship with *constructive* than the trained Yahoo labels, but this could be due to the difference between trained and untrained coders. *Argumentative* has a positive correlation with *constructive* in the Yahoo threads, but a weak negative relationship is found in the IAC. In both domains, threads characterized as *off-topic*, *snarky*, or *flamewars* are more likely to be non-ERICs. Threads with some level of *agreement* characterized as *positive/respectful* are commonly ERICs. A two-tailed z-test shows a significant difference between the number of ERICs and non-ERICs in Yahoo articles in the Arts & Entertainment, Finance, and Lifestyle categories ($p < 0.005$; Figure 5).

5.2   Comment annotations

We next consider the codes assigned by trained annotators to Yahoo comments (Figure 6). The majority of comments are *not persuasive*, *reply to a previous comment*, express *disagreement*, or have *negative sentiment*. More than three times as many comments express disagreement than agreement, and comments are labeled *negative* seven times as frequently as *positive*. Approximately half of the comments express disagreement or a negative sentiment. Very few comments are *funny, positive, sympathetic*, or contain a *personal story* ($< 10\%$). Encouragingly, only 6% of comments are *off-topic with the conversation*, suggesting that participants are attuned to and respectful of the topic. Only 20% of comments are *informative*, indicating that participants infrequently introduce new information to complement the article or discussion.

The only strong correlations are between the binary labels, but the moderate correlations provide insight into the Yahoo threads (Figure 7). Some relationships accord with intuition. For instance, participants tend to go off-topic with the article when they are responding to others and not during broadcast messages; comments expressing disagreement with a commenter are frequently posted in a reply to a commenter; comments expressing agreement tend to be sympathetic and have positive sentiment; and mean comments correlate with negative sentiment. Commenters in this domain also express disagreement without particular nastiness, since there is no correlation between *disagreement* and *mean* or *sarcastic* comments. The *informative* label is moderately correlated with *persuasiveness*, suggesting that comments containing facts and new information are more convincing than those without.

The correlation between comment and thread labels is shown in Figure 7. Many of the relationships are unsurprising, like *off-topic* threads tend to have *off-topic* comments, *personal-story* threads have *personal-story* comments; thread agreement levels correlate with comment-level

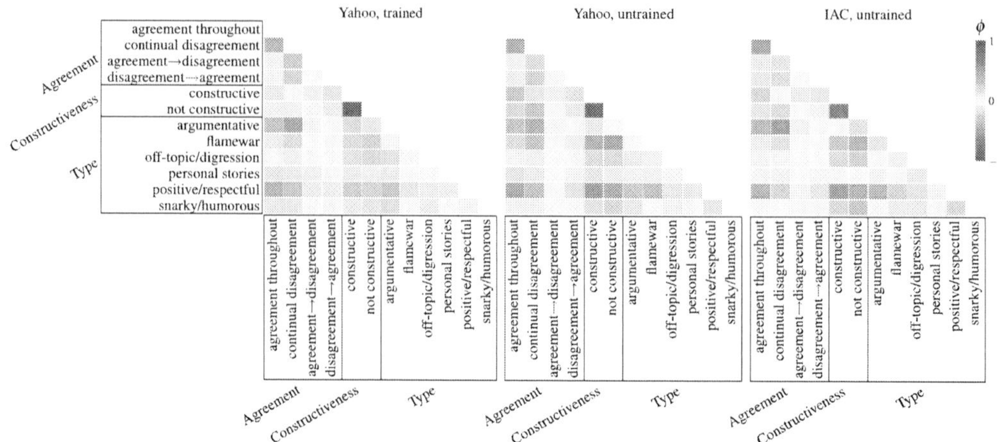

Figure 4: Correlation between thread labels, measured by the phi coefficient (ϕ).

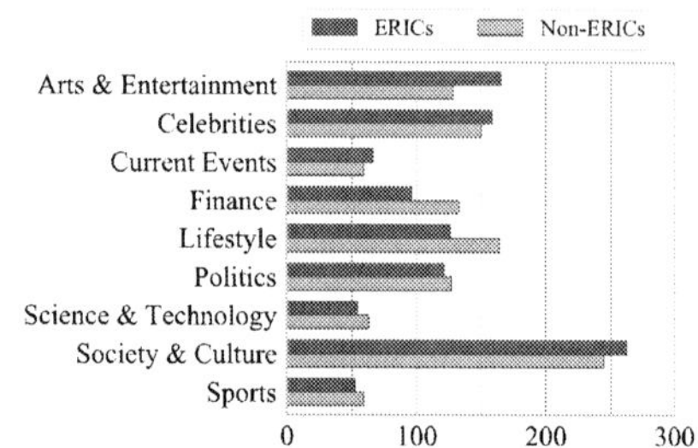

Figure 5: Number of threads by article category.

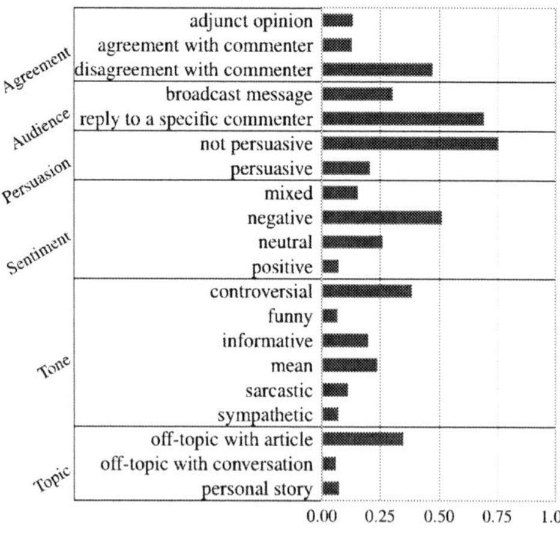

Figure 6: % Yahoo comments assigned each label.

agreements; and *flamewars* are correlated with *mean* comments.

In accord with our definition of ERICs, *constructiveness* is positively correlated with *informative* and *persuasive* comments and negatively correlated with *negative* and *mean* comments. From these correlations one can infer that *argumenta-*

tive threads are generally respectful because, while they are strongly correlated with comments that are *controversial* or express *disagreement* or a *mixed* sentiment, there is no correlation with *mean* and very little with *negative* sentiment. More surprising is the positive correlation between *controversial* comments and *constructive* threads. Controversial comments are more associated with ERICs, not non-ERICs, even though the *controversial* label also positively correlates with *flamewars*, which are negatively correlated with *constructiveness*. The examples in Figures 1–2 both have controversial comments expressing disagreement, but comments in the second half of the non-ERIC veer off-topic and are not persuasive, where the ERIC stays on-topic and persuasive.

5.3 The relationship with social signals

Previous work has taken social signals to be a proxy for thread quality, using some function of the total number of votes received by comments within a thread (e.g., Lee et al. (2014)). Because earlier research has indicated that user votes are not completely independent or objective (Sipos et al., 2014; Danescu-Niculescu-Mizil et al., 2009), we take the use of votes as a proxy for quality skeptically ad perform our own exploration of the relationship between social signals and the presence of ERICs. On Yahoo, users reacted to comments with a *thumbs up* or *thumbs down* and we collected the total number of such reactions for each comment in our corpus. First, we compare the total number of thumbs up (TU) and thumbs down (TD) received by comments in a

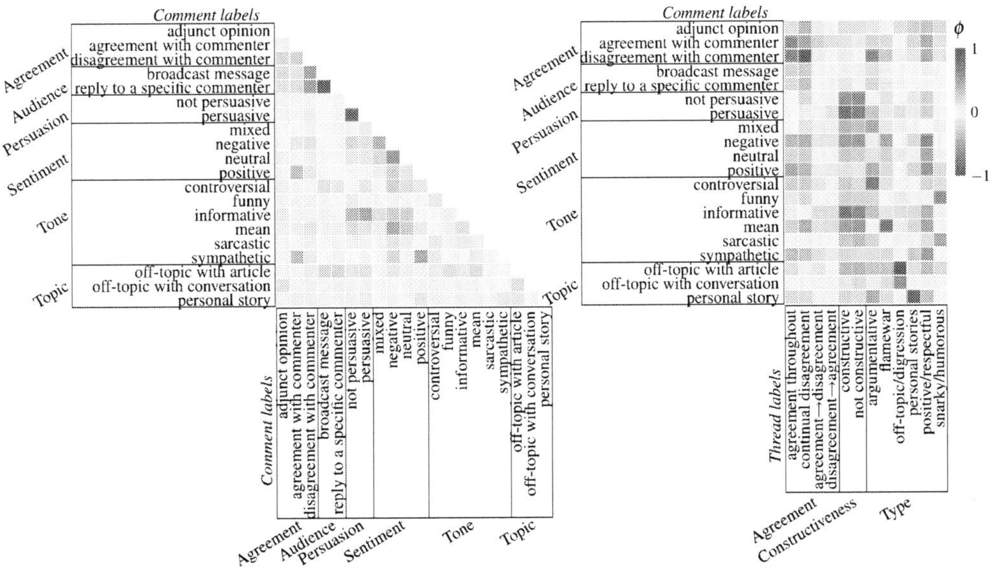

Figure 7: Correlation between comment labels (left) and comment labels and thread labels (right).

thread to the coded labels to determine whether there are any relationships between social signals and threads qualities. We calculate the relationship between labels in each category with TU and TD with Pearson's coefficient for the binary labels and a one-way ANOVA for the *agreement* category. The strongest correlation is between TD and untrained annotators' perception of *flamewars* ($r = 0.21$), and there is a very weak to no correlation (positive or negative) between the other labels and TU, TD, or TU$-$TD. There is moderate correlation between TU and TD ($r = 0.46$), suggesting that threads that elicit reactions tend to receive both thumbs up and down.

The correlation between TU and TD received by each comment is weaker ($r = 0.23$). Comparing the comment labels to the TU and TD received by each comment also show little correlation. Comments that reply to a specific commenter are negatively correlated with TU, TD, and TU$-$TD ($r = 0.30$, -0.25, and -0.22, respectively). The only other label with a non-negligible correlation is *disagreement with a commenter*, which negatively correlates with TU ($r = -0.21$). There is no correlation between social signal and the presence of ERICs or non-ERICs. These results support the findings of previous work and indicate that thumbs up or thumbs down alone (and, presumably, up/down votes) are inappropriate proxies for quality measurements of comments or threads

in this domain.

6 Conclusion

We have developed a coding scheme for labeling "good" online conversations (ERICs) and created the Yahoo News Annotated Comments Corpus, a new corpus of $2.4k$ coded comment threads posted in response to Yahoo News articles. Additionally, we have annotated $1k$ debate threads from the IAC. These annotations reflect several different characteristics of comments and threads, and we have explored their relationships with each other. ERICs are characterized by argumentative, respectful exchanges containing persuasive, informative, and/or sympathetic comments. They tend to stay on topic with the original article and not to contain funny, mean, or sarcastic comments. We found differences between the distribution of annotations made by trained and untrained annotators, but high levels of agreement within each group, suggesting that crowdsourcing annotations for this task is reliable. YNACC will be a valuable resource for researchers in multiple areas of discourse analysis.

Acknowledgments

We are grateful to Danielle Lottridge, Smaranda Muresan, and Amanda Stent for their valuable input. We also wish to thank the anonymous reviewers for their feedback.

References

Rob Abbott, Brian Ecker, Pranav Anand, and Marilyn Walker. 2016. Internet Argument Corpus 2.0: An SQL schema for dialogic social media and the corpora to go with it. In *Proceedings of the Tenth International Conference on Language Resources and Evaluation (LREC 2016)*, pages 4445–4452, Paris, France, May. European Language Resources Association (ELRA).

Jacob Andreas, Sara Rosenthal, and Kathleen McKeown. 2012. Annotating agreement and disagreement in threaded discussion. In *Proceedings of the Eight International Conference on Language Resources and Evaluation (LREC'12)*, pages 818–822, Istanbul, Turkey, May. European Language Resources Association (ELRA).

Emma Barker, Monica Lestari Paramita, Ahmet Aker, Emina Kurtic, Mark Hepple, and Robert Gaizauskas. 2016. The SENSEI annotated corpus: Human summaries of reader comment conversations in on-line news. In *Proceedings of the 17th Annual Meeting of the Special Interest Group on Discourse and Dialogue*, pages 42–52, Los Angeles, September. Association for Computational Linguistics.

Or Biran, Sara Rosenthal, Jacob Andreas, Kathleen McKeown, and Owen Rambow. 2012. Detecting influencers in written online conversations. In *Proceedings of the Second Workshop on Language in Social Media*, pages 37–45, Montréal, Canada, June. Association for Computational Linguistics.

Cristian Danescu-Niculescu-Mizil, Gueorgi Kossinets, Jon Kleinberg, and Lillian Lee. 2009. How opinions are received by online communities: A case study on amazon.com helpfulness votes. In *Proceedings of the 18th International Conference on World Wide Web*, WWW '09, pages 141–150, New York. ACM.

Cristian Danescu-Niculescu-Mizil, Moritz Sudhof, Dan Jurafsky, Jure Leskovec, and Christopher Potts. 2013. A computational approach to politeness with application to social factors. In *Proceedings of the 51st Annual Meeting of the Association for Computational Linguistics (Volume 1: Long Papers)*, pages 250–259, Sofia, Bulgaria, August. Association for Computational Linguistics.

Dmitry Davidov, Oren Tsur, and Ari Rappoport. 2010. Semi-supervised recognition of sarcasm in Twitter and Amazon. In *Proceedings of the Fourteenth Conference on Computational Natural Language Learning*, pages 107–116, Uppsala, Sweden, July. Association for Computational Linguistics.

Nicholas Diakopoulos and Mor Naaman. 2011. Towards quality discourse in online news comments. In *Proceedings of the ACM 2011 Conference on Computer Supported Cooperative Work*, CSCW '11, pages 133–142, New York. ACM.

Nicholas Diakopoulos. 2015. Picking the NYT picks: Editorial criteria and automation in the curation of online news comments. *ISOJ Journal*, 5(1):147–166.

Ethan Fast and Eric Horvitz. 2016. Identifying dogmatism in social media: Signals and models. In *Proceedings of the 2016 Conference on Empirical Methods in Natural Language Processing*, pages 690–699, Austin, Texas, November. Association for Computational Linguistics.

Debanjan Ghosh, Smaranda Muresan, Nina Wacholder, Mark Aakhus, and Matthew Mitsui. 2014. Analyzing argumentative discourse units in online interactions. In *Proceedings of the First Workshop on Argumentation Mining*, pages 39–48, Baltimore, Maryland, June. Association for Computational Linguistics.

Roberto González-Ibánez, Smaranda Muresan, and Nina Wacholder. 2011. Identifying sarcasm in Twitter: A closer look. In *Proceedings of the 49th Annual Meeting of the Association for Computational Linguistics: Human Language Technologies: Short Papers-Volume 2*, pages 581–586. Association for Computational Linguistics.

Ivan Habernal and Iryna Gurevych. 2016. Which argument is more convincing? Analyzing and predicting convincingness of web arguments using bidirectional LSTM. In *Proceedings of the 54th Annual Meeting of the Association for Computational Linguistics (Volume 1: Long Papers)*, pages 1589–1599, Berlin, Germany, August. Association for Computational Linguistics.

Ahmed Hassan, Vahed Qazvinian, and Dragomir Radev. 2010. What's with the attitude? Identifying sentences with attitude in online discussions. In *Proceedings of the 2010 Conference on Empirical Methods in Natural Language Processing*, pages 1245–1255, Cambridge, MA, October. Association for Computational Linguistics.

Hyeju Jang, Mario Piergallini, Miaomiao Wen, and Carolyn Rose. 2014. Conversational metaphors in use: Exploring the contrast between technical and everyday notions of metaphor. In *Proceedings of the Second Workshop on Metaphor in NLP*, pages 1–10, Baltimore, MD, June. Association for Computational Linguistics.

Klaus Krippendorff. 2004. *Content analysis: An introduction to its methodology*. Sage Publications, Thousand Oaks, CA, 2nd edition.

Jung-Tae Lee, Min-Chul Yang, and Hae-Chang Rim. 2014. Discovering high-quality threaded discussions in online forums. *Journal of Computer Science and Technology*, 29(3):519–531.

Macmillan Publishers Ltd. 2009. The online English dictionary: Definition of constructive. `http://www.macmillandictionary.com/dictionary/american/constructive`. Accessed January 20, 2017.

Marco Lui and Timothy Baldwin. 2012. langid.py: An off-the-shelf language identification tool. In *Proceedings of the ACL 2012 System Demonstrations*, pages 25–30, Jeju Island, Korea, July. Association for Computational Linguistics.

Arjun Mukherjee, Vivek Venkataraman, Bing Liu, and Sharon Meraz. 2013. Public dialogue: Analysis of tolerance in online discussions. In *Proceedings of the 51st Annual Meeting of the Association for Computational Linguistics (Volume 1: Long Papers)*, pages 1680–1690, Sofia, Bulgaria, August. Association for Computational Linguistics.

Vlad Niculae and Cristian Danescu-Niculescu-Mizil. 2016. Conversational markers of constructive discussions. In *Proceedings of the 2016 Conference of the North American Chapter of the Association for Computational Linguistics: Human Language Technologies*, pages 568–578, San Diego, California, June. Association for Computational Linguistics.

Chikashi Nobata, Joel Tetreault, Achint Thomas, Yashar Mehdad, and Yi Chang. 2016. Abusive language detection in online user content. In *Proceedings of the 25th International Conference on World Wide Web*, pages 145–153. International World Wide Web Conferences Steering Committee.

Shereen Oraby, Vrindavan Harrison, Lena Reed, Ernesto Hernandez, Ellen Riloff, and Marilyn Walker. 2016. Creating and characterizing a diverse corpus of sarcasm in dialogue. In *Proceedings of the 17th Annual Meeting of the Special Interest Group on Discourse and Dialogue*, pages 31–41, Los Angeles, September. Association for Computational Linguistics.

Bo Pang and Lillian Lee. 2005. Seeing stars: Exploiting class relationships for sentiment categorization with respect to rating scales. In *Proceedings of the 43rd annual meeting on association for computational linguistics*, pages 115–124. Association for Computational Linguistics.

Ruben Sipos, Arpita Ghosh, and Thorsten Joachims. 2014. Was this review helpful to you?: It depends! Context and voting patterns in online content. In *Proceedings of the 23rd International Conference on World Wide Web*, pages 337–348. ACM.

Maria Skeppstedt, Magnus Kerren, Carita Sahlgren, and Andreas Paradis. 2016. Unshared task: (Dis)agreement in online debates. In *3rd Workshop on Argument Mining (ArgMining'16), Berlin, Germany, August 7-12, 2016*, pages 154–159. Association for Computational Linguistics.

Chenhao Tan, Vlad Niculae, Cristian Danescu-Niculescu-Mizil, and Lillian Lee. 2016. Winning arguments: Interaction dynamics and persuasion strategies in good-faith online discussions. In *Proceedings of the 25th International Conference on World Wide Web*, pages 613–624. International World Wide Web Conferences Steering Committee.

Marilyn Walker, Jean Fox Tree, Pranav Anand, Rob Abbott, and Joseph King. 2012. A corpus for research on deliberation and debate. In *Proceedings of the Eight International Conference on Language Resources and Evaluation (LREC'12)*, Istanbul, Turkey, May. European Language Resources Association (ELRA).

Charlie Warzel. 2012. Everything in moderation. *Adweek*, June 18. http://www.adweek.com/digital/everything-moderation-141163/. Accessed February 20, 2017.

Zhongyu Wei, Yang Liu, and Yi Li. 2016. Is this post persuasive? Ranking argumentative comments in online forum. In *Proceedings of the 54th Annual Meeting of the Association for Computational Linguistics (Volume 2: Short Papers)*, pages 195–200, Berlin, Germany, August. Association for Computational Linguistics.

Crowdsourcing discourse interpretations: On the influence of context and the reliability of a connective insertion task

Merel C.J. Scholman
Language Science and Technology
Saarland University
Saarbrücken, Germany

Vera Demberg
Computer Science
Saarland University
Saarbrücken, Germany

{m.c.j.scholman,vera}@coli.uni-saarland.de

Abstract

Traditional discourse annotation tasks are considered costly and time-consuming, and the reliability and validity of these tasks is in question. In this paper, we investigate whether crowdsourcing can be used to obtain reliable discourse relation annotations. We also examine the influence of context on the reliability of the data. The results of the crowdsourced connective insertion task showed that the majority of the inserted connectives converged with the original label. Further, the distribution of inserted connectives revealed that multiple senses can often be inferred for a single relation. Regarding the presence of context, the results show no significant difference in distributions of insertions between conditions overall. However, a by-item comparison revealed several characteristics of segments that determine whether the presence of context makes a difference in annotations. The findings discussed in this paper can be taken as preliminary evidence that crowdsourcing can be used as a valuable method to obtain insights into the sense(s) of relations.

1 Introduction

In order to study discourse coherence, researchers need large amounts of discourse-annotated data, and these data need to be reliable and valid. However, manually coding coherence relations is a difficult task that is prone to individual variation (Spooren and Degand, 2010). Because the task requires a large amount of time and resources, researchers try to find a balance between obtaining reliable data and sparing resources. This has led to the standard practice of using two trained, expert annotators to code data.

Not only is this procedure time-consuming and therefore costly, it also raises questions regarding the reliability and validity of the data. When using trained, expert annotators, they may agree because they share implicit knowledge and know the purpose of the research well, rather than because they are carefully following instructions (Artstein and Poesio, 2008; Riezler, 2014). Krippendorff (2004) therefore notes that the more annotators participate in the process and the less expert they are, the more likely they can ensure the reliability of the data.

In this paper, we investigate how useful crowdsourcing can be in obtaining discourse annotations. We present an experiment in which subjects were asked to insert ("drag and drop") a connecting phrase from a pre-defined list between the two segments of coherence relations. By employing non-trained, non-expert (also referred as naïve) subjects to code the data, large amounts of data can be coded in a short period of time, and it is ensured that the obtained annotations are independent and do not rely on implicit expert knowledge. Instead, the task allows us to tap into the naïve subjects' interpretations directly.

However, crowdsourcing has rarely been used to obtain discourse relation annotations. This could be due to the nature of crowdsourcing: Typically, crowdsourced tasks are small and intuitive tasks. Under these conditions, crowdsourced annotators – unlike expert annotators or in-lab naïve annotators – cannot be asked to code according to a specific framework because this would require them to study manuals. Therefore, rather than asking for relation labels, we ask them to insert a connective from a predefined list. In order to ensure that these connectives are not ambiguous (Asr and Demberg, 2013), we chose connectives based

Proceedings of the 11th Linguistic Annotation Workshop, pages 24–33,
Valencia, Spain, April 3, 2017. ©2017 Association for Computational Linguistics

on a classification of connective substitutability by Knott and Dale (1994). We investigate how reliable the obtained annotations are by comparing them to expert annotations from two existing corpora.

Moreover, we examine the effect of the design of the task on the reliability of the data. Researchers agree that discourse relations should be supplied with linguistic context in order to be annotated reliably but there are no clear guidelines for how much context is needed. The current contribution experimentally examines the influence of context on the interpretation of a discourse relation, with a specific focus on whether there is an interaction between characteristics of the segment and the presence of context.

The contributions of this paper include the following:

- We evaluate a new crowdsourcing method to elicit discourse interpretations and obtain discourse annotations, showing that such a task has the potential to function as a reliable alternative to traditional annotation methods.

- The distributions of inserted connectives per item reveal that, often, annotators converged on two or three dominant interpretations, rather than one single interpretation. We also found that this distribution is replicable with high reliability. This is evidence that relations can have multiple senses.

- We show that the presence of context led to higher annotator agreement when (i) the first segment of a relation refers to an entity or event in the context, or introduces important background information; (ii) the first segment consists of a deranked subordinate clause attaching to the context; or (iii) the context sentence following the relation expands on the second argument of the relation. This knowledge can be used in the design of discourse relation annotation tasks.

2 Background

In recent years, several researchers have set out to investigate whether naïve coders can also be employed to annotate data. Working with such annotators has the practical advantage that they are easier to come by, and it is therefore also easier to employ a larger number of annotators, which decreases the effect of annotator bias (Artstein and Poesio, 2005; Artstein and Poesio, 2008). Studies employing naïve annotators have found high agreement between these annotators and expert annotators for Natural Language tasks (e.g., Snow et al., 2008). Classifying coherence relations, however, is considered to be a different and especially difficult type of task due to the complex semantic interpretations of relations and the fact that textual coherence does not reside in the verbal material, but rather in the readers' mental representation (Spooren and Degand, 2010). Nevertheless, naïve annotators have recently also been employed successfully in coherence relation annotation tasks (Kawahara et al., 2014; Scholman et al., 2016) and connective insertion tasks (Rohde et al., 2015, 2016) similar to the one reported in this paper.

Rohde et al. (2016) showed that readers can infer an additional reading for a discourse relation connected by an adverbial. By obtaining many observations for a single fragment rather than only two, they were able to identify patterns of co-occurring relations; for example, readers can often infer an additional causal reading for a relation marked by *otherwise*. These results highlight a problem with double-coded data: Without a substantial number of observations, differences in annotations might be written off as annotator error or disagreement. In reality, there might be multiple interpretations for a relation, without there being a single correct interpretation. The connective insertion method used by Rohde et al. (2016) is therefore more sensitive to the possibility that relations can have multiple readings.

The current study uses a similar method as Rohde et al. (2016), but applies it to answer a different type of question. Rohde et al. (2016) investigated whether readers can infer an additional sense for a pair of sentences already marked by an adverbial. They did not have any expectations on whether there was a correct answer; rather, they set out to identify specific patters of connective insertions. In the current study, we investigate whether crowdsourcing can be used to obtain annotated data that is similar in quality to data annotated by experts. Crucially, we assume that there is a correct answer, namely the original label that was assigned by expert annotators. We therefore will compare the results from the current study to the original annotations in order to evaluate the usability of the connective insertion method for discourse annotation.

The design of the current study also differs from other connective-based annotation approaches such as Rohde et al. (2016) and the Penn Discourse Treebank (PDTB, Prasad et al., 2008) in that the connectives were selected to unambiguously mark a specific type of relation. Certain connectives are known to mark different types of relations, such as *but*, which can mark CONTRAST, CONCESSION and ALTERNATIVE relations. In the current study, we excluded such ambiguous connectives in order to be able to derive relation types from the insertions. For example, the connecting phrase AS AN ILLUSTRATION is taken to be a dominant marker for INSTANTIATION relations. The procedure for selecting phrases will be explained in Section 3.

Given the limited amount of research into using naïve subjects for discourse relation annotation, it is important to investigate how this task should be designed. One aspect of this design is the inclusion of context. The benefits of context are widely acknowledged in the field of discourse analysis. Context is necessary to ground the discourse being constructed (Cornish, 2009), and the interpretation of any sentence other than the first in a discourse is therefore constrained by the preceding context (Song, 2010). This preceding context has significant effects on essential parts of discourse annotation, such as determining the rhetorical role each sentence plays in the discourse, and the temporal relations between the events described (Lascarides et al., 1992; Spooren and Degand, 2010). The knowledge of context is therefore assumed to be a requirement for discourse analysis.

Although researchers agree that relations should be supplied with linguistic context in order to be annotated reliably, there are no clear guidelines for how much context is needed. As a result, studies have diverged in their methodology. For some annotation experiments, coders annotate the entire text (e.g., Rehbein et al., 2016; Zufferey et al., 2012). In these cases, they automatically take the context of the relation at hand into account when they annotate a text linearly. By contrast, in experiments where the entire text does not have to be annotated, or the task is split into smaller tasks for crowdsourcing purposes, the relations (or connectives) are often presented with a certain amount of context preceding and following the segments under investigation (e.g., Hoek and Zufferey, 2015; Scholman et al., 2016).

Knowing how much context is minimally needed to be able to reliably annotate data will save resources; after all, the less context annotators have to read, the less time they need to spend on the task. The goal of the current experiment is therefore to test the reliability of crowdsourced discourse annotations compared to original corpus annotations, as well as the effect of context on the reliability of the task.

3 Method

Participants were asked to insert connectives into coherence relations. The items were divided into several batches. Each batch contained items with context or without context, but these two types were not mixed.

3.1 Participants

167 native English speakers completed one or more batches of this experiment. They were recruited via Prolific Academic and reimbursed for their participation (2 GBP per batch with context; 1.5 GBP per batch without context). Their education level ranged between an undergraduate degree and a doctorate degree.

3.2 Materials

The experimental passages consisted of 192 implicit and 42 explicit relations from Wall Street Journal texts. These relations are part of both the Penn Discourse Treebank (PDTB, Prasad et al., 2008) and the Rhetorical Structure Theory Discourse Treebank (RST-DT, Carlson et al., 2003), and therefore carry labels that were assigned by the respective expert annotators at the time of the creation of the corpora. The following types of relations were included: 24 CAUSE, 24 CONJUNCTION (additive), 36 CONCESSION, 36 CONTRAST, 54 INSTANTIATION and 60 SPECIFICATION relations. For the first four relation types, the PDTB and RST-DT annotators were in agreement on the label. The latter two types were chosen to accommodate a related experiment, and for most of these, the PDTB and RST-DT annotators were not in agreement. Lower agreement on these relations is therefore also expected in the current experiment.

The 234 items were divided into 12 batches, with 2 CAUSE, 2 CONJUNCTION, 3 CONCESSION, 3 CONTRAST, 4 or 5 INSTANTIATION and

5 SPECIFICATION items per batch. Order of presentation of the items per batch was randomized to prevent order effects. Subjects were allowed to complete more than one batch, but saw every item only once. Average completion time per batch was 16 minutes with context and 12 minutes without context. Due to presentation errors in one CONJUNCTION, two CAUSE, and two CONCESSION items, the final dataset for analysis consists of 229 items.

Connecting phrases – Subjects were presented with a list of connectives and asked to insert the connective that best expresses the relation holding between the textual spans. The connectives were chosen to distinguish between different relation types as unambiguously as possible, based on an investigation on connective substitutability by Knott and Dale (1994). The list of connecting phrases consisted of: *because, as a result, in addition, even though, nevertheless, by contrast, as an illustration* and *more specifically*.

3.3 Procedure

The experiment was hosted on LingoTurk (Pusse et al., 2016). Participants were presented with a box with predefined connectives followed by the text passage. In the context condition, the passage consisted of black and grey sentences. The black sentences were the two arguments of the coherence relation, and the grey sentences functioned as context (two sentences preceding and one following the relation). Subjects were instructed to choose the connecting phrase that best reflected the meaning between the black text elements, but to take the grey text into account. In the no-context condition, the grey sentences were not presented or mentioned.

Punctuation markers following the first argument of the relation were replaced by a double slash (//, cf. Rohde et al., 2015) to avoid participants from being influenced by the original punctuation markers.

In between the two arguments of the coherence relation was a box. Participants were instructed to "drag and drop" the connecting phrase that "best reflected the meaning of the connection between the arguments" (cf. Rohde et al., 2015) into this green box. Participants could also choose two connecting phrases using the option "add another connective". Moreover, they could manually insert a connecting phrase by clicking "none of these".

Participants were allowed to complete more than one batch, but they were never able to complete the same batch in both conditions.

4 Results

Prior to analysis, 5 participants from the context condition and 4 participants from the no-context condition were removed from the analysis because they had very short completion times ($<$10 minutes for 20 passages of 5 sentences each; $<$5 minutes for 20 passages of 2 sentences each) and showed high disagreement compared to other participants. The following analyses do not take the responses of these participants into consideration. In total, each list was completed by 12 to 14 participants.

As with any discourse annotation task, some variation in the distribution of insertions can be expected. We are therefore interested in larger shifts in the distribution of insertions. To evaluate these distributions, we report percentages of agreement (cf. De Kuthy et al., 2016). Typically, annotation tasks are evaluated using Cohen's or Fleiss' Kappa (Cohen, 1960; Fleiss, 1971). However, Kappa is not suitable for the current task because it assumes that all coders annotate all fragments.

Participants were given the option of inserting two connecting phrases if they thought that both phrases reflected the meaning of the relation. 3.4% of all answers consisted of two connecting phrases. For most items that received a double insertion, only one answer consisted of a double insertion. The data on multiple insertions therefore does not allow us to draw any strong conclusions. This will be elaborated on in the discussion.

2% of all insertions were manual answers. There was no clear pattern in these manual answers: Only a few items received manual answers, and these items usually received at most two manual answers. An additional 1% of the data consisted of 'blank insertions': Subjects used the 'manual answer' option to not insert anything. As with the manual answers, there was no clear pattern. We aggregate the class 'manual answer' and 'no answer' for our analyses.

We also aggregated frequencies of the connectives that fell into the same class: *because* and *as a result* were aggregated as causal connectives, and *even though* and *nevertheless* were aggregated as concessive connectives.

In the next section, we first show evidence that

the method is reliable. We then turn to the reliability of the no-context condition in comparison to the context condition to be able to determine whether the presence of context led to higher agreement on the sense(s) of items. Finally, we look at the entropy per item and per condition.

4.1 Overall reliability

The results showed that the method is successful: The connectives inserted by the participants are consistent with the original annotation. This is shown in Figure 1a, with the bars reflecting the inserted connective per original class and condition. Figure 1b shows this distribution in more detail by displaying the percentage of inserted connectives per item for the context condition. The distribution for the no-context condition is not included since it is almost identical to the distribution of the context condition. Every stacked bar on the x-axis represents an item; the colours on the bars represent the inserted connective.

These visualizations reveal several trends. First, for CAUSE and CONCESSION relations, the insertions often converge with the original label. 78% of the inserted connectives in items with a causal original label were causal connectives, and 67% of the inserted connectives in concessive items were concessive connectives. For both classes, the second most frequent category of inserted connectives was the other class: For CAUSE, the second most frequent category was CONCESSION (10%), and for CONCESSION, the second most frequent category was CAUSE (15%). On closer inspection of the items, we find that the disagreement between crowdsourced annotations and original annotations can be traced back to difficulties with specific items, and not to unreliability of the workers: The main cause for the confusion of causal and concessive relations can be attributed to the lack of context and/or background knowledge, especially for items with economic topics. For these topics, it can be very hard to judge whether a situation mentioned in one segment is a consequence of the other segment, or a denied expectation.

The second pattern that Figure 1a reveals concerns the classes CONJUNCTION and CONTRAST. The distribution of inserted connectives for these classes look similar: The expected marker is used most often (40% and 44%, respectively), with the corresponding causal relation as the second most frequent inserted connective type (27% causal insertions and 32% concessive insertions, respectively). A closer look at the annotations for items in these classes reveals that this is due to genuine ambiguity of the relation. For relations originally annotated as additive, we find that oftentimes a causal relation can also be inferred. The same explanation holds for CONTRAST relations: Relations from this class that often receive concessive insertions are characterized by the reference to contrasting expectations. Some confusion between these relations is expected, as it is known that concessive and contrastive relations are relatively difficult to distinguish even for trained annotators (see, for example, Robaldo and Miltsakaki, 2014; Zufferey and Degand, 2013).

Finally, looking at INSTANTIATION and SPECIFICATION relations, we can see that there is more variety in terms of which connective participants inserted. This was expected, as these relations were chosen because original PDTB and RST annotators did not agree on them.

Looking at the no-context condition in Figure 1a, we find a near-perfect replication of the insertions in the context condition. This is further evidence for the reliability of the task. On average, the difference between the conditions on agreement with the original label differed only by 3.7%. Fisher exact tests showed no significant difference in the distribution of responses between conditions for any of the original classes (*Cause*: $p = .61$; *Conjunction*: $p = .62$; *Concession*: $p = .98$; *Contrast*: $p = .88$; *Instantiation*: $p = .93$; *Specification*: $p = .85$).

Another notable pattern, shown in Figure 1b, is that items often did not receive only one type of inserted connective; rather, they received multiple types of insertions. For INSTANTIATION and SPECIFICATION items, for example, participants often converged on two senses: Both the originally annotated sense, as well as a causal reading. This indicates that multiple interpretations are possible for a single relation.

Another way to analyse the data is to assign to each relation the label corresponding to the connective that was inserted most frequently by our participants (in Figure 1b, this corresponds to the largest bar per item). We can then calculate agreement between the dominant response per item and the original label. These results are reported in Table 1.

Table 1 shows that the dominant response con-

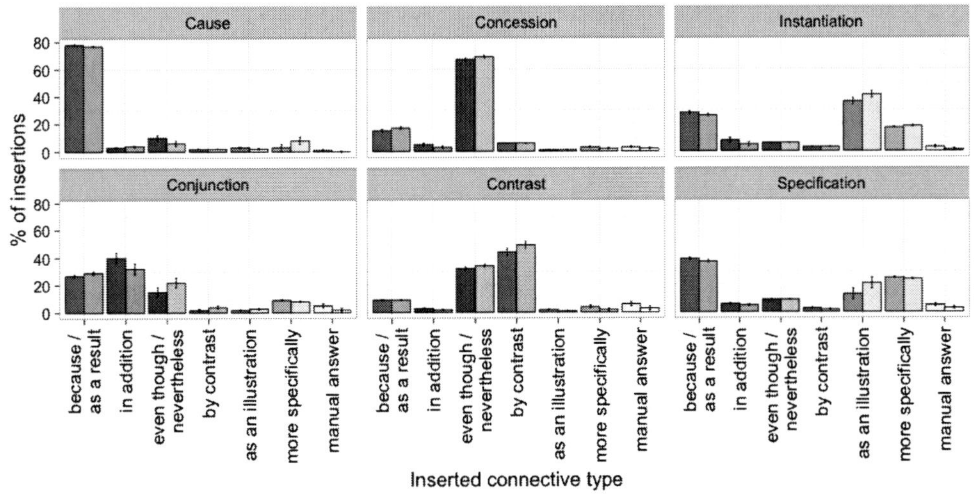

(a) Distributions (%) of inserted connectives per original class. For every type of insertion, darker colours represent the context condition and lighter colours represent the no-context condition.

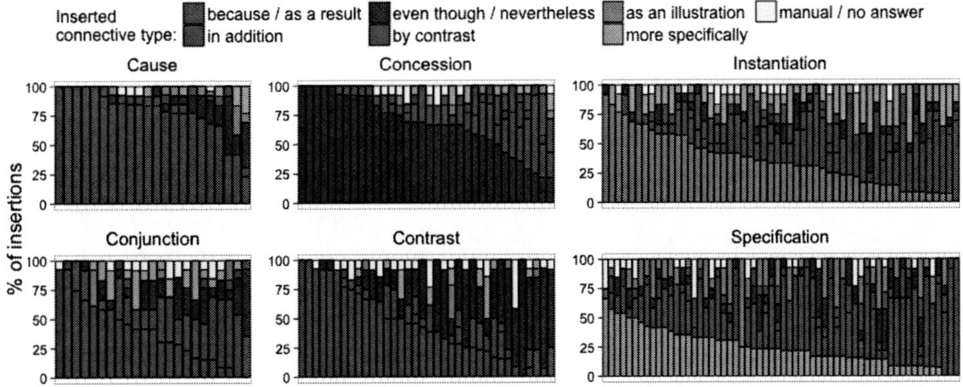

(b) By-item distributions (%) for the context condition. Every bar represents a single item; the colours on the bars represent the inserted connective. Plots are arranged according to the amount of dominant insertions corresponding to the original label.

Figure 1: Distributions (%) of inserted connectives per original class.

Original class	Context	No context
CAUSE	91	95
CONJUNCTION	52	35
CONCESSION	85	79
CONTRAST	53	58
INSTANTIATION	54	46
SPECIFICATION	25	20

Table 1: Percentage agreement between the original label and the dominant response per condition.

verges with the original label often for CAUSE and CONCESSION relations and a majority of the time for CONJUNCTION (in the context condition), CONTRAST and INSTANTIATION relations (in the context condition). The dominant response for SPECIFICATION items hardly converges with their original classification. This is as expected, as PDTB and RST-DT annotators also showed little agreement on SPECIFICATION relations.

Looking at the effect of context, we see that agreement between the dominant response and the original label is slightly higher when context is present for four of six types of relations (CONCESSION, INSTANTIATION and SPECIFICATION relations). For CONJUNCTION relations, the agreement is even 17% higher in the context condition compared to the no-context condition. These results suggest that presence of context does have an influence on the subjects' interpretations of the relations. In the next sections, we will look at the distribution of individual items in more detail.

4.2 Effect of context: Dominant response per item

For 9% of the items, the dominant response shifts from one category to another depending on the presence of context. Manual inspection of these items revealed several characteristics that they have in common. First, it was found that often the topic is introduced in the context, and the (lack of) knowledge of the topic influenced the subject's interpretation of the relation. This is illustrated using the following CONJUNCTION example:

(1)   Quite the contrary – it results from years of work by members of the National Council on the Handicapped, all appointed by President Reagan. You depict the bill as something Democratic leaders "hoodwinked" the administration into endorsing.
Arg1: The opposite is true: It's the product of many meetings with administration officials, Senate staffers, advocates, and business and transportation officials //
Arg2: many congressmen are citing the compromise on the Americans With Disabilities Act of 1989 as a model for bipartisan deliberations.
Most National Council members are themselves disabled or are parents of children with disabilities.   wsj_694

In Example 1, the context introduces the topic. The first argument (Arg1) then presents one argument for the claim that the bill results from years of hard work (as mentioned in the context), and the second argument (Arg2) is another argument for this claim. However, without the context, Arg2 can be taken as a result of Arg1. While this interpretation might be true, it does not seem to be the intended purpose of the relation. In the context condition, subjects interpreted the relation as a CONJUNCTION relation (58% of insertions were *in addition*. In the no-context condition, however, the dominant response was causal (58% of insertions), and the conjunctive *in addition* only accounted for 17% of all insertions.

Another common characteristic in items for which the presence or absence of context changes the dominant response, is that the context sentence following the relation expands on Arg2, thereby changing the probability distribution of that relation. This is common in INSTANTIATION and SPECIFICATION relations, where the second argument provides an example or specification of Arg1. Often, the sentence following Arg2 also provides an example or further specification, which emphasizes the INSTANTIATION/SPECIFICATION sense of the relation between Arg1 and Arg2. However, in relations for which Arg2 can also be seen as evidence for Arg1, the following context sentence can also function to emphasize the causal sense of the relation by expanding on the argument in Arg2. Consider Example 2, taken from the class SPECIFICATION.

(2)   Like Lebanon, and however unfairly, Israel is regarded by the Arab world as a colonial aberration. Its best hope of acceptance by its neighbours lies in reaching a settlement with the Palestinians.
Arg1: Like Lebanon, Israel is being remade by demography //
Arg2: in Greater Israel more than half the children under six are Muslims.
Within 25 years Jews will probably be the minority.   wsj_1141

In this example, the context sentence following Arg2 expands on Arg2. Together, they convey the information that although Jews are the majority now, within 25 years Muslims will be the majority. Without the context, one could imagine that the text would go on to list more instances of how the demography is changing. Subjects in the no-context condition indeed seem to have interpreted it this way: 75% of the inserted connective phrases were *as an illustration*, and the remaining insertions were *even though* and *because*. By contrast, in the context condition subjects mainly interpreted a causal relation (64% of insertions), together with the specification sense (17%). The marker *as an illustration* only accounted for 7% of completions. Hence, with context present subjects interpreted Arg2 as providing evidence for Arg1, but without context it was interpreted as an INSTANTIATION relation.

4.3 Effect of context: Entropy per item

Another way of analyzing the influence of the presence of context on the participants' response, is to look at the entropy of the distribution of insertions. In the context of the current study, entropy is defined as a measure of the consistency of connective insertions. When the majority of insertions for a certain item are the same, the entropy will be low, but when a certain item receives many different types of insertions, the entropy will be high.

For every item, we calculated Shannon's entropy. We then compared the conditions to determine whether entropy of an item increased or decreased depending on the presence of the context. Here we discuss items that have a difference of at least 1 bit of entropy between the conditions. This set consists of 18 items. Interestingly, presence of context only leads to lower entropy (higher agreement) in 10 items. For the other 8 items, subjects showed more agreement when the context was not presented.

When context is beneficial An analysis of items for which presence of context led to higher agreement has revealed two common characteristics. First, similar to what we found in the previous section, presence of context is helpful when the context introduces important background information, or when the first argument refers to an entity or event in the context.

Second, we observed that agreement was higher in the context condition when Arg1 consists of a subordinate clause that attaches to another clause in the context. In these cases, the dependancy of Arg1 to the context possibly hinders a correct interpretation of Arg1. Consider the following SPECIFICATION relation:

(3) The spun-off concern "clearly will be one of the dominant real estate development companies with a prime portfolio," he said. For the last year, Santa Fe Pacific has redirected its real estate operations toward longer-term development of its properties, **Arg1:** hurting profits that the parent had generated in the past from periodic sales from its portfolio //
Arg2: real estate operating income for the first nine months fell to $71.9 million from $143 million a year earlier.
In a statement late yesterday, Santa Fe Pacific's chairman, Robert D. Krebs, said that Santa Fe Pacific Realty would re-

pay more than $500 million in debt owed to the parent before the planned spinoff. wsj_1330

In this example, Arg1 is a deranked subordinate clause, which cannot be used as an independent clause. All subjects in the context condition inserted a causal connective. However, in the no-context condition only 58% inserted a causal connective, and 33% of inserted connectives were *in addition*. Hence, the dominant response remained the same, but the amount of agreement decreased when the context was absent.

When context is disadvantageous Of the 8 items for which absence of context led to more agreement, 7 had a common characteristic: The relation between the context and Arg1 is not strong, for example because Arg1 is also the start of a new paragraph, or because there is a topic change. It is likely that in these cases, the presence of context took the focus away from the relation.

5 Discussion

The annotations obtained using the connective insertion task have the potential to better reflect the average readers' interpretations because the naïve annotators don't rely on implicit expert knowledge. Moreover, it is easier, more affordable and faster to obtain many annotations for the same item via crowdsourcing than via traditional annotation methods. Collecting a large number of annotations for the same item furthermore reveals a probability distribution over relation senses. This can give researchers more insight into the readings of ambiguous relations, and into how dominant each sense is for a specific relation.

The procedures of traditional annotation methods often lead to implicit annotation biases that are implemented to achieve inter-annotator agreement (see, for example, Rehbein et al., 2016). However, annotations that contain biases are less useful from a linguistic or machine learning perspective, as relevant information about a second or third interpretation is obscured. Asking a single, trained annotator to annotate several senses also does not solve this issue: The annotations would still depend on expert knowledge and the annotation process would take more time. In this paper, we have shown that crowdsourcing can be a solution.

However, it should be noted that the design of the experiment was somewhat simplified compared to traditional annotation tasks, largely due to two factors. First, all items were known to be related to one of the six senses under investigation, that is, participants were not presented with items that did not actually contain a relation (similar to PDTB's NOREL), or that belonged to a different class from those under investigation (for example, TEMPORAL relations). A second constraint on the current study is that participants were presented with tokens that only marked the six classes under investigation. Including more classes and therefore also more connectives in an annotation study could result in lower agreement between the coders. Future research will therefore focus on whether other relations (including NOREL) can also be annotated reliably by naïve coders.

Crowdsourcing the data also presents possible confounding factors for the design of an annotation study. More specifically, one has to be aware of the effect of motivation on the results. For example, we found that the participants rarely inserted multiple connectives for the same relation. It is possible that motivation played a role in this. Participants were only required to insert one connecting phrase; the second one was optional. Since inserting a second phrase takes more time, participants might have neglected to do so, even if they interpreted multiple readings for some relations. For future experiments, this effect can be avoided by asking subjects to explicitly indicate that they don't see a second reading.

Regarding the influence of context, the findings from our experiment do not support the general consensus that presence of context is a necessary requirement for discourse annotation. The lack of a clear positive effect of context on agreement could be due to general ambiguity of language. As Spooren and Degand (2010) note, "establishing a coherence relation in a particular instance requires the use of contextual information, which in itself can be interpreted in multiple ways and hence is a source of disagreement." Nevertheless, we do suggest to include context in discourse annotation tasks if time and resources permit it. Generally context does not lead to worse annotations when the fragments are presented in their original formatting, and the presence of context might facilitate the inference of the intended relation.

6 Conclusion

The current paper addresses the question of whether a crowdsourcing connective insertion task can be used to obtain reliable discourse annotations, and whether the presence of context influence the reliability of the data.

Regarding the influence of context, the results showed that the presence of context influenced the annotations when the fragments contained at least one of the following characteristics: (i) the context introduced the topic, (ii) the context sentence following the relation expands on the second argument of the relation; or (iii) the first argument of the relation is a subordinate clause that attaches to the context. The presence of context led to less agreement when the connection between the context and the first argument was not strong due to a paragraph break or a topic change.

Regarding the reliability of the task, we found that the method is reliable for acquiring discourse annotations: The majority of inserted connectives converged with the original label, and this convergence was almost perfectly replicable, in the sense that a similar pattern was found in both conditions. The results also showed that subjects often converged on two types of insertions. This indicates that multiple interpretations are possible for a single relation. Based on these results, we argue that annotation by many (more than 2) annotators is necessary, because it provides researchers with a probability distribution of all the senses of a relation. This probability distribution reflects the true meaning of the relation better than a single label assigned by an annotator according to a specific framework.

Acknowledgements

This research was funded by the German Research Foundation (DFG) as part of SFB 1102 "Information Density and Linguistic Encoding" and the Cluster of Excellence "Multimodal Computing and Interaction" (EXC 284).

References

Ron Artstein and Massimo Poesio. 2005. Bias decreases in proportion to the number of annotators. *Proceedings of the Conference on Formal Grammar and Mathematics of Language (FG-MoL)*, pages 141–150.

Ron Artstein and Massimo Poesio. 2008. Inter-coder agreement for computational linguistics. *Computational Linguistics*, 34(4):555–596.

Fatemeh Torabi Asr and Vera Demberg. 2013. On the information conveyed by discourse markers. In *Proceedings of the Fourth Annual Workshop on Cognitive Modeling and Computational Linguistics, pages 84–93.

Lynn Carlson, Daniel Marcu, and Mary Ellen Okurowski. 2003. Building a discourse-tagged corpus in the framework of Rhetorical Structure Theory. In Current and new directions in discourse and dialogue, pages 85–112. Springer.

Jacob Cohen. 1960. A coefficient of agreement for nominal scales. Educational and Psychological Measurement, 20(1):37–46.

Francis Cornish. 2009. "Text'' and "discourse" as context. Working Papers in Functional Discourse Grammar (WP-FDG-82): The London Papers I, 2009, pages 97–115.

Kordula De Kuthy, Ramon Ziai, and Detmar Meurers. 2016. Focus annotation of task-based data: Establishing the quality of crowd annotation. In Proceedings of the Linguistic Annotation Workshop (LAW X), pages 110–119.

Joseph L. Fleiss. 1971. Measuring nominal scale agreement among many raters. Psychological bulletin, 76(5):378–382.

Jet Hoek and Sandrine Zufferey. 2015. Factors influencing the implicitation of discourse relations across languages. In Proceedings 11th Joint ACL-ISO Workshop on Interoperable Semantic Annotation (isa-11), pages 39–45. TiCC, Tilburg center for Cognition and Communication.

Daisuke Kawahara, Yuichiro Machida, Tomohide Shibata, Sadao Kurohashi, Hayato Kobayashi, and Manabu Sassano. 2014. Rapid development of a corpus with discourse annotations using two-stage crowdsourcing. In Proceedings of the International Conference on Computational Linguistics (COLING), pages 269–278.

Alistair Knott and Robert Dale. 1994. Using linguistic phenomena to motivate a set of coherence relations. Discourse Processes, 18(1):35–62.

Klaus Krippendorff. 2004. Reliability in content analysis. Human communication research, 30(3):411–433.

Alex Lascarides, Nicholas Asher, and Jon Oberlander. 1992. Inferring discourse relations in context. In Proceedings of the 30th annual meeting on Association for Computational Linguistics, pages 1–8. Association for Computational Linguistics.

Rashmi Prasad, Nikhil Dinesh, Alan Lee, Eleni Miltsakaki, Livio Robaldo, Aravind K. Joshi, and Bonnie Webber. 2008. The Penn Discourse TreeBank 2.0. In Proceedings of the International Conference on Language Resources and Evaluation (LREC). Citeseer.

Florian Pusse, Asad Sayeed, and Vera Demberg. 2016. LingoTurk: Managing crowdsourced tasks for psycholinguistics. In Proceedings of the North American Chapter of the Association for Computational Linguistics: Human Language Technologies (NAACL-HLT).

Ines Rehbein, Merel C. J. Scholman, and Vera Demberg. 2016. Annotating discourse relations in spoken language: A comparison of the PDTB and CCR frameworks. In Proceedings of the Tenth International Conference on Language Resources and Evaluation (LREC), Portoroz, Slovenia. European Language Resources Association (ELRA).

Stefan Riezler. 2014. On the problem of theoretical terms in empirical computational linguistics. Computational Linguistics, 40(1):235–245.

Livio Robaldo and Eleni Miltsakaki. 2014. Corpus-driven semantics of concession: Where do expectations come from? Dialogue & Discourse, 5(1):1–36.

Hannah Rohde, Anna Dickinson, Nathan Schneider, Christopher Clark, Annie Louis, and Bonnie Webber. 2016. Filling in the blanks in understanding discourse adverbials: Consistency, conflict, and context-dependence in a crowdsourced elicitation task. In Proceedings of the Linguistic Annotation Workshop (LAW X), pages 49–58.

Merel C. J. Scholman, Jacqueline Evers-Vermeul, and Ted J. M. Sanders. 2016. Categories of coherence relations in discourse annotation: Towards a reliable categorization of coherence relations. Dialogue & Discourse, 7(2):1–28.

Rion Snow, Brendan O'Connor, Daniel Jurafsky, and Andrew Y Ng. 2008. Cheap and fast—but is it good?: Evaluating non-expert annotations for natural language tasks. In Proceedings of the Conference on Empirical Methods in Natural Language Processing (EMNLP), pages 254–263. Association for Computational Linguistics.

Lichao Song. 2010. The role of context in discourse analysis. Journal of Language Teaching and Research, 1(6):876–879.

Wilbert P. M. S. Spooren and Liesbeth Degand. 2010. Coding coherence relations: Reliability and validity. Corpus Linguistics and Linguistic Theory, 6(2):241–266.

Sandrine Zufferey and Liesbeth Degand. 2013. Annotating the meaning of discourse connectives in multilingual corpora. Corpus Linguistics and Linguistic Theory, 1:1–24.

Sandrine Zufferey, Liesbeth Degand, Andrei Popescu-Belis, and Ted J. M. Sanders. 2012. Empirical validations of multilingual annotation schemes for discourse relations. In Proceedings of the 8th Joint ISO-ACL/SIGSEM Workshop on Interoperable Semantic Annotation, pages 77–84.

A Code-Switching Corpus of Turkish-German Conversations

Özlem Çetinoğlu
IMS, University of Stuttgart
Germany
`ozlem@ims.uni-stuttgart.de`

Abstract

We present a code-switching corpus of Turkish-German that is collected by recording conversations of bilinguals. The recordings are then transcribed in two layers following speech and orthography conventions, and annotated with sentence boundaries and intersentential, intrasentential, and intra-word switch points. The total amount of data is 5 hours of speech which corresponds to 3614 sentences. The corpus aims at serving as a resource for speech or text analysis, as well as a collection for linguistic inquiries.

1 Introduction

Code-switching (CS) is mixing two (or more) languages in spoken and written communication (Myers-Scotton, 1993; Poplack, 2001; Toribio and Bullock, 2012) and is quite common in multilingual communities (Auer and Wei, 2007). With the increase in multilingual speakers worldwide, CS becomes more prominent.

In parallel, the interest in processing mixed language is on the rise in the Computational Linguistics community. Researchers work on core tasks such as normalisation, language identification, language modelling, part-of-speech tagging as well as downstream ones such as automatic speech recognition and sentiment analysis (Çetinoğlu et al., 2016). The majority of the corpora used in these tasks come from social media (Nguyen and Doğruöz, 2013; Barman et al., 2014; Vyas et al., 2014; Solorio et al., 2014; Choudhury et al., 2014; Jamatia et al., 2015; Samih and Maier, 2016; Vilares et al., 2016; Molina et al., 2016).

Social media has the advantage of containing vast amount of data and easy access. Depending on the medium, however, limitations might arise.

For instance, Twitter, the most popular source so far, allows the distribution of tweet IDs rather than tweets themselves, which can be deleted. Hence it is hard to use the full resource, reproduce previous results or compare to them. Moreover the character limit and idiosyncratic language of social media bring extra challenges of processing in addition to challenges coming from code-switching.

Spoken data has also been a popular source in computational CS research (Solorio and Liu, 2008; Lyu and Lyu, 2008; Chan et al., 2009; Shen et al., 2011; Li et al., 2012; Lyu et al., 2015; Yilmaz et al., 2016). There are no limitations on the length of sentences, idiosyncrasies are less pronounced. Despite such advantages, it is almost solely used in speech analysis. To our knowledge, only Solorio and Liu (2008) have used transcriptions of CS speech in text analysis. One reason that researchers processing CS text prefer social media could be that it is already text-based, and it requires much less time and effort than speech collection transcription. For the existing speech corpora, discrepancies between the speech transcriptions and the input text processing tools expect could be a drawback. For instance the SEAME corpus (Lyu et al., 2015) does not use punctuation, capitalisation, or sentence boundaries in transcriptions, yet standard text processing tools (POS taggers, morphological analysers, parsers) are trained on edited text, hence make use of orthographic cues.

In this paper, we introduce a Turkish-German code-switching corpus of conversations and their two layers of transcriptions following speech and orthography conventions. The data is annotated with sentence boundaries and intersentential, intrasentential, and intra-word switch points. Our aim is to provide a resource that could be used by researchers from different backgrounds, e.g., for speech recognition and language identification in

Proceedings of the 11th Linguistic Annotation Workshop, pages 34–40,
Valencia, Spain, April 3, 2017. ©2017 Association for Computational Linguistics

speech, for language identification and predicting CS points in text, and as a corpus of empirical evidence for linguistically interesting structures.

2 Related Work

Creating code-switching corpora for speech analysis has started with reading designed text rather than spontaneous speech. Lyu and Lyu (2008) use a Mandarin-Taiwanese test set for their language identification system that consist of 4.8 hours of speech corresponding to 4600 utterances. The set is designed to have Mandarin as the main language with one or two Taiwanese words replaced with their Mandarin counterparts. Chan et al. (2009) introduce a Cantonese-English corpus of read speech of 3167 manually designed sentences. English is inserted into Cantonese as segments of one or more words. Another read speech corpus is created by Shen et al. (2011) for Mandarin-English and consists of 6650 utterances. Li et al. (2012) collected 5 hours of code-switched Mandarin-English speech from conversational and project meetings. Intersentential and intrasentential switches add up to 1068 in total.

Lyu et al. (2015) present the largest CS speech resource, the SEAME corpus, which has 192 hours of transcribed Mandarin-English interviews and conversations in the latest version.[1] The code-switching points naturally occur in the text, as both languages are written in their own scripts. A recent corpus of 18.5 hours is introduced by Yilmaz et al. (2016) on Frisian-Dutch broadcasts. CS points are marked in the transcriptions but not on the audio level.

Solorio and Liu (2008) recorded a conversation of 40 minutes among Spanish-English bilinguals. The transcribed speech contains 922 sentences with 239 switch points among them. The authors used this data to train machine learning algorithms that predict CS points of an incrementally given input.

Speech collections have always been the primary source in sociolinguistic and pyscholinguistic research. We list some of these spoken corpora that employ code-switching instances of Turkish and German, mixed with other languages or with each other. The "Emigranto" corpus (Eppler, 2003) documents conversations with Jewish refugees settled in London in 1930s, who mix

Austrian German with British English. In this corpus, Eppler (2011) looks into mixed dependencies where a dependent and its head are from different languages. She observes that dependents with a mixed head have on average longer dependencies than ones with a monolingual head.

In a similar fashion, Tracy and Lattey (2009) present more than 50 hours of recordings of elderly German immigrants in the U.S. The data is fully transcribed and annotated, yet each session of recordings is transcribed as a single file with no alignment between transcript utterences and their corresponding audio parts, and annotations use Microsoft Word markings, e.g. bold, italic, underline, or different font sizes, thus require format conversions to be processed by automatic tools that accept text-based inputs.

Kallmeyer and Keim (2003) investigate the communication characteristics between young girls in Mannheim, mostly of Turkish origin, and show that with peers, they employ a mixed form of Turkish and German. Rehbein et al. (2009) and Herkenrath (2012) study the language acquisition of Turkish-German bilingual children. On the same data Özdil (2010) analyses reasons of code-switching decisions. The Kiezdeutsch corpus (Rehbein et al., 2014) consists of conversations among native German adolescents with a multiethnic background, including Turkish. As a result, it also contains a small number of Turkish-German mixed sentences.

3 Data

The data collection and annotation processes are handled by a team of five Computational Linguistics and Linguistics students. In the following sections we give the details of these processes.

3.1 Collection

The data collection is done by the annotators as conversation recordings. We asked the annotators to approach Turkish-German bilinguals from their circle for an informal setting, assuming this might increase the frequency of code-switching. Similarly we recommended the annotators to open topics that might induce code-switching, such as work and studies (typically German-speaking environments) if a dialogue started in Turkish, or Turkish food and holidays in Turkey (hence Turkish-specific words) in a German-dominated conversation.

---

[1] https://catalog.ldc.upenn.edu/LDC2015S04

28 participants (20 female, 8 male) took part in the recordings. The majority of the speakers are university students. Their ages range from 9 to 39, with an average of 24 and a mode of 26. We also asked the participants to assign a score from 1 to 10 for their proficiency in Turkish and German. 18 of the participants think their German is better, 5 of them think their Turkish is better, and the remaining 5 assigned an equal score. The average score for German is 8.2, and for Turkish 7.5.[2]

3.2 Annotation

The annotation and transcriptions are done using Praat.[3] We created six tiers for each audio file: `spk1_verbal`, `spk1_norm`, `spk2_verbal`, `spk2_norm`, `lang`, `codesw`. The first four tiers contain the verbal and normalised transcription of speakers 1 and 2. The tier `lang` corresponds to the language of intervals and can have TR for Turkish, DE for German, and LANG3 for utterances in other languages. The first five tiers are intervals, while the last one is a point tier that denotes sentence and code-switching boundaries. The labels on the boundaries are SB when both sides of the boundary are in the same language, SCS when the language changes from one sentence to the next (intersentential), WCS when the switch is between words within a sentence (intrasentential). Figure 1 shows a Praat screenshot that demonstrates the tiers and exemplifies SCS and WCS boundaries.

Since Turkish is agglutinative and case markers determine the function of NPs, non-Turkish common and proper nouns with Turkish suffixes are commonly observed in CS conversations. We mark such words in the `codesw` tier as a intra-word switch and use the symbol § following Çetinoğlu (2016). Example (1) depicts the representation of a mixed word where the German compound *Studentenwohnheim* 'student accommodation' is followed by the Turkish locative case marker *-da* (in bold).

(1) Studentenwohnheim   § **da**
     student accommodation § **Loc**

     'in the student accommodation'

For many proper names, Turkish and German orthography are identical. Here, the speech data in parallel becomes an advantage, and the language is decided according to the pronunciation. If the proper name is pronounced in German, and followed by a Turkish suffix a § switch point is inserted. Otherwise it follows Turkish orthography.

3.3 Transcription

For speech analysis it is important to transcribe utterances close to how they are pronounced. In some transcription guidelines, capitalisation and punctuation are omitted (e.g. in the SEAME corpus (Lyu et al., 2015)[4]), in some others they are used to mark speech information (e.g. in the Kiezdeutsch corpus (Rehbein et al., 2014)[5]). Text analysis on the other hand generally relies on standard orthography. This raises a conflict between two tasks on how to transcribe speech. To avoid this problem, we introduced two tiers of transcription. The verbal tier follows the speech conventions. If a speaker uses a contraction, the word is transcribed as contracted. The acronyms are written as separate characters. Numbers are spelled out. Recurring characters are represented with the single character followed by a colon. The normalised tier follows the edited text conventions. Words obey the orthographic rules of standard Turkish and German, e.g. characters of acronyms are merged back. Punctuation is added to the text, obeying the tokenisation standards (i.e. separated from the preceding and following tokens with a space).

Example (2) gives a sentence showing the verbal and normalised tiers for a Turkish sentence. The *r* sound in the progressive tense suffix *-yor* is not pronounced, hence omitted in the verbal tier. The vowel of the interjection *ya* is extended during speech, and the colon representation is used to reflect it in the verbal tier, yet the normalised tier has the standard form. Also, the question mark is present in the normalised tier.

(2) `verbal`: ne   diyosun   ya**:**
     `norm`:   Ne   diyorsun   ya ?
             What say.Prog.2PSg Intj.

      'What do you say??'

If a made-up word is uttered, it is preceded with an asterisk mark in the transcription. Note that dialectal pronunciation or using a valid word in

---

[2]The metadata is also available in the CMDI format at the IMS Clarin repository.

[3]www.fon.hum.uva.nl/praat

[4]https://catalog.ldc.upenn.edu/docs/ LDC2015S04/SEAME.V4.0.pdf

[5]http://www.kiezdeutschkorpus. de/files/kidko/downloads/ KiDKo-Transkriptionsrichtlinien.pdf

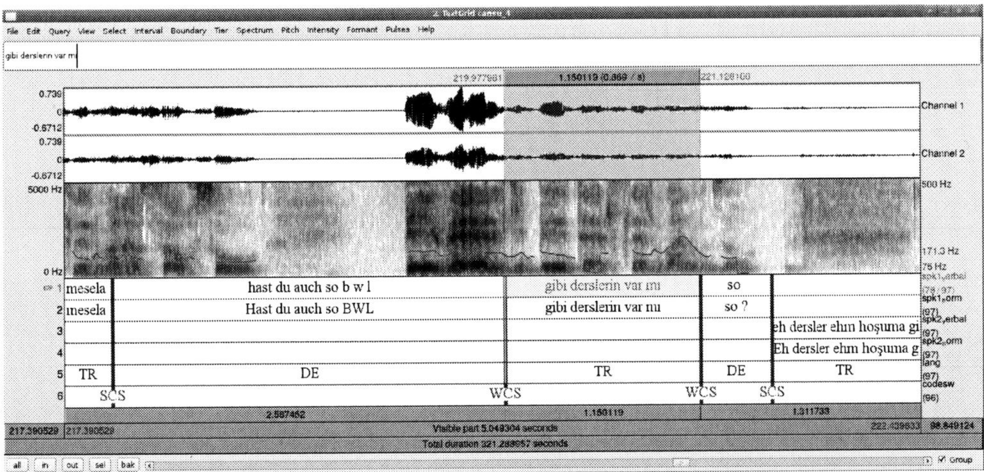

Figure 1: A screenshot example from Praat annotations. It shows part of a Turkish sentence and a full mixed sentence from speaker 1, and part of a Turkish sentence from speaker 2.

wrong context is not considered within this class. Partial words are marked with two hyphens instead of the common use of one hyphen, as the latter is used in German to denote the initial part of a compound when two compounds share a common part and the first compound is written only as the unshared part (e.g. *Wohn- und Schlafzimmer* 'living room and bedroom').

We also marked `[silence]`, `[laugh]`, `[cough]`, `[breathe]`, `[noise]`, and put the remaining sounds into the `[other]` category. Overlaps occur usually when one speaker is talking and the other is uttering backchannel signals and words of acknowledgement. There are also cases both speakers tend to speak at the same time. In all such cases, both voices are transcribed, one speaker is chosen to be the main speaker, and an `[overlap]` marker is inserted to the secondary speaker's verbal and normalised tiers. The `codesw` and `lang` tiers are decided according to the main speaker's transcription.

3.4 Quality Control

Once the Praat annotation is completed its output files are converted to a simpler text format for easier access from existing tools and for easier human readability. [6] We ran simple quality control scripts that check if all the tiers are present and non-

empty, if the `lang` and `codesw` tiers have values from their label sets, and if the `lang` and `codesw` labels are meaningful, for instance, if there are TR labels on both sides of a SCS (intersentential CS) boundary, either the boundary should be corrected to SB or one of the language labels should be DE or LANG3. Any mistakes are corrected by the annotators on a second pass.

For the quality control of the transcriptions we employed Turkish and German morphological analysers (Oflazer, 1994; Schmid et al., 2004) and analysed all the tokens in the normalised tier according to their languages. We then created a list of tokens unknown to the analysers, which are potentially mispelled words. The annotators went through the list and corrected their mistakes in both the verbal and normalised tiers. The remaining list also gives us the words unknown to the morphological analysers.

4 Statistics and Observations

The durations of recordings range from 20 seconds to 16 minutes. There are 47 transcribed files with a total of 5 hours. Each file is accompanied with a metadata file that contains speaker information, that could be used to filter the corpus according to age intervals, education levels, language proficiency etc.

Table 1 gives the basic statistics on the normalised version of the transcriptions. The token count includes punctuation and interjections, and excludes paralinguistic markers and overlaps.

---

[6]The format of the text files is given with an example in `http://www.ims.uni-stuttgart.de/ institut/mitarbeiter/ozlem/LAW2017.html` The script that converts Praat .TextGrid files to that format is also provided.

sentences	3614
tokens	41056
average sent. length	11.36
sentence boundaries (SB)	2166
intersentential switches (SCS)	1448
intrasentential switches (WCS)	2113
intra-word switches (§)	257
switches in total	3818
sent. with at least one WCS	1108

Table 1: Basic statistics about the data.

Switch	Language Pair	#	%
SB	DE → DE	1356	62.60
	TR → TR	809	37.35
	LANG3 → LANG3	1	0.05
SCS	TR → DE	754	52.07
	DE → TR	671	46.34
	LANG3 → TR	7	0.48
	LANG3 → DE	6	0.41
	DE → LANG3	5	0.35
	TR → LANG3	5	0.35
WCS	TR → DE	1082	51.20
	DE → TR	914	43.26
	DE → LANG3	34	1.61
	TR → LANG3	31	1.47
	LANG3 → DE	28	1.33
	LANG3 → TR	24	1.14
§	DE → TR	246	95.72
	LANG3 → TR	11	4.28

Table 2: Breakdown of switches from one language to another, and their percentages within their switch type.

Switch points split mixed tokens into two in the transcriptions for representational purposes, but they are counted as one token in the statistics.

The majority of the switches are intrasentential and the language of the conversation changes when moving from one sentence to another in 40% of the time. They also correspond to the 55.3% of all switches. 38% of them happen between words, and the remaining 6.7% are within a word. Table 2 shows the breakdown of switches. There are 614 overlaps and 648 paralinguistic markers.[7]

We have observed that many CS instances fall into the categories mentioned in Çetinoğlu (2016), like German verbs coupled with Turkish light verbs *etmek* 'do' or *yapmak* 'make'; Turkish lexicalised expressions and vocatives in German sentences, and vice versa; subordinate clauses and conjuctions in the one language while the remaining of the sentence is in the other language. One category we have seen more prominent in speech data is non-standard syntactic constructions, perhaps due to spontaneity. For instance, Example

(3), which is also given as Figure 1, is a question with two verbs (Turkish in bold). Both German *hast du* and Turkish *var mı* corresponds to 'do you have'.

(3) Hast du auch so BWL **gibi**
Have you also like business studies **like**
derslerin var mı so?
class.Poss2Sg exist Ques like?
'Do you also have classes like business studies?'

5 Conclusion

We present a corpus collected from Turkish-German bilingual speakers, and annotated with sentence and code-switching boundaries in audio files and their corresponding transcriptions which are carried out as both verbal and normalised tiers. In total, it is 5 hours of speech and 3614 sentences.

Transcriptions are available for academic research purposes.[8] The licence agreement can be found at `http://www.ims.uni-stuttgart.de/institut/mitarbeiter/ozlem/LAW2017.html` along with transcription examples. Audio files will be manipulated before distribution in order to conceal speakers' identity, to comply with the German data privacy laws[9].

Acknowledgements

We thank Sevde Ceylan, Uğur Kostak, Hasret el Sanhoury, Esra Soydoğan, and Cansu Turgut for the data collection and annotation. We also thank anonymous reviewers for their insightful comments. This work was funded by the Deutsche Forschungsgemeinschaft (DFG) via SFB 732, project D2.

References

Peter Auer and Li Wei. 2007. *Handbook of multilingualism and multilingual communication*, volume 5. Walter de Gruyter.

Utsab Barman, Amitava Das, Joachim Wagner, and Jennifer Foster. 2014. Code mixing: A challenge for language identification in the language of social media. In *Proceedings of the First Workshop on Computational Approaches to Code Switching*,

---

[7]laugh: 279, noise: 148, silence: 113, breath: 74, other: 25, cough: 9.

[8]If parts of data contain information that can reveal the identity of a specific person, they are anonymised.

[9]National: `https://www.datenschutz-wiki.de/Bundesdatenschutzgesetz`, State: `https://www.baden-wuerttemberg.datenschutz.de/landesdatenschutzgesetz-inhaltsverzeichnis/`

pages 13–23, Doha, Qatar, October. Association for Computational Linguistics.

Özlem Çetinoğlu, Sarah Schulz, and Ngoc Thang Vu. 2016. Challenges of computational processing of code-switching. In *Proceedings of the Second Workshop on Computational Approaches to Code Switching*, pages 1–11, Austin, Texas, November. Association for Computational Linguistics.

Özlem Çetinoğlu. 2016. A Turkish-German code-switching corpus. In *The 10th International Conference on Language Resources and Evaluation (LREC-16)*, Portorož, Slovenia.

Joyce YC Chan, Houwei Cao, PC Ching, and Tan Lee. 2009. Automatic recognition of Cantonese-English code-mixing speech. *Computational Linguistics and Chinese Language Processing*, 14(3):281–304.

Monojit Choudhury, Gokul Chittaranjan, Parth Gupta, and Amitava Das. 2014. Overview of FIRE 2014 track on transliterated search. In *Forum for Information Retrieval Evaluation*, Bangalore,India, December.

Eva Eppler. 2003. Emigranto data: A dependency approach to code-mixing. In Pereiro Carmen C., Anxo M.L. Suarez, and XoÃąn P Rodriguez-Yanez, editors, *Bilingual communities and individuals.*, pages 652–63. Vigo: Servicio de Publicacions da Universidade de Vigo, 1.

Eva Duran Eppler. 2011. The dependency distance hypothesis for bilingual code-switching. In *Proceedings of the International Conference on Dependency Linguistics*.

Annette Herkenrath. 2012. Receptive multilingualism in an immigrant constellation: Examples from Turkish–German children's language. *International Journal of Bilingualism*, pages 287–314.

Anupam Jamatia, Björn Gambäck, and Amitava Das. 2015. Part-of-speech tagging for code-mixed English-Hindi Twitter and Facebook chat messages. In *Proceedings of the International Conference Recent Advances in Natural Language Processing*, pages 239–248, Hissar, Bulgaria, September. INCOMA Ltd. Shoumen, BULGARIA.

Werner Kallmeyer and Inken Keim. 2003. Linguistic variation and the construction of social identity in a German-Turkish setting. *Discourse constructions of youth identities*, 110:29.

Ying Li, Yue Yu, and Pascale Fung. 2012. A Mandarin-English code-switching corpus. In Nicoletta Calzolari, Khalid Choukri, Thierry Declerck, Mehmet Uğur Doğan, Bente Maegaard, Joseph Mariani, Jan Odijk, and Stelios Piperidis, editors, *Proceedings of the Eighth International Conference on Language Resources and Evaluation (LREC-2012)*, pages 2515–2519, Istanbul, Turkey, May. European Language Resources Association (ELRA). ACL Anthology Identifier: L12-1573.

Dau-Cheng Lyu and Ren-Yuan Lyu. 2008. Language identification on code-switching utterances using multiple cues. In *Interspeech*, pages 711–714.

D.-C. Lyu, T.-P. Tan, E.-S. Chng, and H. Li. 2015. Mandarin–English code-switching speech corpus in South-East Asia: SEAME. *LRE*, 49(3):581–600.

Giovanni Molina, Fahad AlGhamdi, Mahmoud Ghoneim, Abdelati Hawwari, Nicolas Rey-Villamizar, Mona Diab, and Thamar Solorio. 2016. Overview for the second shared task on language identification in code-switched data. In *Proceedings of the Second Workshop on Computational Approaches to Code Switching*, pages 40–49, Austin, Texas, November. Association for Computational Linguistics.

C. Myers-Scotton. 1993. *Duelling languages: Grammatical structure in codeswitching*. Oxford University Press.

Dong Nguyen and A. Seza Doğruöz. 2013. Word level language identification in online multilingual communication. In *Proceedings of the 2013 Conference on Empirical Methods in Natural Language Processing*, pages 857–862, Seattle, Washington, USA, October. Association for Computational Linguistics.

Kemal Oflazer. 1994. Two-level description of Turkish morphology. *Literary and Linguistic Computing*, 9(2):137–148.

Erkan Özdil. 2010. *Codeswitching im zweisprachigen Handeln*. Waxmann Verlag.

Shana Poplack. 2001. Code-switching (linguistic). *International encyclopedia of the social and behavioral sciences*, pages 2062–2065.

Jochen Rehbein, Annette Herkenrath, and Birsel Karakoç. 2009. Turkish in Germany on contact-induced language change of an immigrant language in the multilingual landscape of europe. *STUF-Language Typology and Universals Sprachtypologie und Universalienforschung*, 62(3):171–204.

Ines Rehbein, Sören Schalowski, and Heike Wiese. 2014. The KiezDeutsch korpus (KiDKo) release 1.0. In *The 9th International Conference on Language Resources and Evaluation (LREC-14), Reykjavik, Iceland*.

Younes Samih and Wolfgang Maier. 2016. An Arabic-Moroccan Darija code-switched corpus. In *Proceedings of the Tenth International Conference on Language Resources and Evaluation (LREC 2016)*, Portorož, Slovenia, may.

Helmut Schmid, Arne Fitschen, and Ulrich Heid. 2004. SMOR: A German computational morphology covering derivation, composition and inflection. In *Proceedings of the IVth International Conference on Language Resources and Evaluation (LREC 2004*, pages 1263–1266.

Han-Ping Shen, Chung-Hsien Wu, Yan-Ting Yang, and Chun-Shan Hsu. 2011. Cecos: A chinese-english code-switching speech database. In *Speech Database and Assessments (Oriental COCOSDA), 2011 International Conference on*, pages 120–123. IEEE.

Thamar Solorio and Yang Liu. 2008. Part-of-speech tagging for English-Spanish code-switched text. In *Proceedings of the 2008 Conference on Empirical Methods in Natural Language Processing*, pages 1051–1060, Honolulu, Hawaii, October. Association for Computational Linguistics.

Thamar Solorio, Elizabeth Blair, Suraj Maharjan, Steven Bethard, Mona Diab, Mahmoud Ghoneim, Abdelati Hawwari, Fahad AlGhamdi, Julia Hirschberg, Alison Chang, and Pascale Fung. 2014. Overview for the first shared task on language identification in code-switched data. In *Proceedings of the First Workshop on Computational Approaches to Code Switching*, pages 62–72, Doha, Qatar, October. Association for Computational Linguistics.

Almeida Jacqueline Toribio and Barbara E Bullock. 2012. *The Cambridge handbook of linguistic code-switching*. Cambridge University Press.

Rosemarie Tracy and Elsa Lattey. 2009. It wasn't easy but irgendwie äh da hat sich's rentiert, net?: a linguistic profile. In Michaela Albl-Mikasa, Sabine Braun, and Sylvia Kalina, editors, *Dimensionen der Zweitsprachenforschung. Dimensions of Second Language Research*. Narr.

David Vilares, Miguel A. Alonso, and Carlos Gomez-Rodriguez. 2016. EN-ES-CS: An English-Spanish code-switching twitter corpus for multilingual sentiment analysis. In Nicoletta Calzolari (Conference Chair), Khalid Choukri, Thierry Declerck, Sara Goggi, Marko Grobelnik, Bente Maegaard, Joseph Mariani, Helene Mazo, Asuncion Moreno, Jan Odijk, and Stelios Piperidis, editors, *Proceedings of the Tenth International Conference on Language Resources and Evaluation (LREC 2016)*, Paris, France, may. European Language Resources Association (ELRA).

Yogarshi Vyas, Spandana Gella, Jatin Sharma, Kalika Bali, and Monojit Choudhury. 2014. Pos tagging of English-Hindi code-mixed social media content. In *Proceedings of the 2014 Conference on Empirical Methods in Natural Language Processing (EMNLP)*, pages 974–979, Doha, Qatar, October. Association for Computational Linguistics.

Emre Yilmaz, Maaike Andringa, Sigrid Kingma, Jelske Dijkstra, Frits Van der Kuip, Hans Van de Velde, Frederik Kampstra, Jouke Algra, Henk van den Heuvel, and David van Leeuwen. 2016. A longitudinal bilingual Frisian-Dutch radio broadcast database designed for code-switching research. In Nicoletta Calzolari (Conference Chair), Khalid Choukri, Thierry Declerck, Sara Goggi, Marko Grobelnik, Bente Maegaard, Joseph Mariani, Helene Mazo, Asuncion Moreno, Jan Odijk, and Stelios Piperidis, editors, *Proceedings of the Tenth International Conference on Language Resources and Evaluation (LREC 2016)*, Paris, France, May. European Language Resources Association (ELRA).

Annotating omission in statement pairs

Héctor Martínez Alonso[1]   **Amaury Delamaire**[2,3]   **Benoît Sagot**[1]

1. Inria (ALMAnaCH), 2 rue Simone Iff, 75012 Paris, France
2. École des Mines de Saint-Étienne, 158 cours Fauriel, 42000 Saint-Étienne, France
3. Storyzy (Trooclick), 130 rue de Lourmel, 75015 Paris, France

`{hector.martinez-alonso,benoit.sagot}@inria.fr`
`amaury.delamaire@trooclick.com`

Abstract

In this piece of industrial application, we focus on the identification of omission in statement pairs for an online news platform. We compare three annotation schemes, namely two crowdsourcing schemes and an expert annotation. The simplest of the two crowdsourcing approaches yields a better annotation quality than the more complex one. We use a dedicated classifier to assess whether the annotators' behaviour can be explained by straightforward linguistic features. However, for our task, we argue that expert and not crowdsourcing-based annotation is the best compromise between cost and quality.

1 Introduction

In a user survey, the news aggregator Storyzy[1] found out that the two main obstacles for user satisfaction when accessing their site's content were redundancy of news items, and missing information respectively. Indeed, in the journalistic genre that is characteristic of online news, editors make frequent use of citations as prominent information; yet these citations are not always in full. The reasons for leaving information out are often motivated by the political leaning of the news platform.

Existing approaches to the detection of political bias rely on bag-of-words models (Zhitomirsky-Geffet et al., 2016) that examine the words present in the writings. Our goal is to go beyond such approaches, which focus on what is said, by instead focusing on what is omitted. Thus, this method requires a pair of statements; an original one, and a shortened version with some deleted words or spans. The task is then to determine whether the information left out in the second statement conveys substantial additional information. If so, the pair presents an omission; cf. Table 1.

Omission detection in sentence pairs constitutes a new task, which is different from the recognition of textual entailment—cf. (Dagan et al., 2006)—because in our case we are certain that the longer text entails the short one. What we want to estimate is whether the information not present in the shorter statement is relevant. To tackle this question, we used a supervised classification framework, for which we require a dataset of manually annotated sentence pairs.

We conducted an annotation task on a sample of the corpus used by the news platform (Section 3). In this corpus, reference statements extracted from news articles are used as long 'reference' statements, whereas their short 'target' counterparts were selected by string and date matching.

We followed by examining which features help identify cases of omission (Section 4). In addition to straightforward measures of word overlap (the Dice coefficient), we also determined that there is a good deal of lexical information that determines whether there is an omission. This work is, to the best of our knowledge, the first empirical study on omission identification in statement pairs.[2]

2 Related work

To the best of our knowledge, no work has been published about omission detection as such. However, our work is related to a variety of questions of interest that resort both to linguistics and NLP.

Segment deletion is one of the most immediate forms of paraphrase, cf. Vila et al. (2014) for a survey. Another phenomenon that also presents the notion of segment deletion, although in a very

---

[1]`http://storyzy.com`

[2]We make all data and annotations are freely available at `github.com/hectormartinez/verdidata`.

Proceedings of the 11th Linguistic Annotation Workshop, pages 41–45,
Valencia, Spain, April 3, 2017. ©2017 Association for Computational Linguistics

different setting, is ellipsis. In the case of an ellipsis, the deleted segment can be reconstructed given a discourse antecedent in the same document, be it observed or idealized (Asher et al., 2001; Merchant, 2016). In the case of omission, a reference and a target version of a statement are involved, the deleted segment in one version having an antecedent in the other version of the statement, in another document, as a result of editorial choices.

Our task is similar to the problem of omission detection in translations, but the bilingual setting allows for word-alignment-based approaches (Melamed, 1996; Russell, 1999), which we cannot use in our setup. Omission detection is also related to hedge detection, which can be achieved using specific lexical triggers such as vagueness markers (Szarvas et al., 2012; Vincze, 2013).

3 Annotation Task

The goal of the annotation task is to provide each reference–target pair with a label: *Omission*, if the target statement leaves out substantial information, or *Same* if there is no information loss.

Corpus We obtained our examples from a corpus of English web newswire. The corpus is made up of aligned reference-target statement pairs; cf. Table 1 for examples. These statements were aligned automatically by means of word overlap metrics, as well as a series of heuristics such as comparing the alleged speaker and date of the statement given the article content, and a series of text normalization steps. We selected 500 pairs for annotation. Instead of selecting 500 random pairs, we selected a contiguous section from a random starting point. We did so in order to obtain a more natural proportion of reference-to-target statements, given that reference statements can be associated with more than one target.[3]

Annotation setup

Our first manual annotation strategy relies on the AMT crowdsourcing platform. We refer to AMT annotators as *turkers*. For each statement pair, we presented the turkers with a display like the one in Figure 1.

We used two different annotation schemes, namely OM_p, where the option to mark an omission is "Text B leaves out some *substantial* information", and OM_e, where it is "Text B leaves out

---

[3]The full distribution of the corpus documentation shall provide more details on the extraction process.

something *substantial*, such as **time**, **place**, **cause**, **people** involved or important **event** information."

The OM_p scheme aims to represent a naive user intuition of the relevance of a difference between statements, akin to the intuition of the users mentioned in Section 1, whereas OM_e aims at capturing our intuition that relevant omissions relate to missing key news elements describable in terms of the 5-W questions (Parton et al., 2009; Das et al., 2012). We ran AMT task twice, once for each scheme. For each scheme, we assigned 5 turkers per instance, and we required that the annotators be Categorization Masters according to the AMT scoring. We paid 0.05$ per instance.

Moreover, in order to choose between OM_p and OM_e, two experts (two of the authors of this article) annotated the same 100 examples from the corpus, yielding the OE annotation set.

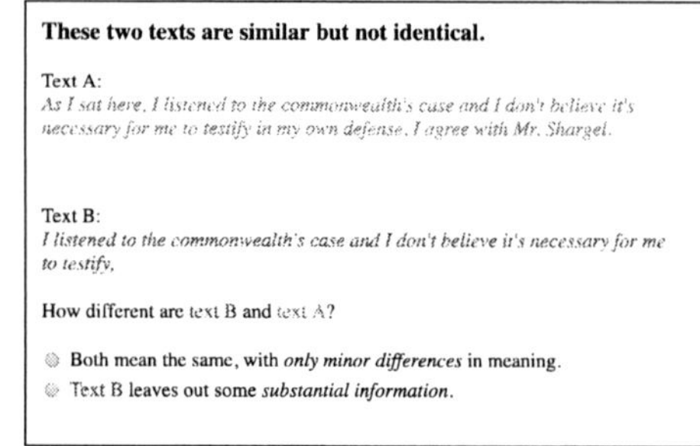

Figure 1: Annotation scheme for OM_p

Annotation results The first column in Table 2 shows the agreement of the annotation tasks in terms of Krippendorff's α coefficient. A score of e.g. 0.52 is not a very high value, but is well within what can be expected on crowdsourced semantic annotations. Note, however, the chance correction that the calculation of α applies to a skewed binary distribution is very aggressive (Passonneau and Carpenter, 2014). The conservativeness of the chance-corrected coefficient can be assessed if we compare the raw agreement between experts (0.86) with the α of 0.67. OM_e causes agreement to descend slightly, and damages the agreement of Same, while Omission remains largely constant. Moreover, disagreement is not evenly distributed across annotated instances, i.e. some instances show perfect agreement, while other instances have maximal disagreement.

We also measured the median annotation time per instance for all three methods; OM_e is almost twice as slow as OM_p (42s vs. 22s), while

Instance	OM_p	OM_e	OE
Example 1 *Interior Minister Chaudhry Nisar Ali Khan on Friday said* no Pakistani can remain silent over the atrocities being committed against the people of the occupied Kashmir by the Indian forces.	0	1	1
Example 2 *I don't feel guilty. I cannot tell you how humiliated I feel.* "I feel robbed emotionally. But we're coming from the east (eastern Europe), we're too close to Russia .."	.8	.2	0
Example 3 The tusks resemble the prehistoric sabre-tooth tiger, but of course, they are not related. *It could make wildlife watching in Sabah more interesting. The rare elephant's reversed tusks might create some problems when it comes to jostling with other elephants. The tusks resemble the prehistoric sabre-tooth tiger, but of course, they are not related*	.6	.4	.5

Table 1: Examples of annotated instances. The 'Instance' column contains the full reference statement, with the elements not present in the target statement marked in italics. The last three columns display the proportion of *Omission* labels provided by the three annotation setups.

Dataset	α	$\tilde{t}$	% Om.	Vote	MACE
Full OM_p	0.52	22	61.72	.65	.63
Full OM_e	0.49	41	63.48	.69	.61
100 OM_p	0.52	22	62.42	.64	.62
100 OM_e	0.54	42	60.00	.61	.58
100 OE	0.67	16	70.87	....	.62

Table 2: Dataset, Krippendorff's α, median annotation time, raw proportion of *Omision*, and label distribution using voting and MACE.

the the expert annotation time in OE is 16s. The large time difference between OM_p and OM_e indicates that changing the annotation guidelines has indeed an effect in annotation behavior, and that the agreement variation is not purely a result of the expectable annotation noise in crowdsourcing.

The fourth and fifth columns in Table 2 show the label distribution after adjudication. While the distribution of *Omission-Same* labels is very similar after applying simple majority voting, we observe that the distribution of the agreement does change. In OM_p, approx. 80% of the *Same*-label instances are assigned with a high agreement (at least four out of five votes), whereas only a third of the *Same* instances in OM_e have such high agreement. Both experts have a similar perception of omission, albeit with a different threshold: in the 14 where they disagree, one of the annotators shows a systematic preference for the *Omission* label.

We also use MACE to evaluate the stability of the annotations. Using an unsupervised expectation-maximization model, MACE assigns confidence to annotators, which are used to estimate the resulting annotations (Hovy et al., 2013). While we do not use the label assignments from

MACE for the classification experiments in Section 4, we use them to measure how much the proportion of omission changes with regards to simple majority voting. The more complex OM_e scheme has, parallel to lower agreement, a much higher fluctuation—both in relative and absolute terms—with regards to OM_p, which also indicates this the former scheme provides annotations that are more subject to individual variation. While this difference is arguably of a result of genuine linguistic reflection, it also indicates that the data obtained by this method is less reliable as such.

To sum up, while the label distribution is similar across schemes, the *Same* class drops in overall agreement, but the *Omission* class does not.

In spite of the variation suggested by their α coefficient, the two AMT annotated datasets are very similar. They are 85% identical after label assignment by majority voting. However, the cosine similarity between the example-wise proportions of omission labels is 0.92. This difference is a consequence of the uncertainty in low-agreement examples. The similarity with OE is 0.89 for OM_p and 0.86 for OM_e; OM_p is more similar to the expert judgment. This might be related to the fact that the OM_e instructions prime turkers to favor named entities, leading them to pay less attention to other types of substantial information such as modality markers. We shall come back to the more general role of lexical clues in Section 4.

Given that it is more internally consistent and it matches better with OE, we use the OM_p dataset for the rest of the work described in this article.

4 Classification experiments

Once the manually annotated corpus is built, we can assess the learnability of the *Omission–Same* decision problem, which constitutes a binary classification task. We aimed at measuring whether the annotators' behavior can be explained by simple proxy linguistic properties like word overlap or length of the statements and/or lexical properties.

Features: For a reference statement r, a target statement t and a set M of the words that only appear in r, we generate the following feature sets:

1. **Dice** (F_a): Dice coefficient between r and t.
2. **Length** (F_b): The length of r, the length of t, and their difference.
3. **BoW** (F_c): A bag of words (BoW) of M.
4. **DWR** (F_d): A dense word representation is word-vector representation of M built from the average word vector for all words in M. We use the representations from GloVe (Pennington et al., 2014).
5. **Stop proportion** (F_e): The proportion of stop words and punctuation in M.
6. **Entities** (F_f): The number of entities in M predicted by the 4-class Stanford Named Entity Recognizer (Finkel et al., 2005).

Table 3 shows the classification results. We use all exhaustive combinations of these feature sets to train a discriminative classifier, namely a logistic regression classifier, to obtain a best feature combination. We consider a feature combination to be the best when it outperforms the others in both accuracy and F1 for the *Omission* label. We compare all systems against the most frequent label (MFL) baseline. We evaluate each feature twice, namely using five-cold cross validation (CV-5 OM_p), and in a split scenario where we test on the 100 examples of OE after training with the remaining 400 examples from OM_p (Test OE). The three best systems (i.e. non-significantly different from each other when tested on OM_p) are shown in the lower section of the table. We test for significance using Student's two-tailed test and $p < 0.05$.

As expected, the overlap (F_a) and length metrics (F_b) make the most competitive standalone features. However, we want to measure how much of the labeling of omission is determined by *which* words are left out, and not just by *how many*.

The system trained on BoW outperforms the system on DWR. However, BoW features contain a proxy for statement length, i.e. if n words are different between ref and target, then n features will fire, and thus approximate the size of M. A distributional semantic model such as GloVe is however made up of non-sparse, real-valued vec-

	CV-5 OM_p		Test OE	
	acc.	F1	acc.	F1
MFL	.69	.81	.73	.84
F_a	.79	.81	.76	.83
F_b	.80	.85	.74	.82
F_c	.76	.83	.76	.82
F_d	.74	.84	.76	.84
F_e	.69	.81	.73	.84
F_f	.69	.81	.73	.84
F_{abe}	.83	.87	.74	.81
F_{bf}	.83	.85	.79	.85
F_{cdf}	.81	.86	.82	.88

Table 3: Accuracy and F1 for the *Omission* label for all feature groups, plus for the best feature combination in both evaluation methods. Systems significantly under baseline are marked in grey.

tors, and does not contain such a proxy for word density. If we examine the contribution of using F_d as a feature model, we see that, while it falls short of its BoW counterpart, it beats the baseline by a margin of 5-10 points. In other words, regardless of the size of M, there is lexical information that explains the choices of considering an omission.

5   Conclusion

We have presented an application-oriented effort to detect omissions between statement pairs. We have assessed two different AMT annotation schemes, and also compared them with expert annotations. The extended crowdsourcing scheme is defined closer to the expert intuition, but has lower agreement, and we use the plain scheme instead. Moreover, if we examine the time need for annotation, our conclusion is that there it is in fact detrimental to use crowdsourcing for this annotation task with respect to expert annotation. Chiefly, we also show that simple linguistic clues allow a classifier to reach satisfying classification results (0.86–0.88 F1), which are better than when solely relying on the straightforward features of different length and word overlap.

Further work includes analyzing whether the changes in the omission examples contain also changes of uncertainty class (Szarvas et al., 2012) or bias type (Recasens et al., 2013), as well as expanding the notion of omission to the detection of the loss of detail in paraphrases. Moreover, we want to explore how to identify the most omission-prone news types, in a style similar to the characterization of unreliable users in Wei et al. (2013).

References

Nicholas Asher, Daniel Hardt, and Joan Busquets. 2001. Discourse parallelism, ellipsis, and ambiguity. *Journal of Semantics*, 18(1):1–25.

Ido Dagan, Oren Glickman, and Bernardo Magnini. 2006. The pascal recognising textual entailment challenge. In *Machine learning challenges. evaluating predictive uncertainty, visual object classification, and recognising tectual entailment*, pages 177–190. Springer.

Amitava Das, Sivaji Bandyaopadhyay, and Björn Gambäck. 2012. The 5w structure for sentiment summarization-visualization-tracking. In *International Conference on Intelligent Text Processing and Computational Linguistics*, pages 540–555. Springer.

Jenny Rose Finkel, Trond Grenager, and Christopher Manning. 2005. Incorporating non-local information into information extraction systems by gibbs sampling. In *Proceedings of the 43rd Annual Meeting on Association for Computational Linguistics*, pages 363–370. Association for Computational Linguistics.

Dirk Hovy, Taylor Berg-Kirkpatrick, Ashish Vaswani, and Eduard Hovy. 2013. Learning whom to trust with MACE. In *Proceedings of the 2013 Conference of the North American Chapter of the Association for Computational Linguistics: Human Language Technologies*, pages 1120–1130.

I. Dan Melamed. 1996. Automatic detection of omissions in translations. In *Proceedings of the 16th Conference on Computational Linguistics - Volume 2*, COLING '96, pages 764–769, Copenhagen, Denmark.

Jason Merchant. 2016. Ellipsis: A survey of analytical approaches. `http://home.uchicago.edu/ merchant/pubs/ellipsis.revised.pdf`. Manuscript for Jeroen van Craenenbroeck and Tanja Temmerman (eds.), Handbook of ellipsis, Oxford University Press: Oxford, United Kingdom.

Kristen Parton, Kathleen R McKeown, Bob Coyne, Mona T Diab, Ralph Grishman, Dilek Hakkani-Tür, Mary Harper, Heng Ji, Wei Yun Ma, Adam Meyers, et al. 2009. Who, what, when, where, why?: comparing multiple approaches to the cross-lingual 5W task. In *Proceedings of the Joint Conference of the 47th Annual Meeting of the ACL and the 4th International Joint Conference on Natural Language Processing of the AFNLP*, pages 423–431.

Rebecca J Passonneau and Bob Carpenter. 2014. The benefits of a model of annotation. *Transactions of the Association for Computational Linguistics*, 2:311–326.

Jeffrey Pennington, Richard Socher, and Christopher D. Manning. 2014. GloVe: Global Vectors for Word Representation. In *Proceedings of the 2014 Conference on Empirical Methods in Natural Language Processing (EMNLP)*, pages 1532–1543, Doha, Qatar.

Marta Recasens, Cristian Danescu-Niculescu-Mizil, and Dan Jurafsky. 2013. Linguistic models for analyzing and detecting biased language. In *Proceedings of the 51th Annual Meeting of the ACL*, pages 1650–1659, Sofia, Bulgaria.

Graham Russell. 1999. Errors of Omission in Translation. In *Proceedings of the 8th International Conference on Theoretical and Methodological Issues in Machine Translation (TMI 99)*, pages 128–138, University College, Chester, England.

György Szarvas, Veronika Vincze, Richárd Farkas, György Móra, and Iryna Gurevych. 2012. Cross-genre and cross-domain detection of semantic uncertainty. *Computational Linguistics*, 38(2):335–367.

Marta Vila, M Antònia Martí, Horacio Rodríguez, et al. 2014. Is this a paraphrase? what kind? paraphrase boundaries and typology. volume 4, page 205. Scientific Research Publishing.

Veronika Vincze. 2013. Weasels, Hedges and Peacocks: Discourse-level Uncertainty in Wikipedia Articles. In *Proceedings of the International Joint Conference on Natural Language Processing*, pages 383–391, Nagoya, Japan.

Zhongyu Wei, Junwen Chen, Wei Gao, Binyang Li, Lanjun Zhou, Yulan He, and Kam-Fai Wong. 2013. An empirical study on uncertainty identification in social media context. In *Proceedings of the 51th Annual Meeting of the ACL*, pages 58–62, Sofia, Bulgaria.

Maayan Zhitomirsky-Geffet, Esther David, Moshe Koppel, Hodaya Uzan, and GE Gorman. 2016. Utilizing overtly political texts for fully automatic evaluation of political leaning of online news websites. *Online Information Review*, 40(3).

Annotating Speech, Attitude and Perception Reports

Corien Bary, Leopold Hess, Kees Thijs,
Radboud University Nijmegen
Department of Philosophy,
Theology and Religious Studies
Nijmegen, the Netherlands
`l.hess,k.thijs,c.bary`
`@ftr.ru.nl`

Peter Berck and Iris Hendrickx
Radboud University Nijmegen
Centre for Language & Speech Technology /
Centre for Language Studies,
Nijmegen, the Netherlands
`p.berck,i.hendrickx`
`@let.ru.nl`

Abstract

We present REPORTS, an annotation scheme for the annotation of speech, attitude and perception reports. The scheme makes it possible to annotate the various text elements involved in such reports (e.g. embedding entity, complement, complement head) and their relations in a uniform way, which in turn facilitates the automatic extraction of information on, for example, complementation and vocabulary distribution. We also present the Ancient Greek corpus RAG (Thucydides' *History of the Peloponnesian War*), to which we have applied this scheme using the annotation tool BRAT. We discuss some of the issues, both theoretical and practical, that we encountered, show how the corpus helps in answering specific questions about narrative perspective and the relation between report type and complement type, and conclude that REPORTS fitted in well with our needs.

1 Introduction

Both in our daily communication and in narratives we often refer to what other people said, thought and perceived. Take as an example (1) which has a speech, attitude and perception report in the first, second and third sentence, respectively:

(1) John came to Mary, bent on his knees, and asked her 'Will you marry me?' He was afraid that Mary didn't like him enough. He didn't look at her face.

Notice that not only does the type of the report differ (speech, attitude, perception), we also see different kinds of complements: a direct complement *'Will you marry me?'*, an indirect complement *that Mary didn't like him enough* and an NP complement *her face*. (Throughout this paper, by 'reports' we understand reports of speech acts, attitudes and perceptions - i.e., such things that can in principle have *propositional contents*, even if in a given case the report complement is only an NP. *John came to Mary* is not a report in this sense.)

The relation between the report type and the complement type (direct, indirect (further divided into e.g. complementizer + finite verb, participle, infinitive), NP) has been a major topic of research in semantics (Portner, 1992; Verspoor, 1990), syntax (Bresnan, 1970; Haumann, 1997), and language typology (Givón, 1980; Cristofaro, 2003; Cristofaro, 2008) alike.

A corpus annotated for speech, attitude and perception reports is a convenient tool to study this relation since it makes it possible to extract relevant information automatically. For a dead language like Ancient Greek - for which we developed our annotation scheme REPORTS in the first place - such a corpus is even more important, as the research is corpus-based by necessity.

In addition to the linguistic question of understanding the relation between report type and complement type, a corpus annotated for speech, attitude and perception reports is also of great use for questions of a more narratological nature. Narratology is the study of narratives, and one of the big topics here is that of *narrative perspective*, the phenomenon whereby literary texts often present events through the eyes of one of the characters in the story. Such a perspective emerges from the intricate interplay of all kinds of linguistic expressions, with an important role for speech, attitude and perception reports (whose thoughts and perceptions we read and what form they have).

In order to ultimately understand how narrative perspective works, a first step is a corpus annotated for speech, attitude and perception reports. Within the Perspective project,[1] we created such

---

[1] `www.ru.nl/ncs/perspective`

46

Proceedings of the 11th Linguistic Annotation Workshop, pages 46–56,
Valencia, Spain, April 3, 2017. ©2017 Association for Computational Linguistics

a corpus for Ancient Greek, RAG (Reports in Ancient Greek). Ancient Greek authors often create shifts to the perspectives of characters. Thucydides, for example, whose *History of the Peloponnesian War* (books 6 and 7) is the first corpus we annotated, was already in ancient times famous for this (Plutarch, *De Gloria* 3). How these authors achieved these perspective shifts is however an unsolved puzzle. We aim to shed light on these issues using the RAG corpus. Both the annotation guidelines and the annotated corpus are publicly available.[2]

RAG makes it possible to extract certain information about reports automatically, which will contribute to answering questions at both the linguistic and the narratological side. Although we developed the annotation scheme primarily with Ancient Greek in mind, we expect that it can be used for corpora in many other languages as well (see the evaluation below). A corpus annotated according to this scheme makes it for example easy to see which report types occur with which complement types. Here we distinguish not only between reports of speech, attitude and perception, but also annotate certain further subdivisions such as that between normal and manipulative speech reports (as in English *tell that* vs. *tell to*) which can be expected to be relevant.

In addition to extracting information about the combinations of report types and complement types, RAG (and other corpora that use the scheme) also makes it possible to search for certain words in report complements only. An interesting class here is for example that of attitudinal particles such as Ancient Greek δή, μήν, and που. These small words express the attitude of the actual speaker towards his utterance (e.g. (un)certainty, confirming expectations, countering the assumptions of the addressee (Thijs, 2017)). In reports, however, they can also be anchored to the reported speaker. Both in light of a better understanding of these notoriously elusive words themselves (e.g. which layer of meaning they target), and in light of their role in creating a certain narrative perspective (whose point of view they express) (Eckardt, 2012), the behavior of particles in reports deserves special attention (Döring, 2013), the study of which is strongly facilitated by a corpus annotated for reports.

In parallel with RAG, we developed an Ancient Greek lemmatizer, GLEM, and POS tagger. This combination increases the possibilities for data extraction considerably, as we will see. An interesting application of the lemmatizer for the narratological question lies in determining the vocabulary distribution of a certain text. Are there for example significant differences between the words the narrator uses when speaking for himself and those in the complements of other people's speeches, attitudes and perceptions (and how does this differ for the different kinds of reports and complements)? The lemmatizer makes it possible to extract this information at the level of the lemma rather than the individual word form. If we apply the scheme REPORTS to other authors, we can also study differences between authors in this respect, for example, whether Herodotus has a stronger distinction between vocabularies, while in Thucydides this is more blurred. This could then explain why it is especially Thucydides that stands out as the author who creates especially sophisticated narrative effects.

A characteristic feature of Ancient Greek speech reports is that they are often quite long. Even indirect reports seem to easily extend to several sentences (rather than just clauses). RAG is also useful for a better linguistic understanding of these constructions. We can for example search for clitic words that are taken to come exclusively at the peninitial position within a sentence, e.g. connective particles such as γάρ (Goldstein, 2016), to see whether it is indeed justified to speak about 'complements' consisting of more than one sentence (and hence, in the case of infinitive complements, of sentences without a finite verb!).

In this paper we discuss related annotation work (section 2), and describe the annotation tool BRAT which we used (section 3) and our annotation scheme REPORTS (section 4). In section 4 we also discuss some choices we made regarding the implementation of REPORTS in our corpus RAG. The corpus is further described in section 5, where we also discuss the application of the lemmatizer and POS tagger and present the results of a small experiment testing inter-annotator agreement. We evaluate BRAT and REPORTS in section 6, including a discussion of the extendability of REPORTS to other languages. Section 7 concludes with final remarks.

---

[2] `https://github.com/GreekPerspective`

2 Related work

Previous attempts at corpus annotation for related topics include the annotation of committed belief for English (Diab et al., 2009) and the annotation of direct and indirect speech in Portuguese (Freitas et al., 2016). Our project differs from the former in its focus on complementation (rather than information retrieval) and from the latter in its broader scope (reports in general rather than only speech).

Also related are the annotation schemes for modality such as (McShane et al., 2004; Hendrickx et al., 2012). These schemes aim to grasp the attitude of the actual speaker towards the proposition and label such attitudes as for example belief or obligation. In contrast to modality annotation, which focuses on the attitude of the actual speaker, we are interested in speech, attitude and perception acriptions in general, including ascriptions to other people than the actual speaker. Another difference is our focus on the linguistic constructions used. In that respect our scheme also differs from (Wiebe et al., 2005), which, like RAG, annotates what we call reports, but without differentiating between e.g. different kinds of complements.

3 BRAT rapid annotation tool

BRAT is an open source web-based tool for text annotation (Stenetorp et al., 2012)[3] and is an extension of *stav*, a visualization tool that was designed initially for complex semantic annotations for information extraction in the bio-medical domain including entities, events and their relations (Ohta et al., 2012; Neves et al., 2012). BRAT has been used in many different linguistic annotation projects that require complex annotation such as ellipsis (Anand and McCloskey, 2015), co-reference resolution (Kilicoglu and Demner-Fushman, 2016), and syntactic chunks (Savkov et al., 2016).

As BRAT uses a server-based web interface, annotators can access it in a web browser on their own computer without the need for further installation of software. All annotations are conveniently stored on the server.

We considered several other possible annotation tools for our project, such as MMAX2 (Müller and Strube, 2006), GATE Teamware (Bontcheva et al., 2013) and Arethusa[4]. The main reasons for se-

lecting BRAT as tool for the implementation of our annotation scheme were its web interface and its flexibility: BRAT accommodates the annotation of discontinuous spans as one entity and supports different types of relations and attributes.

Furthermore, BRAT offers a simple search interface and contains a tool for comparison of different versions of annotations on the same source text. BRAT also includes conversion scripts to convert several input formats such as the CoNNL shared task format, MALT XML[5] for parsing and the BIO format (Ramshaw and Marcus, 1995).

BRAT stores the annotation in a rather simple plain text standoff format that is merely a list of character spans and their assigned labels and relations, but that can easily be converted to other formats for further exploitation or search. We plan to port the annotated corpus to the ANNIS search tool (Krause and Zeldes, 2016) in a later stage to carry out more complex search queries.

4 REPORTS: an annotation scheme for speech, attitude and perception reports

4.1 The scheme

The annotation scheme REPORTS consists of entities, events and attributes of both.

Entities are (possibly discontinuous) spans of text. Let's start with two central ones, the **attitude/ speech/ perception embedding entity**, like *confessed* in (2), and the report **complement**, here *that he was in love*.

(2) John confessed that he was in love.

The attitude/speech/perception embedding entity is most typically a verb form, as in (2), but may also be a noun phrase (e.g. *the hope that*).[6] The embedding entity and the complement stand in the two-place relation **report**, which we implemented as an event in BRAT.

Because this complement is internally complex in some cases – consisting of a series of connected complement clauses – we use as a third entity the **complement chunk**. Chunks are all of the individual complement clauses that are syntactically dependent upon one and the same embedding entity. In (3) we have one complement *that he was in love and had not slept for three nights*, which

---

[3] http://brat.nlplab.org
[4] http://www.perseids.org/tools/ arethusa/app/#/

[5] https://stp.lingfil.uu.se/~nivre/ research/treebank.xsd.txt
[6] Hence the term *embedding entity*, rather than just *verb*.

consists of two chunks *that he was in love* and *and had not slept for three nights*:

(3) John confessed that he was in love and had not slept for three nights.

The complement chunks stand in the **chunk-of** relation to the complement they are part of. Complement chunks have a **head**, the final entity we annotate. Heads are always verbs. It is the verb that is directly dependent on the embedding entity and can be either a finite verb, an infinitive or a participle, depending on the specific subordinating construction used. In (3) the heads are *was* and *had*. As one would expect they stand in the **head-of** relation to the chunk. Table 1 lists all the entities and events.

The table also shows the attributes assigned within each class. The attributes of the embedding entities concern its semantic type. Within the class of speech report we distinguish (i) normal speech, involving neutral expressions such as *say, answer, report*; (ii) manner of speech, which are restricted to entities that refer to the physical properties of the speech act (e.g. *scream, cry, whisper*); (iii) manipulative speech, which is reserved for speech entities that are meant to lead to future actions of the addressee, such as *order/persuade/beg someone to*. The attitude embedding entities (which cover a broadly construed range of propositional attitudes) are further subdivided into (i) knowledge (e.g. *know, understand that*), (ii) belief (e.g. *think, believe, assume that*), (iii) voluntative (e.g. *want, intend, hope, fear to*) and (iv) other (mostly emotional attitudes such as *be ashamed, be grieved, rejoice*). Entities of perception (e.g. *see, hear*) do not have a further subdivision.

The complement type is also specified by means of an attribute. Here, there are five options: (i) direct, (ii) indirect, (iii) mixed, (iv) NP and (v) preposed NP. The mixed category is used for those cases where a combination of direct and indirect speech is used – embedding constructions in Ancient Greek sometimes shift or slip from one construction into the other (Maier, 2015). The NP-category covers instances of complements which do not have a propositional (clausal) character, but only consist of an NP-object. An English example would be *he expects a Spartan victory*.

The category of preposed NPs is typical of Ancient Greek. In case of finite complement clauses, a constituent that semantically belongs to this complement is sometimes placed in a position preceding the complementizer, i.e. syntactically outside of the complement clause. This happens for reasons of information structure – Ancient Greek is a discourse-configurational language, in which word order is determined mainly by information-structural concepts like topic and focus (Allan, 2014; Goldstein, 2016). It may even happen that this constituent is syntactically marked as a main clause argument – this phenomenon is called prolepsis in the literature (Panhuis, 1984). As a whole, constructions like these are annotated as containing two complements – a preposed NP and an indirect one – as well as two report relations.

Let's consider some Ancient Greek examples from RAG.

(4) οἱ   δὲ   ἄλλοι   ἐψηφίσαντό
     the.NOM PRT others.NOM vote.PST.3PL
     τε   ξυμμαχίαν   τοῖς   Ἀθηναίοις
     PRT alliance.ACC the.DAT Athenians.DAT
     καὶ τό   ἄλλο   στράτευμα
     and the.ACC   other.ACC army.ACC
     ἐκέλευον   ἐκ   Ῥηγίου   κομίζειν
     invite.PST.3PL from   Rhegium.GEN   fetch.INF
     'the others voted for an alliance with the
     Athenians and invited them to fetch the rest of
     their army from Rhegium.'   (Thuc. 6.51.2)

Figure 1 shows the visualization of (4) (with some context) as it is annotated in BRAT. Here, we have a manipulative speech verb (ἐκέλευον) that governs a discontinuous infinitival complement that consists of one chunk (τὸ ἄλλο στράτευμα ... ἐκ Ῥηγίου κομίζειν); its head is the infinitive κομίζειν.

Our second example is more complicated. The annotations in BRAT are shown in Figure 2, again with some context.

(5) [A ship went from Sicily to the
     Peloponnesus with ambassadors,]

     οἵπερ   τά   τε   σφέτερα
     who.REL.NOM   the.ACC PRT   own.affairs.ACC
     φράσουσιν   ὅτι   ἐν   ἐλπίσιν   εἰσὶ
     tell.FUT.3PL   that in   hopes.DAT be.PRS.3PL
     καὶ τὸν   ἐκεῖ πόλεμον ἔτι μᾶλλον
     and the.ACC   there war.ACC even more
     ἐποτρυνοῦσι   γίγνεσθαι
     incite.PRS.3PL become.INF
     'who should tell that their own affairs were
     hopeful, and should incite [the Peloponnesians]
     to prosecute the war there even more
     actively.'   (Thuc. 7.25.1)

Entities		
embedding entity[a]	speech	normal
		manner of speech
		manipulative
	attitude	knowledge
		belief
		voluntative
		other
		perception
complement		direct
		indirect
		mixed
		noun phrase
		preposed noun
		phrase
complement chunk		
head of complement chunk	finite, not optative	
	finite, optative	
	infinitive	
	participle	

Events (relations)		
report		
chunk-of		
head-of		

Table 1: RAG's entities, events and their attributes

[a]In the implementation in BRAT there actually is no such entity as an underspecified embedding entity, instead we go straight to the speech, attitude and perception embedded entities. The reason is that BRAT does not allow attributes of attributes, which we would otherwise need for the attributes normal etc.

Figure 1: visualization of annotation in BRAT of the sentence in (4) with some preceding context

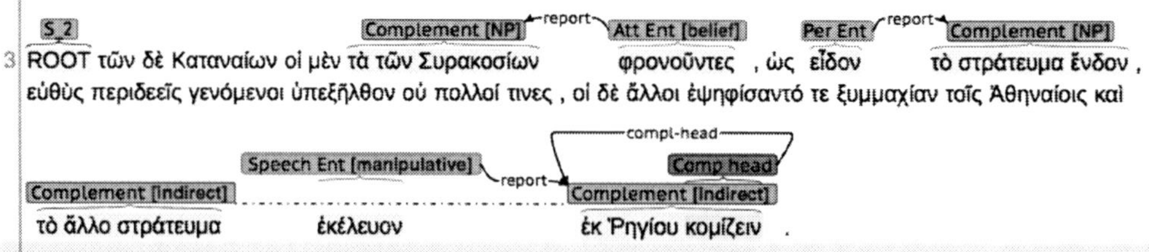

Here τά σφέτερα is a preposed NP, the complement clause being marked by the complementizer ὅτι 'that'. In the second part of the example, however, we find an infinitive construction instead of a finite clause with a complementizer and the whole complement clause is annotated as one (discontinuous) complement span again, like in (4).

4.2 Choices that we made

This basic scheme can be felicitously used for a great deal of the actual data in our corpus, but we also encountered on the one hand practical and on the other hand more complex issues that asked for additional annotation rules. The issues were discussed in the test phase and the rules were spelled out in an elaborate annotation manual. Some examples of the choices we made are the following.

Figure 2: visualization of annotation in BRAT of the sentence in (5)

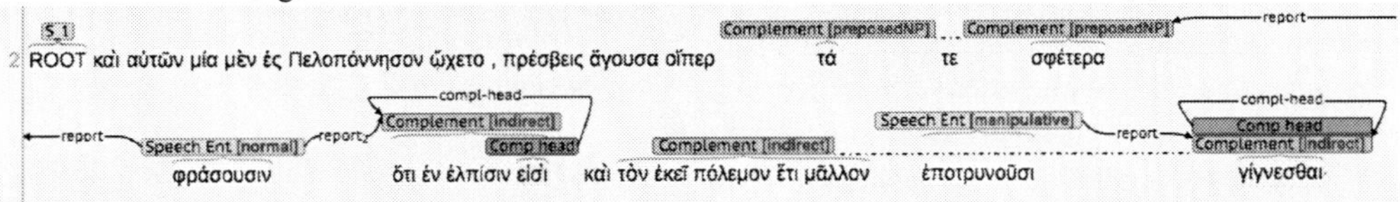

NPs We only made annotations when a complement is explicitly present. In other words, speech or attitude verbs used in an absolute sense (*he spoke for a long time*) are left out. We did include, however, NP-complements that have a prepositional form, as in περὶ τῆς ἀρχῆς εἰπεῖν (*to speak about the empire*) or ἐς Συρακοσίους δέος (*fear of the Syracusans*). With regard to NP-complements in general, we excluded instances of indefinite and demonstrative pronominal NP-objects (e.g. *he expects something/this*), since they are not interesting for our present research goals due to their lack of meaningful content.

chunks and heads As follows from the definition of a chunk as a subordinated clause, we did not annotate chunks in the case of NP and direct complements (nor heads, since a head is always head of a chunk).

attributes of the head We did not make manual annotation for the attributes of the complement head, i.e. whether it is an indicative, optative, infinitive or participle form. Instead, we used the output from the independently-trained POS tagger (see section 5).

UID As mentioned in the introduction, Ancient Greek reports, even indirect ones, can be very long. Quite frequently we find what is called Unembedded Indirect Discourse (Bary and Maier, 2014), as in (6).

(6) [A general sends messengers to his allies,]

ὅπως   μὴ   διαφρήσωσι
in.order.that   not   let.through.SBJV.3PL
τοὺς   πολεμίους   ἀλλὰ
the.ACC   enemies.ACC   but
ξυστραφέντες   κωλύσωσι
combine.PTCP.PASS   prevent.SBJV.3PL
διελθεῖν. ἄλλη   γὰρ αὐτοὺς   οὐδὲ
pass.INF elsewhere   for   them.ACC   not.even
πειράσειν.
try.INF.FUT

'in order that they would not let the enemies through, but would combine themselves and prevent them from passing; for [he said]

elsewhere they would not even attempt it.'
(Thuc. 7.32.1)

UID has a form that is usually associated with a dependent construction (infinitive or the Ancient Greek reportative mood called the optative), but in cases like the second sentence in (6) there is no embedding verb it is syntactically dependent on. As the clause with the infinitive or optative expresses the content of the report, we do annotate it as a complement (although the term complement may be misleading in this case).

parenthetical reports We made a different choice in the case of parenthetical report constructions, *Xerxes builds a bridge, as it is said* (ὡς λέγεται in Greek). Although here we do annotate the parenthetical verbs (since they have an important narrative function – the narrator attributes a thought or story to someone other than himself), we do not annotate the main clause *Xerxes builds a bridge* as a complement because there is no report morphology (infinitive or optative). In such cases the boundaries of the complement are also often very vague. Thus, while UID is annotated as a report complement without an embedding entity (or report relation), a parenthetical verb is annotated as an embedding entity without a complement.

defaults for ambiguous cases Some of the embedding entities have multiple meanings, which belong to different semantic categories in our classification of attributes. In some of these cases the choice of the attribute depends on the construction used for the complement clause. Just as English *tell*, mentioned in the introduction, εἶπον with a bare infinitive means *tell someone to* and is classified as a manipulative speech verb, whereas εἶπον with a subordinated *that*-clause means *say that* and belongs to the category of normal speech. In case of speech verbs governing an accusative constituent and an infinitive, however, there may still be an ambiguity in interpretation between the so-called Accusative plus Infinitive-construction (*He told that Xerxes builds a bridge*), where the accusative constituent functions exclusively as the subject of the complement infinitive clause, and a construction with an accusative object and a bare infinitive (*He told Xerxes to build a bridge*) (cf. (Rijksbaron, 2002)). Usually a decision can be easily made by looking at the surrounding context (as is the case in (4) above).

In other cases, the semantics of embedding entities is truly ambiguous between two categories, irrespective of the complement construction. Perception verbs like *see*, for instance, can easily mean *understand* or *know*. For verbs like these, we have made default classification rules such as the following: 'a perception entity is annotated as such by default; only if an interpretation of direct physical perception is not possible in the given discourse context it is annotated as an attitude knowledge entity.' Moreover, a list was made of all embedding entities and their (default) classification.

personal passive report constructions If the embedding entity is a passive verb of speech or thought, as in *Xerxes is said to build a bridge*, its subject is coreferential with the subject of the complement clause. (This is the so-called Nominative plus Infinitive construction (Rijksbaron, 2002)). What is reported here, of course, is the fact that Xerxes builds a bridge. However, we have decided not to include the subject constituent within the annotated complement in these cases, mainly to warrant consistency with other constructions with coreferential subjects for which it is more natural to exclude the subject from the complement (as in *Xerxes promised to build a bridge/that he would build a bridge*). There is a similar rule for constructions like δοκεῖ μοι 'X seems to me' and φαίνομαι 'to appear'.

complement boundaries In complex, multi-clause report complements, which are not rare in Ancient Greek, it is sometimes difficult to tell which parts actually belong to the report and which are interjections by the reporting speaker. As a default rule, we only treat material within the span of a report complement as an interjection (i.e. not annotate it as part of the complement) if it is a syntactically independent clause. Thus, for instance, relative clauses in non-final positions always belong to the span of the complement.

These and similar choices that we made in the progress of fine-tuning our annotation were motivated primarily by practical considerations, but they already led to a better conceptualization of some substantial questions, such as complement boundaries or relevant kinds of syntactic and semantic ambiguities.

5 RAG: a Greek corpus annotated for reports

So far we have annotated Thucydides' *History of the Peloponnesian War*, books 6 and 7, which consists of 807 sentences and 30891 words. In addition to Thucydides, we are also currently working on Herodotus' *Histories*.

The Thucydides digital text is provided by the Perseus Digital Library (Crane, 2016). As it was in betacode we converted it into unicode (utf8) using a converter created by the Classical Language Toolkit (Johnson and others, 2016).[7]

As mentioned before, we combine the manual reports annotation with automated POS-tagging and lemmatization (Bary et al., 2017), which we developed independently and which is open source.

The POS tagger made life easier for the annotator. We only annotated what is the head of the complement chunk and let it to the POS tagger to decide automatically whether this head is e.g. an infinitive, participle or finite verb and if finite, whether it has indicative mood or for example the reportative optative mood.

The lemmatizer enables us to discover whether a specific verb (e.g. all forms of λέγω 'to say') occurs with, say, a complement which contains the particle μήν or a complement with an oblique optative, without having to specify the (first, second, third person etc) forms of the verb manually.

For Herodotus, we can also adapt the manual annotations (including syntactic dependencies) made in the PROIEL project (Haug and Jøhndal, 2008; Haug et al., 2009),[8] whose text we use.

All of the corpus has been annotated by two annotators (PhD students with MA in Classics) working independently. An inventory of differences has been made for every chapter by a student assistant (partly extracted from BRAT automatically using the built-in comparison tool). All the errors and differences were then reviewed by

---

[7] https://github.com/cltk/cltk/blob/ master/cltk/corpus/greek/beta_to_ unicode.py

[8] http://www.hf.uio.no/ifikk/english/ research/projects/proiel/

the annotators (the most difficult issues were discussed in project meetings) to arrive at a common and final version. Most often differences between annotators concerned two types of issues, where clear-cut criteria are impossible to define: categorization of embedding verbs and syntactic structure ambiguities. The former issue involved verbs which could, depending on interpretation, be annotated with two or more different attributes. For example, ἐλπίζω may be a 'voluntative' verb ('to hope') or a 'belief' verb ('to expect'), (cf. discussion of εἶπον above); some verbs are ambiguous between factive ('knowledge' attitude entity category) and non-factive ('belief' category) senses etc. Even with the use of the more specific rules in the manual, different readings were often possible. The latter issue involved many kinds of ambiguities, most typically concerning relation between the complement clause and other subordinate and coordinate clauses. For example, a final relative clause whose antecedent is within the scope of the complement may, depending on interpretation, belong to the complement as well (its content is part of the content of the reported speech act or attitude) or be an external comment. (Purpose and conditional clauses give rise to similar issues.)

A small selection of the results are listed in Table 2. Here we see for example that γάρ, which is taken to come exclusively at the second position within a sentence, quite frequently occurs within a non-direct complement, suggesting that in these cases we have to do with main clauses rather than dependent clauses. Likewise we can easily search for the particle δή within complements to investigate whose perspective it expresses.

Inter annotator agreement

We performed a small experiment to measure the inter annotator agreement for labeling the main labels in this annotation task. We compared the span annotations of the following sample: book one of Thucydides, chapters 138-146, which contain 1932 words and 56 sentences. We counted the main labels (complement, complement chunk, head of chunk, attitude, speech and perception entities). We wielded a strict form of agreement: both the span length and span labels had to match to count as agreement. One annotator labeled 192 spans while the other labeled 182 spans leading to an inter annotator agreement of 83.4% mutual F-score (Hripcsak and Rothschild, 2005).

# embedding entities	670
speech	189
attitude	441
perception	40
# complements	702
indirect	543
direct	15
NP	138
preposed NP	19
with speech embedding entities	186
with attitude embedding entities	460
with perception embedding entities	39
unembedded	17
# δή/δὴ in non-direct complements	10
# multisentential complements	9
# γάρ/γὰρ after sentence-boundary in non-direct complements	12
total # words in complements[a]	17.836
average # of words per complement	25.41
indirect	14.25
direct	630.60
NP	4.09
preposed NP	3.89

Table 2: Some numbers for RAG

[a]Embedded ones counted twice.

6 Evaluation

In this section we evaluate both the BRAT tool and the REPORTS scheme with respect to their convenience and usefulness.

BRAT is a convenient annotation tool, offering perspicuous visualization and easy to use without any prior training or IT skills (although such skills are needed, of course, to set up an annotation scheme in BRAT). It does not even require typing any commands - after selecting a span of text, a window opens from which the annotation can be chosen with a click of the mouse. However, it has its limitations. The following remarks can be seen as suggestions for future versions or extensions of the program.

For example, with complex annotations involving multiple entities and relations (where often one report is embedded in another) the visualization ceases to be easily legible. In this respect, it seems that an annotation scheme of the complexity of

REPORTS reaches the limits of BRAT's usefulness. Also, since it is currently impossible to assign attributes to attributes, we could not have speech, attitude and perception as attributes of the category embedding entities (see the footnote in Table 1). As a result we need to query the conjunction of speech, attitude and perception entities if we want to draw conclusions about this class in general.

Deleting and correcting complex annotations is not straightforward. Crossing and overlapping spans frequently give rise to errors, which are then impossible to repair from the level of BRAT's interface and require manual access to source files.

A useful function would be that of creating different annotation layers that could be switched on and off in the visual representation - which is possible in e.g. MMAX2 (Müller and Strube, 2006) and would be helpful in this project to use for the annotations of POS and lemma information.

Finally, it would have been convenient if it had been possible to formulate default features, such as the attribute 'normal' in the case of speech embedding entities.

As for the annotation scheme itself, it involves a relatively small number of entities, relations and attributes, but its application is not straightforward and it necessitated the creation of additional documents (described above): a manual containing explicit rules for annotation and a list of embedding verbs in the different categories. Both documents have been extended and amended in the course of work on the annotation. Annotators also required time to get accustomed to the scheme. Nonetheless, after the initial period it was possible to achieve a good level of inter-annotator agreement, as shown by the experiment mentioned above.

The annotation scheme is easily extendable to other languages which share the same typology of complements (direct vs. indirect vs. NP) in speech, attitude and perception reports (that includes at least all major European languages). The categorization of embedding verbs should be universally applicable. Some simplifications are possible in many languages, e.g. removing the category of preposed NP complements or the additional layer of complement chunks (which may not be as useful for many languages as it is for Ancient Greek, where complements often contain several clauses of different types). For modern literary languages it would probably be necessary to create a category for Free Indirect Discourse (but perhaps this would not require more than adding a new attribute of complement entities - the scheme already supports unembedded reports). More substantial changes would be needed for languages which have different typologies of reports (e.g. with no strict distinction between direct and indirect reports) or use other constructions besides embedding verbs to convey reports (e.g. evidential morphemes).

7 Conclusion

BRAT, despite some limitations, is a useful annotation tool that made it possible to implement an annotation scheme which covers all the categories and distinctions that we had wanted to include.

Our annotation scheme REPORTS serves its purpose well, as it makes it possible to easily extract from the corpus information that is relevant to a variety of research questions, concerning e.g. relations between semantics of embedding entities and syntax of complement clauses, factive presuppositions, distribution of vocabulary (including special subsets such as discourse particles, evaluative expressions, deictic elements) in different types of report complements and outside of them, narrative perspective and focalization etc. Both the corpus and the annotation scheme, which are made publicly available, can therefore be a valuable resource for both linguists and literary scholars.

Acknowledgments

This research is supported by the EU under FP7, ERC Starting Grant 338421-Perspective. We thank Anke Kersten, Celine Teeuwen and Delano van Luik for their help.

References

Rutger Allan. 2014. Changing the topic: Topic position in Ancient Greek word order. *Mnemosyne*, 67(2):181–213.

Pranav Anand and Jim McCloskey. 2015. Annotating the implicit content of sluices. In *The 9th Linguistic Annotation Workshop held in conjuncion with NAACL 2015*, pages 178–187.

Corien Bary and Emar Maier. 2014. Unembedded Indirect Discourse. *Proceedings of Sinn und Bedeutung*, 18:77–94.

Corien Bary, Peter Berck, and Iris Hendrickx. 2017. A memory-based lemmatizer for Ancient Greek. Manuscript.

Kalina Bontcheva, Hamish Cunningham, Ian Roberts, Angus Roberts, Valentin Tablan, Niraj Aswani, and Genevieve Gorrell. 2013. Gate teamware: a web-based, collaborative text annotation framework. *Language Resources and Evaluation*, 47(4):1007–1029.

Joan W. Bresnan. 1970. *On Complementizers: Toward a Syntactic Theory of Complement Types*. Springer, Dordrecht.

Gregory R. Crane. 2016. Perseus Digital Library. `http://www.perseus.tufts.edu`. [Online; accessed Dec 16, 2016].

Sonia Cristofaro. 2003. *Subordination*. Oxford University Press, Oxford.

Sonia Cristofaro. 2008. A constructionist approach to complementation: Evidence from Ancient Greek. *Linguistics*, 46(3):571–606.

Mona T. Diab, Lori S. Levin, Teruko Mitamura, Owen Rambow, Vinodkumar Prabhakaran, and Weiwei Guo. 2009. Committed Belief Annotation and Tagging. In *Third Linguistic Annotation Workshop*, pages 68–73, Singapore. The Association for Computer Linguistics.

Sophia Döring. 2013. Modal particles and context shift. In *Beyond expressives: Explorations in use-conditional meaning*, pages 95–123, Leiden. Brill.

Regine Eckardt. 2012. Particles as speaker indexicals in Free Indirect Discourse. *Sprache und Datenverarbeitung*, 36(1):1–21.

Cláudia Freitas, Bianca Freitas, and Diana Santos. 2016. Quemdisse? Reported speech in Portuguese. In *Proceedings of the Tenth International Conference on Language Resources and Evaluation (LREC 2016)*, pages 4410–4416, Paris. European Language Resources Association (ELRA).

Talmy Givón. 1980. The binding hierarchy and the typology of complements. *Studies in Language*, 4(3):333–377.

David Goldstein. 2016. *Classical Greek Syntax: Wackernagel's Law in Herodotus*. Brill, Leiden.

Dag Haug and Marius Jøhndal. 2008. Creating a parallel treebank of the old Indo-European Bible translations. In *Proceedings of the Language Technology for Cultural Heritage Data Workshop (LaTeCH 2008), Marrakech, Morocco, 1st June 2008*, pages 27–34.

Dag Haug, Marius Jøhndal, Hanne Eckhoff, Eirik Welo, Mari Hertzenberg, and Angelika Müth. 2009. Computational and linguistic issues in designing a syntactically annotated parallel corpus of Indo-European languages. *Traitement Automatique des Langues (TAL)*, 50(2):17–45.

Dagmar Haumann. 1997. *The Syntax of Subordination*. Max Niemeyer, Tübingen.

Iris Hendrickx, Amália Mendes, and Silvia Mencarelli. 2012. Modality in Text: a Proposal for Corpus Annotation. In *LREC'2012 – Eighth International Conference on Language Resources and Evaluation*, pages 1805–1812, Istanbul, Turkey, May. European Language Resources Association (ELRA).

George Hripcsak and Adam S. Rothschild. 2005. Agreement, the f-measure, and reliability in information retrieval. *Journal of the American Medical Informatics Association (JAMIA)*, 12(3):296–298.

Kyle P. Johnson et al. 2016. CLTK: The Classical Languages Toolkit. `https://github.com/cltk/cltk`. [Online; accessed Nov 12, 2016].

Halil Kilicoglu and Dina Demner-Fushman. 2016. Bio-SCoRes: A Smorgasbord Architecture for Coreference Resolution in Biomedical Text. *PLoS ONE*, 11(3).

Thomas Krause and Amir Zeldes. 2016. Annis3: A new architecture for generic corpus query and visualization. *Digital Scholarship in the Humanities*, 31(1):118–139.

Emar Maier. 2015. Reported speech in the transition from orality to literacy. *Glotta: Zeitschrift für griechische und lateinische Sprache*, 91E(1):152–170.

Marjorie McShane, Sergei Nirenburg, and Ron Zacharski. 2004. Mood and modality: out of theory and into the fray. *Natural Language Engineering*, 10(01):57–89.

Christoph Müller and Michael Strube. 2006. Multilevel annotation of linguistic data with MMAX2. In Sabine Braun, Kurt Kohn, and Joybrato Mukherjee, editors, *Corpus Technology and Language Pedagogy: New Resources, New Tools, New Methods*, pages 197–214. Peter Lang, Frankfurt a.M.

Mariana Neves, Alexander Damaschun, Andreas Kurtz, and Ulf Leser. 2012. Annotating and evaluating text for stem cell research. In *Third Workshop on Building and Evaluation Resources for Biomedical Text Mining (BioTxtM 2012) at Language Resources and Evaluation (LREC)*.

Tomoko Ohta, Sampo Pyysalo, Jun'ichi Tsujii, and Sophia Ananiadou. 2012. Open-domain anatomical entity mention detection. In *Proceedings of the Workshop on Detecting Structure in Scholarly Discourse*, pages 27–36. Association for Computational Linguistics.

Dirk Panhuis. 1984. Prolepsis in Greek as a discourse strategy. *Glotta: Zeitschrift für griechische und lateinische Sprache*, 62:26–39.

Paul Portner. 1992. Situation theory and the semantics of propositional expressions. Ph.D. Dissertation, University of Massachusetts, Amherst.

L.A. Ramshaw and M.P. Marcus. 1995. Text chunking using transformation-based learning. In *Proceedings of the Third Workshop on Very Large Corpora*, pages 82–94.

Albert Rijksbaron. 2002. *The Syntax and Semantics of the Verb in Classical Greek: An Introduction.* Gieben, Amsterdam.

A. Savkov, J. Carroll, R. Koeling, and J. Cassell. 2016. Annotating patient clinical records with syntactic chunks and named entities: the Harvey Corpus. *Language Resources and Evaluation*, 50:523–548.

Pontus Stenetorp, Sampo Pyysalo, Goran Topic, Tomoko Ohta, Sophia Ananiadou, and Jun'ichi Tsujii. 2012. BRAT: a web-based tool for NLP-assisted text annotation. In *Proceedings of the Demonstrations at the 13th Conference of the European Chapter of the Association for Computational Linguistics*, pages 102–107.

Kees Thijs. 2017. The Attic particle μήν: intersubjectivity, contrast and polysemy. *Journal of Greek Linguistics*.

Marjolijn Verspoor. 1990. Semantic criteria in English complement selection. Ph.D. Dissertation, Rijksuniversiteit Leiden.

Janyce Wiebe, Theresa Wilson, and Claire Cardie. 2005. Annotating expressions of opinions and emotions in language. *Language resources and evaluation*, 39(2):165–210.

Consistent Classification of Translation Revisions:
A Case Study of English-Japanese Student Translations

Atsushi Fujita
NICT
atsushi.fujita@nict.go.jp

Kikuko Tanabe
Kobe College
kikukotanabe@gmail.com

Chiho Toyoshima
Kansai Gaidai University
c.toyoshima1113@gmail.com

Mayuka Yamamoto
Honyaku Center Inc.
yamamoto.mayuka
@honyakuctr.co.jp

Kyo Kageura
University of Tokyo
kyo@p.u-tokyo.ac.jp

Anthony Hartley
Rikkyo University
A.Hartley@rikkyo.ac.jp

Abstract

Consistency is a crucial requirement in text annotation. It is especially important in educational applications, as lack of consistency directly affects learners' motivation and learning performance. This paper presents a quality assessment scheme for English-to-Japanese translations produced by learner translators at university. We constructed a revision typology and a decision tree manually through an application of the OntoNotes method, i.e., an iteration of assessing learners' translations and hypothesizing the conditions for consistent decision making, as well as reorganizing the typology. Intrinsic evaluation of the created scheme confirmed its potential contribution to the consistent classification of identified erroneous text spans, achieving visibly higher Cohen's κ values, up to 0.831, than previous work. This paper also describes an application of our scheme to an English-to-Japanese translation exercise course for undergraduate students at a university in Japan.

1 Introduction

Assessing and assuring translation quality is one of the main concerns for translation services, machine translation (MT) industries, and translation teaching institutions.[1] The assessment process for a given pair of source document (SD) and its translation, i.e., target document (TD), consists of two tasks. The first task is to identify erroneous text spans in the TD. In professional settings, when assessors consider a text span in a TD as erroneous,

they generally suggest a particular revision proposal (Mossop, 2014). For instance, in example (1), a transliteration error is corrected.

(1) SD: Mark <u>Potok</u> is a senior fellow at the Southern Poverty Law Center.
TD: マーク・ポッドック (⇒ ポトク) 氏は南部貧困法律センターの上級研究員だ。
(Podok ⇒ Potok)

Henceforth, we refer to a marked text span reflecting the identification of a particular error or deficiency as an *issue*. The second task is to classify each identified issue into an abstract *issue type*, such as "omission" or "misspelling."

An inherent problem concerning translation quality assessment is that it inevitably involves human judgments, and thus is subjective.[2] The first task, i.e., identifying issues in TDs, relies heavily on assessors' translation and linguistic competence, as may the subsequent step of making a revision proposal for them, depending on the subtlety of the issue. It therefore seems impractical to create an annotation scheme that enables even inexperienced translators to perform this task at a comparable level to mature translators.

For regulating the second task, several typologies, such as those reviewed in Secară (2005), the Multilingual e-Learning in Language Engineering (MeLLANGE) error typology (Castagnoli et al., 2006), and Multidimensional Quality Metrics (MQM),[3] have been proposed. Existing issue typologies show diversity in their granularity and their organization of issue types, owing to the fact that the scope and granularity of issues depend

---

[1] These include both private companies and translation-related departments in colleges and universities.

[2] While automated metrics for MT quality evaluation are often presented as objective, many, including BLEU (Papineni et al., 2002), rely on comparison with a one or more human reference translations whose quality and subjectivity are merely assumed and not independently validated.

[3] http://www.qt21.eu/launchpad/content/multidimensional-quality-metrics

Proceedings of the 11th Linguistic Annotation Workshop, pages 57–66,
Valencia, Spain, April 3, 2017. ©2017 Association for Computational Linguistics

on the purpose of translations and the aim of human assessments (e.g., formative or summative). However, the typology alone does not necessarily guarantee consistent human assessments (Lommel et al., 2015). For instance, while one may classify the issue in (1) as an "incorrect translation of term," it could also be regarded as a "misspelling."

In this paper, we focus on the quality assessment of learners' translations. Motivated by the increasing demand for translation, translation teaching institutions have been incorporating best practices of professionals into their curricula. When teaching the revision and review processes in such institutions, the assessor's revision proposal is normally not provided, in order to prevent learners believing that it is the only correct solution (Klaudy, 1996). Thus, issue type plays a crucial role in conveying the assessors' intention to learners, and its consistency is especially important, since lack of consistency directly affects learners' motivation and learning performance. Besides the consistency, the applicability of an assessment tool to a wide range of translations is also important. To the best of our knowledge, however, none of the existing typologies have been validated for translations between languages whose structures are radically different, such as English and Japanese. Neither have their applicability to translations produced by less advanced learners, such as undergraduate students, been fully examined.

Aiming at (i) a consistent human assessment, (ii) of English-to-Japanese translations, (iii) produced by learner translators, we manually constructed a scheme for classifying identified issues. We first collected English-to-Japanese translations from learners in order to assure and validate the applicability of our scheme (§3). We then manually created an issue typology and a decision tree through an application of the OntoNotes method (Hovy et al., 2006), i.e., an iteration of assessing learners' translations and updating the typology and decision tree (§4). We adopted an existing typology, that of MNH-TT (Babych et al., 2012), as the starting point, because its origin (Castagnoli et al., 2006) was tailored to assessing university student learners' translations and its applicability across several European languages had been demonstrated. We evaluated our scheme with inter-assessor agreement, employing four assessors and an undergraduate learner translator (§5).

We also implemented our scheme in an English-to-Japanese translation exercise course for undergraduate students at a university in Japan, and observed tendencies among absolute novices (§6).

2 Previous Work

To the best of our knowledge, the error typology in the Multilingual e-Learning in Language Engineering (MeLLANGE) project (Castagnoli et al., 2006) was the first tool tailored to assessing learners' translations. It had been proved applicable to learners' translations across several European languages, including English, German, Spanish, French, and Italian. The MeLLANGE typology distinguished more than 30 types of issues, grouped into Transfer (TR) issues, whose diagnosis requires reference to both SD and TD, and Language (LA) issues, which relate to violations of target language norms. This distinction underlies the widespread distinction between adequacy and fluency, the principal editing and revision strategies advocated by Mossop (2014), and the differentiation between (bilingual) revision and (monolingual) reviewing specified in ISO/TC27 (2015). Designed for offering formative assessment by experienced instructors to university learner translators, it provided a fine-grained discrimination seen also in, for instance, the framework of the American Translators Association (ATA) with 23 categories.[4]

The MeLLANGE typology was simplified by Babych et al. (2012), who conflated various subcategories and reduced the number of issue types to 16 for their translation training environment, MNH-TT, which differs from MeLLANGE in two respects. First, it is designed for feedback from peer learners acting as revisers and/or reviewers, whose ability to make subtle distinctions is reduced. Second, it is embedded in a project-oriented translation scenario that simulates professional practice and where more coarse-grained, summative schemes prevail.[5,6] In our pilot test, however, we found that even the MNH-TT typology did not necessarily guarantee consistent human assessments. When we identified 40 issues

---

[4]`http://www.atanet.org/certification/aboutexams_error.php`

[5]SAE J2450, the standard for the automotive industry, has only seven categories. `http://standards.sae.org/j2450_200508/`

[6]The latest MQM (as of February 21, 2017) has eight top-level issue types (dimensions) and more than 100 leaf nodes. `http://www.qt21.eu/mqm-definition/`

Level 1: **Incompleteness**	Translation is not finished.
Level 2: **Semantic errors**	The contents of the SD are not properly transferred.
Level 3: **TD linguistic issues**	The contents of the SD are transferred, but there are some linguistic issues in the TD.
Level 4: **TD felicity issues**	The TD is meaning-preserving and has no linguistic issues, but have some flaws.
Level 5: **TD register issues**	The TD is a good translation, but not suitable for the assumed text type.

Table 1: Priority of coarse-grained issue types for translation training for novices.

in an English-to-Japanese translation by a learner and two of the authors separately classified them, only 17 of them (43%) resulted in agreement on the classification, achieving Cohen's κ (Cohen, 1960) of 0.36. This highlighted the necessity of a navigation tool, such as a decision tree, for consistent human decision making, especially given that the issue type serves as feedback to learners.

Multidimensional Quality Metrics (MQM) has been widely used in the MT community and translation industries. However, the consistency of classifying issues had not been guaranteed when only its issue typology was used. Lommel et al. (2014) measured the inter-assessor agreement of identifying erroneous text spans in MT outputs and classifying them, using the MQM typology comprising 20 types. Having obtained low Cohen's κ values, 0.18 to 0.36, and observed several types of ambiguities, they pointed out the lack of decision making tool. Motivated by this study, MQM later established a decision tree (Burchardt and Lommel, 2014). Nevertheless, MQM has not been validated as applicable to learners' translations, especially those between distant languages.

3 Collecting English-to-Japanese Translations by Learners

Our study began with collecting English-to-Japanese translations produced by learner translators. Assuming novice learner translators and the very basic competences to teach, we selected journalistic articles as the text type. As the SDs in English, 18 articles with similar conceptual and linguistic difficulties were sampled from the column page of a news program "Democracy Now!"[7] by a professional translator, who also had significant experience in teaching English-to-Japanese translation at universities. The average number of words in the SDs was 781. Then, 30 students (12 undergraduate and 18 graduate students) were employed to translate one of the SDs into Japanese.[8]

---

[7] http://www.democracynow.org/blog/
category/weekly_column/

[8] Some of the SDs were separately translated by more than one student.

All these participants were native Japanese speakers and had attended translation classes at a university in Japan. They were asked to produce a TD that served as a Japanese version of the original article.

The collected pairs of SD and TD were divided into the following three partitions.

Development: Three randomly selected document pairs were used to develop our scheme (§4).

Validation 1: Another 17 sampled document pairs were used to gauge the inter-assessor agreement of the issue classification task, given the identified issues (§5.1).

Validation 2: The remaining ten document pairs were used to examine the stability of identifying erroneous text spans in the TDs, as well as the inter-assessor agreement between a learner and an experienced assessor (§5.2).

4 Development of an Issue Classification Scheme

To alleviate potential inconsistencies, we structuralized the issue types in the MNH-TT typology (Babych et al., 2012), introducing a decision tree. We chose a decision tree as a navigation tool for human decision making, as in MQM (Burchardt and Lommel, 2014), because the resulting issues will be used not only by the instructors in order to evaluate the translation quality but also by learners in order to understand the diagnoses. We also considered that explicit explanation for decisions is critical in such scenarios.

We first determined the priorities of issue types through in-depth interviews with two professional translators, who also had ample experience in teaching English-to-Japanese translation at universities. These priorities were based on both the work-flow of the professionals and the nature of the issues they found in grading learners' translations. Table 1 shows the coarse-grained figure resulting from the two translators' agreement. Obvious incompleteness of translations are captured

Issue types in our typology		MeLLANGE	MQM
Level 1: Incompleteness			
X4a	Content-SD-intrusion-untranslated:	TR-SI-UT	Untranslated
	The TD contains elements of the SD left untranslated in error		
X6	Content-indecision:	TR-IN	n/a
	The TD contains alternative choices left unresolved by the translator		
Level 2: Semantic errors			
X7	Lexis-incorrect-term: Item is a non-term, incorrect, inconsistent with the glossary or inconsistent within the TD	LA-TL-{IN,NT,IG,IT}	Terminology
X1	Content-omission:	TR-OM	Omission
	Content present in the SD is wrongly omitted in the TD		
X2	Content-addition:	TR-AD	Addition
	Content not present in the SD is wrongly added to the TD		
X3	Content-distortion:	TR-DI, TR-TI-*, TR-TL-IN	Mistranslation
	Content present in the SD is misrepresented in the TD		
Level 3: TD linguistic issues			
X8	Lexis-inappropriate-collocation: Item is not a usual collocate of a neighbor it governs or is governed by	LA-TL-IC	n/a
X10	Grammar-preposition/particle:	LA-PR	Grammar
	Incorrect preposition or (Japanese) particle		
X11	Grammar-inflection: Incorrect inflection or agreement for tense, aspect, number, case, or gender	LA-IA-*	Grammar
X12	Grammar-spelling: Incorrect spelling	LA-HY-SP	Spelling
X13	Grammar-punctuation: Incorrect punctuation	LA-HY-PU	Punctuation
X9	Grammar-others: Other grammatical and syntactic issues in the TD	n/a	Grammar
Level 4: TD felicity issues			
X16	Text-incohesive: Inappropriate use or non-use of anaphoric expressions, or wrong ordering of given and new elements of information	n/a	n/a
X4b	Content-SD-intrution-too-literal:	TR-SI-TL	Overly literal
	The TD contains elements of the SD that are translated too literally		
X15	Text-clumsy: Lexical choice or phrasing is clumsy, tautologous, or unnecessarily verbose	LA-ST-*	Awkward
Level 5: TD register issues			
X14	Text-TD-inappropriate-register: Lexical choice, phrasing, or style is inappropriate for the intended text type of the TD	LA-RE-*	Style (except "Awkward"), Local convention, Grammatical register

Table 2: Our issue typology, with prefixes (context, lexis, grammar, and text) indicating their coarse-grained classification in the MNH-TT typology (Babych et al., 2012). The two rightmost columns show the corresponding issue types in the MeLLANGE typology (Castagnoli et al., 2006) and those in MQM (Lommel et al., 2015), respectively, where "n/a" indicates issue types that are not covered explicitly.

at Level 1. While Level 2 covers issues related to misunderstandings of the SD, Levels 3 and 4 highlight issues in the language of the TD. Level 5 deals with violation of various requirements imposed by the text type of the translated document.

Regarding Table 1 as a strict constraint for the shape of the decision tree, and the 16 issue types in the MNH-TT typology as the initial issue types, we developed our issue classification scheme, using the OntoNotes method (Hovy et al., 2006). In other words, we performed the following iteration(s).

Step 1. Annotate issues in the TDs for development, using the latest scheme.

Step 2. Terminate the iteration if we meet a satisfactory agreement ratio (90%, as in Hovy et al. (2006)).

Step 3. Collect disagreed issues among assessors, including those newly found, and discuss the factors of consistent decision making.

Step 4. Update the scheme, including the definition of each issue type, the conditions for decision making, and their organization in the form of a decision tree. Record marginal examples in the example list.

Step 5. Go back to Step 1.

Three of the authors conducted the above process using the three document pairs (see §3), which resulted in the issue typology in Table 2 and the decision tree in Table 3. A total of 52 typical and marginal examples were also collected.

It is noteworthy that our issue typology preserves almost perfectly the top-level distinction of the MeLLANGE typology, i.e., the TR (trans-

ID	Question	Determined type or next question	
		True	False
Q1a	Is it an unjustified copy of the SD element?	X4a	Q1b
Q1b	Do multiple options remain in the TD?	X6	Q2a
Q2a	Is all content in the SD translated in proper quantities in a proper way?	Q3a	Q2b
Q2b	Is the error related to a term in the given glossary?	X7	X1/X2/X3
Q3a	Is it a grammatical issue?	Q3b	Q4a
Q3b	Is it predefined specific type?	X8/X10/X11/X12/X13	X9
Q4a	Does it hurt cohesiveness of the TD?	X16	Q4b
Q4b	Does it hurt fluency?	Q4c	Q5a
Q4c	Is it too literal?	X4b	X15
Q5a	Is it unsuitable for the intended text type of the TD?	X14	Q6a
Q6a	Is it anyways problematic?	"Other issue"	"Not an issue"

Table 3: Our decision tree for classifying a given issue: we do not produce questions for distinguishing X1/X2/X3, and X8/X10/X11/X12/X13, considering that their definitions are clear enough.

fer) and LA (language) issues, described in §2. The priority of the former over the latter, implicitly assumed in the MeLLANGE typology, is also largely preserved; the sole exceptions are X7 (incorrect translations of terms) and X4b (too literal). Table 2 also shows that our typology includes the following three issue types that are not covered by MQM.

- X6 (indecision) captures a student habit of offering more than one translation for a given text, which is not observed in professional translators.

- X8 (collocation) employs a more specific, linguistic terminology for diagnosing one subtype of X15 (clumsy).

- X16 (incohesive), which is also absent from the MeLLANGE typology but present in the ATA framework, appears not applicable in the common (commercial) situation where sentences are translated without reference to their context.

During the development process, we decided to identify and classify only the first occurrence of *identical issues* in a single TD. For instance, other incorrect translations of "ポッドック" for "Potok" in the same TD as example (1) will not be annotated repeatedly. This is because annotations are made and used by humans, i.e., assessors and learners, and persistent indications of identical issues may waste the time of assessors and discourage learners. This practice differs from ordinary linguistic annotation, especially that aiming to develop training data for machine learning methods, which requires exhaustive annotation of the phenomena of interest within given documents. Although there have been several studies on the use

of partial/incomplete annotation, e.g., Tsuboi et al. (2008), our procedure is nevertheless different from these in the sense that we leave issues "unannotated" only when identical ones are already annotated.

5 Intrinsic Evaluation of the Scheme

It is hard to make a fair and unbiased comparison between different annotation schemes that target the same phenomena, employing the same assessors. We thus evaluated whether our issue classification scheme leads to sufficiently high level of inter-assessor agreement, regarding those poor results described in §2 as baselines, and analyzed the tendencies of disagreements and the distribution of issues.

5.1 Validation 1: Classification of Identified Issues

5.1.1 Inter-Assessor Agreement

We gauged the consistency of classifying identified issues by the inter-assessor agreement.

First, three of the authors who developed our scheme identified erroneous text spans in the 17 TDs (see §3) and made a revision proposal for each, through discussion. Then, four assessors were independently asked to classify each of the resulting 575 issues into one of the 16 issue types, "other issue," and "not an issue," following our decision tree in Table 3. Two of them were anonymous paid workers (A and B), while the others (C and D) were two of the above three authors. All four assessors were native Japanese speakers with a strong command of English and an understanding of our scheme and translation-related notions. While they were asked to adhere to our decision

ID	Background	Agreement ratio [%]				Cohen's κ			
		vs A	vs B	vs C	vs D	vs A	vs B	vs C	vs D
A	Bachelor of Engineering (now translation editor)	-	67.7	63.3	57.9	-	0.613	0.554	0.490
B	Master of Japanese Pedagogy (now translator)	67.7	-	67.1	61.4	0.613	-	0.592	0.523
C	Master of Translation Studies	63.3	67.1	-	86.6	0.554	0.592	-	0.831
D	Ph.D in Computational Linguistics	57.9	61.4	86.6	-	0.490	0.523	0.831	-

Table 4: Inter-assessor agreement on the identified 575 issues.

tree, no dictionary or glossary was provided.

Table 4 summarizes the agreement ratio and Cohen's κ (Cohen, 1960). The most consistent pair was C and D who agreed on 86.6% (498/575) of the issues and achieved almost perfect agreement, $\kappa = 0.831$, although it is indisputable that they had some advantages, having been engaged in developing the scheme and identifying the issues. Both of the two measures draw a clear distinction between the anonymous and identified assessors. As our analysis below illustrates, the anonymous workers made many careless mistakes, presumably because the human resource agency did not offer substantial incentive to pursue accurate and consistent annotations. Nevertheless, even the lowest κ value in our experiment, 0.490, was visibly higher than those achieved using the typologies with the same level of granularity but without a tool for consistent decision making (see §2).

Table 5 shows the most frequent disagreement patterns between each anonymous worker and the two authors (C and D) on the 498 issues about which the authors have agreed. The most typical disagreement was between X3 (distortion) and X4b (too literal). For instance, "has passed" in example (2) was mistakenly translated into "通過した ([bill] passed [legislature])," resulting in two exclusive subjects marked with nominative case marker "が," i.e., "各州政府 (state after state)" and "農業口封じ法 (Ag-Gag laws)."

(2)   SD: State after state <u>has passed</u> so-called Ag-Gag laws.

      TD: 各州政府がいわゆる農業口封じ法<u>が通過した</u> (⇒ を可決した)。
([bill] passed [legislature] ⇒ [legislature] passed [bill])

As the TD does not convey the original meaning in the SD, both C and D classified this issue into X3 (distortion). In contrast, both A and B regarded them as X4b (too literal), presumably considering that both of the original translation "通過した" and the revision proposal "可決した" were appropriate lexical translations for "has passed" when

A, B	C&D	A	B
X4b (Level 4)	X3 (Level 2)	37	8
X3 (Level 2)	X4b (Level 4)	11	24
X1 (Level 2)	X3 (Level 2)	13	10
X1 (Level 2)	X4b (Level 4)	6	5
X1 (Level 2)	X16 (Level 4)	6	4
X1 (Level 2)	X7 (Level 2)	5	4

Table 5: Frequent disagreements between anonymous workers (A and B) and two of the authors (C and D) among the 498 identified issues that C and D classified consistently.

separated from the context. The above results, and the fact that X3 (distortion) and X4b (too literal) also produced the most frequent disagreements between C and D (11 out of 77 disagreements), suggested that question Q2a in Table 3 should be defined more clearly. We plan to make this precise in our future work.

The other frequent disagreements concerned the issues classified as X1 (omission) by A and B, whereas C and D classified them as other types. For instance, both C and D classified the issue in (3) as X3 (distortion) since the original word "sailors" was incorrectly translated as "soldiers," and the issue in (4) as X7 (incorrect translation of terms) since named entities compose a typical subclass of term.

(3)   SD: We have filed a class action for approximately a hundred <u>sailors</u>.

      TD: およそ100人の<u>兵士</u> (⇒ 海兵兵士) のための集団訴訟を起こした。(soldiers ⇒ sailors)

(4)   SD: <u>President Ronald Reagan</u> vetoed the bill, but, . . .

      TD: <u>レーガン大統領</u> (⇒ ロナルド・レーガン大統領) はその法案を拒否したが、. . .
(President Reagan ⇒ President Ronald Reagan)

These disagreements imply that the anonymous workers might not have strictly adhered to our decision tree, and classified them as X1 after merely

Issue type		n	undergrad. (6)		grad. (11)	
			avg.	s.d.	avg.	s.d.
Level 1	X4a	3	0.04	0.11	0.01	0.04
	X6	0	0.00	0.00	0.00	0.00
Level 2	X7	33	0.39	0.18	0.26	0.31
	X1	53	0.73	0.54	0.34	0.29
	X2	28	0.33	0.26	0.26	0.32
	X3	240	2.67	1.26	2.24	1.41
Level 3	X8	16	0.19	0.23	0.16	0.24
	X10	22	0.27	0.24	0.21	0.32
	X11	10	0.13	0.11	0.07	0.11
	X12	8	0.11	0.15	0.07	0.11
	X13	18	0.21	0.15	0.17	0.20
	X9	10	0.08	0.10	0.12	0.12
Level 4	X16	18	0.20	0.23	0.14	0.14
	X4b	92	0.87	0.69	1.05	0.93
	X15	14	0.09	0.07	0.21	0.25
Level 5	X14	28	0.34	0.14	0.25	0.32
Total		593	6.63	2.35	5.58	3.35

Table 6: Total frequency and relative frequency of each issue type (macro average and standard deviation over TDs).

comparing the marked text span with the revision proposal at the surface level.

5.1.2 Coverage of the Issue Typology

Through a discussion, the disagreements between C and D on the 77 issues were resolved and 18 newly identified issues were also classified. We then calculated relative frequency RF of each issue type, t, in each TD, d, as follows:

$$RF(t, d) = \frac{\text{(frequency of } t \text{ in } d)}{(\text{\# of words in the SD of } d)/100}.$$

Table 6 summarizes the frequency of each issue type; the "n" column shows their total frequency across all TDs and the remaining columns compares macro average and standard deviation of the relative frequencies over TDs produced by each group of students. All the identified issues were classified into one of the 16 issue types in our typology, confirming that the MNH-TT typology had also covered various types of issues appearing in English-to-Japanese translations produced by learners. As reviewed in §2 and §4, both of our typology and the MNH-TT typology cover a broader range of issues than the MeLLANGE typology. Thus, we can even insist that our scheme is applicable to translations between several European languages that Castagnoli et al. (2006) have investigated. In our preliminary experiments on assessing English-to-Chinese and Japanese-to-Korean translations using our scheme, we have not observed any novel type of issues.

X3 (distortion) occurred significantly more frequently than the others. This is consistent with the previous investigation based on the MeLLANGE typology (Castagnoli et al., 2006), considering that X3 (distortion) in our typology corresponds to parts of the most frequent type, LA-TL-IN (Language, terminology and lexis, incorrect), and the second-ranked TR-DI (Transfer, distortion). The other frequent types were X4b (too literal) and X1 (omission), which are both listed in the two existing typologies in Table 2, and also frequently observed in the learners' translations between European languages (Castagnoli et al., 2006).

The annotation results revealed that the graduate students produced issues at Level 2 less frequently than the undergraduate students, while producing more Level 4 issues. Although the relative frequencies of issues vary greatly between individuals, we speculate that less experienced students are more likely to struggle at Level 2, i.e., properly understanding content in SDs.

5.2 Validation 2: Annotation by a Novice Learner Translator

We also evaluated our issue classification scheme in a more realistic setting: the comparison of an undergraduate learner translator with an experienced assessor.

The learner involved in this experiment, referred to as assessor E, was also a native Japanese speaker and had attended some translation classes at a university. The other assessor was D, who had participated in the first experiment. The two assessors separately identified erroneous text spans in the ten TDs (see §3) with a revision proposal, and classified them following our decision tree.

As a result, D and E respectively annotated 561 and 406 issues. Among these, 340 were for identical text spans, with not necessarily identical but similar revision proposals. They consistently classified 289 issues out of 340 (85.0%), achieving a substantial and notably high agreement, $\kappa = 0.794$. These are substantially higher than those achieved by the anonymous workers A and B (see Table 4), although they worked on different TDs. This fact indicates that the identified assessors in the first experiment (C and D) did not necessarily have an advantage. More importantly, this experiment verified the understandability of our scheme by actual learner translators. We expect that learner translators would be able

D	E	# of issues
X4b (Level 4)	X3 (Level 2)	6
X3 (Level 2)	X15 (Level 4)	6
X4b (Level 4)	X15 (Level 2)	5
X1 (Level 2)	X3 (Level 2)	3

Table 7: Frequent disagreements between a learner translator (E) and one of the authors (D) among the 340 issues they identified consistently.

to perform peer reviewing of their draft translations, once they have acquired a certain level of understanding of our scheme. Consequently, as Kiraly (2000) mentions, they would be able to effectively develop their translation skills through playing various roles in the translation work-flow, including that of assessor.

Typical disagreement patterns are shown in Table 7. Similarly to the first experiment, disagreement between X3 (distortion) and X4b (too literal) was frequently observed. E also classified as X15 (clumsy) 11 issues which D classified as X3 (distortion) or X4b (too literal). To answer question Q4c consistently, the literalness needs to be confirmed, for instance, by using dictionaries.

There were 221 and 66 issues identified only by D or E, respectively; 171 and 41 out of these were ignored by the other, including missed issues and accepted translations, reflecting the different levels of sensitivity of the assessors. The other 38 and 14 mismatches suggested the necessity of a guideline to consistently annotate *single issues*. For instance, E identified one X3 (distortion) issue in (5), while D annotated two issues there: "情報が豊富な (with rich information)" as X2 (addition) and "お天気アプリ (weather application)" as X3 (distortion).

(5) SD: I put the question to Jeff Masters, co-founder at Weather Underground, <u>an Internet weather information service.</u>

TD: 情報量が豊富なお天気アプリ (⇒ 気象情報を提供するウェブサービス)、ウェザー・アンダーグラウンドの共同設立者であるジェフ・マスターズ氏に質問を投げかけた。(a weather application with rich information ⇒ a Web service which provides weather information)

6 Translation Exercise at a University

Having created and validated an annotation scheme, we should ultimately verify its usefulness in actual practice. We implemented our scheme in an English-to-Japanese translation exercise course for undergraduate students at a university in Japan.

6.1 Course Design

Two different types of English texts were used: travel guides from "Travellerspoint"[9] (henceforth, "Travel") and columns from "Democracy Now!" as in §3 (henceforth, "Column"). For each text type, the instructor of the course sampled three documents with similar conceptual and linguistic difficulties, and excerpted roughly the first 550 words of each document as SDs.

A total of 27 undergraduate students participated in the course held over 15 weeks, from April to July 2015. All of them were native Japanese speakers; eight had attended translation classes at a university, while the other 19 were absolute novices. Each student selected one of the sampled SDs for each text type. Before starting translation, they prepared a glossary and collected background information by themselves, and the instructor added any missing information. Each student first translated a "Travel" SD into Japanese over six weeks, referring to the corresponding glossary and background information, and then a "Column" SD in the same manner.

During the process of translating one SD, students' translations were assessed every two weeks (three times per SD); a teaching assistant identified erroneous text spans with a revision proposal, and classified them following our decision tree; and then the instructor double-checked them. While the identified erroneous text spans and the assigned issue types were fed back to the students, revision proposals were not shown (Klaudy, 1996). When the instructor fed back the assessment results to the students, she also explained our issue typology (Table 2) and decision tree (Table 3), also using the examples collected during the development process.

6.2 Observations

Through the course, 54 TDs were annotated with 1,707 issues, all of which fell into one of the 16 types in our issue typology. Table 8 summarizes the relative frequency of each issue type. X3 (distortion) occurred significantly more frequently than the others in translating both types of SDs, as in the results in Table 6 and previous work (Castagnoli et al., 2006). In other words, transfer-

---

[9] http://www.travellerspoint.com/

Issue type		Travel		Column	
		avg.	s.d.	avg.	s.d.
Level 1	X4a	0.03	0.07	0.03	0.07
	X6	0.00	0.00	0.00	0.00
Level 2	X7	1.14	0.79	0.53	0.39
	X1	0.47	0.42	0.49	0.31
	X2	0.09	0.13	0.16	0.19
	X3	2.20	0.95	2.91	1.03
Level 3	X8	0.11	0.11	0.13	0.18
	X10	0.19	0.24	0.18	0.27
	X11	0.07	0.09	0.12	0.15
	X12	0.15	0.16	0.11	0.11
	X13	0.09	0.16	0.17	0.21
	X9	0.22	0.34	0.03	0.08
Level 4	X16	0.07	0.11	0.03	0.07
	X4b	0.53	0.53	0.24	0.22
	X15	0.10	0.18	0.08	0.13
Level 5	X14	0.30	0.25	0.45	0.31
Total		5.76	2.17	5.65	1.84

Table 8: Relative frequency of each issue type (macro average and standard deviation over TDs).

ring content of the given SD is the principal issue for learner translators in general.

Table 8 also highlights that the relative frequencies of X7 (incorrect translations of terms) and X4b (too literal) are drastically different for the "Travel" and "Column" SDs. A student-wise comparison of the relative frequencies in Figure 1 revealed that the students who made these two types of issues more frequently in translating "Travel" SDs (shown in the right-hand side in the figure) produced these types of issues significantly less frequently during translating "Column" SDs. Due to the difference in text types, we cannot claim that this demonstrates students' growth in learning to translate and that this has been promoted by our scheme. Nevertheless, our scheme is clearly useful for quantifying the characteristics of such students.

7 Conclusion

To consistently assess human translations, especially focusing on English-to-Japanese translations produced by learners, we manually created an improved issue typology accompanied by a decision tree through an application of the OntoNotes method. Two annotation experiments, involving four assessors and an actual learner translator, confirmed the potential contribution of our scheme to making consistent classification of identified issues, achieving Cohen's κ values of between 0.490 (moderate) to 0.831 (almost perfect). We also used our scheme in a translation exercise course at a university in order to assess

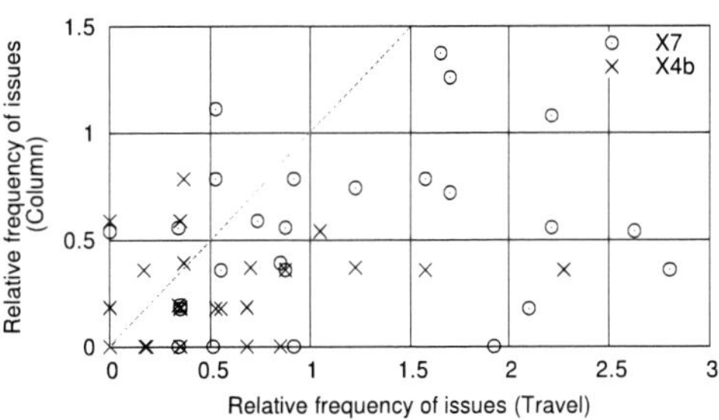

Figure 1: Student-wise comparison of relative frequencies of X7 (incorrect translations of terms) and X4b (too literal).

learners' translations. The predefined 16 issue types in our typology covered all the issues that appeared in English-to-Japanese translations produced by undergraduate students, supporting the applicability of our issue typology to real-world translation training scenarios.

Our plans for future work include further improvements of our issue classification scheme, such as clarifying questions in the decision tree and establishing a guideline for annotating single issues. Its applicability will further be validated using other text types and other language pairs. From the pedagogical point of view, monitoring the effects of assessment is also important (Orozco and Hurtado Albir, 2002). Given the high agreement ratio in our second experiment (§5.2), we are also interested in the feasibility of peer reviewing (Kiraly, 2000). Last but not least, with a view to efficient assessment with less human labor, we will also study automatic identification and classification of erroneous text spans, referring to recent advances in the field of word- and phrase-level quality estimation for MT outputs.[10]

Acknowledgments

We are deeply grateful to anonymous reviewers for their valuable comments. This work was partly supported by JSPS KAKENHI Grant-in-Aid for Scientific Research (A) 25240051.

References

Bogdan Babych, Anthony Hartley, Kyo Kageura, Martin Thomas, and Masao Utiyama. 2012. MNH-TT: a collaborative platform for translator training. In *Proceedings of Translating and the Computer 34*.

---

[10]`http://www.statmt.org/wmt16/`
`quality-estimation-task.html`

Aljoscha Burchardt and Arle Lommel. 2014. QT-LaunchPad supplement 1: Practical guidelines for the use of MQM in scientific research on translation quality. http://www.qt21.eu/downloads/MQM-usage-guidelines.pdf.

Sara Castagnoli, Dragos Ciobanu, Kerstin Kunz, Natalie Kübler, and Alexandra Volanschi. 2006. Designing a learner translator corpus for training purpose. In *Proceedings of the 7th International Conference on Teaching and Language Corpora*.

Jacob Cohen. 1960. A coefficient of agreement for nominal scales. *Educational and Psychological Measurement*, 20(1):37–46.

Eduard Hovy, Mitchell Marcus, Martha Palmer, Lance Ramshaw, and Ralph Weischedel. 2006. OntoNotes: The 90% solution. In *Proceedings of the Human Language Technology Conference of the North American Chapter of the Association for Computational Linguistics (HLT-NAACL) Short Papers*, pages 57–60.

ISO/TC27. 2015. ISO 17100:2015 translation services: Requirements for translation services.

Donald Kiraly. 2000. *A Social Constructivist Approach to Translator Education: Empowerment from Theory to Practice*. Routledge.

Kinga Klaudy. 1996. Quality assessment in school vs professional translation. In Cay Dollerup and Vibeke Appel, editors, *Teaching Translation and Interpreting 3: New Horizons: Papers from the Third Language International Conference*, pages 197–203. John Benjamins.

Arle Lommel, Maja Popović, and Aljoscha Burchardt. 2014. Assessing inter-annotator agreement for translation error annotation. In *Proceedings of the LREC MTE Workshop on Automatic and Manual Metrics for Operational Translation Evaluation*.

Arle Lommel, Attila Görög, Alan Melby, Hans Uszkoreit, Aljoscha Burchardt, and Maja Popović. 2015. QT21 deliverable 3.1: Harmonised metric. http://www.qt21.eu/wp-content/uploads/2015/11/QT21-D3-1.pdf.

Brian Mossop. 2014. *Revising and Editing for Translators (3rd Edition)*. Routledge.

Mariana Orozco and Amparo Hurtado Albir. 2002. Measuring translation competence acquisition. *Translators' Journal*, 47(3):375–402.

Kishore Papineni, Salim Roukos, Todd Ward, and Wei-Jing Zhu. 2002. BLEU: A method for automatic evaluation of machine translation. In *Proceedings of the 40th Annual Meeting of the Association for Computational Linguistics (ACL)*, pages 311–318.

Alina Secară. 2005. Translation evaluation: A state of the art survey. In *Proceedings of the eCoLoRe/MeLLANGE Workshop*, pages 39–44.

Yuta Tsuboi, Hisashi Kashima, Shinsuke Mori, Hiroki Oda, and Yuji Matsumoto. 2008. Training conditional random fields using incomplete annotations. In *Proceedings of the 22nd International Conference on Computational Linguistics (COLING)*, pages 897–904.

Representation and Interchange of Linguistic Annotation
An In-Depth, Side-by-Side Comparison of Three Designs

Richard Eckart de Castilho[♣], Nancy Ide[♠], Emanuele Lapponi[♡], Stephan Oepen[♡],
Keith Suderman[♠], Erik Velldal[♡], and Marc Verhagen[♢]

[♣] Technische Universität Darmstadt, Department of Computer Science
[♠] Vassar College, Department of Computer Science
[♡] University of Oslo, Department of Informatics
[♢] Brandeis University, Linguistics and Computational Linguistics

Abstract

For decades, most self-respecting linguistic engineering initiatives have designed and implemented *custom representations* for various layers of, for example, morphological, syntactic, and semantic analysis. Despite occasional efforts at harmonization or even standardization, our field today is blessed with a multitude of ways of encoding and exchanging linguistic annotations of these types, both at the levels of 'abstract syntax', naming choices, and of course file formats. To a large degree, it is possible to work within and across design plurality by *conversion*, and often there may be good reasons for divergent design reflecting differences in use. However, it is likely that some abstract commonalities across choices of representation are obscured by more superficial differences, and conversely there is no obvious procedure to tease apart what actually constitute contentful vs. mere technical divergences. In this study, we seek to conceptually align three representations for common types of morpho-syntactic analysis, pinpoint what in our view constitute contentful differences, and reflect on the underlying principles and specific requirements that led to individual choices. We expect that a more in-depth understanding of these choices across designs may lead to increased harmonization, or at least to more informed design of future representations.

1 Background & Goals

This study is grounded in an informal collaboration among three frameworks for 'basic' natural language processing, where *workflows* can combine the outputs of processing tools from different developer communities (i.e. software repositories), for example a sentence splitter, tokenizer, lemmatizer, tagger, and parser—for morpho-syntactic analysis of running text. In large part owing to divergences in input and output representations for such tools, it tends to be difficult to connect tools from different sources: Lacking interface standardization, thus, severely limits *interoperability*.

The frameworks surveyed in this work address interoperability by means of a common representation—a uniform framework-internal convention—with mappings from tool-specific input and output formats. Specifically, we will take an in-depth look at how the results of morpho-syntactic analysis are represented in (a) the DKPro Core component collection[1] (Eckart de Castilho and Gurevych, 2014), (b) the Language Analysis Portal[2] (LAP; Lapponi et al. (2014)), and (c) the Language Application (LAPPS) Grid[3] (Ide et al., 2014a). These three systems all share the common goal of facilitating the creation of complex NLP workflows, allowing users to combine tools that would otherwise need input and output format conversion in order to be made compatible. While the programmatic interface of DKPro Core targets more technically inclined users, LAP and LAPPS are realized as web applications with a point-and-click graphical interface. All three have been under active development for the past several years and have—in contemporaneous, parallel work—designed and implemented framework-specific representations. These designs are rooted in related but interestingly different traditions; hence, our side-by-side discussion of these particular frameworks provides a good initial sample of observable commonalities and divergences.[4]

2 Terminological Definitions

A number of closely interrelated concepts apply to the discussion of design choices in the repre-

---

[1]https://dkpro.github.io/dkpro-core
[2]https://lap.clarino.uio.no
[3]https://www.lappsgrid.org

[4]There are, of course, additional designs and workflow frameworks that we would ultimately hope to include in this comparison, as for example the representations used by CONCRETE, WebLicht, and FoLiA (Ferraro et al., 2014; Heid et al., 2010; van Gompel and Reynaert, 2013), to name just a few. However, some of these frameworks are at least abstractly very similar to representatives in our current sample, and also for reasons of space we need to restrict this in-depth comparison to a relatively small selection.

Proceedings of the 11th Linguistic Annotation Workshop, pages 67–75,
Valencia, Spain, April 3, 2017. ©2017 Association for Computational Linguistics

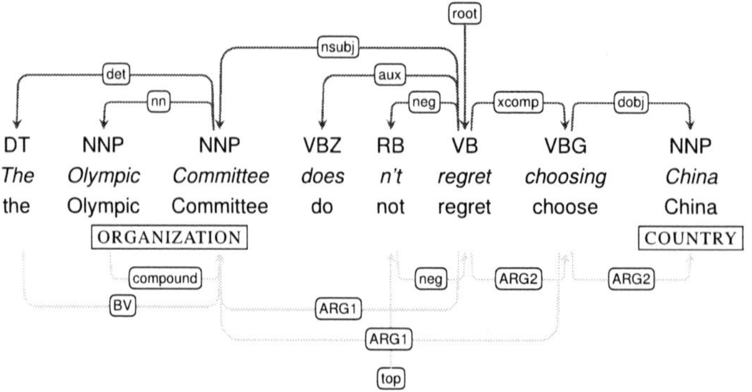

Figure 1: Running example, in 'conventional' visualization, with five layers of annotation: syntactic dependencies and parts of speech, above; and lemmata, named entities, and semantic dependencies, below.

sentations for linguistic annotations. Albeit to some degree intuitive, there is substantial terminological variation and vagueness, which in turn reflects some of the differences in overall annotation scheme design across projects and systems. Therefore, with due acknowledgement that no single, definitive view exists we provide informal definitions of relevant terms as used in the sections that follow in order to ground our discussion.

Annotations For the purposes of the current exercise we focus on annotations of language data in textual form, and exclude consideration of other media such as speech signals, images, and video. An *annotation* associates linguistic information such as morpho-syntactic tags, syntactic roles, and a wide range of semantic information with one or more spans in a text. Low-level annotations typically segment an entire text into contiguous spans that serve as the base units of analysis; in text, these units are typically sentences and tokens. The association of an annotation to spans may be direct or indirect, as an annotation can itself be treated as an object to which other (higher level) annotations may be applied.

Vocabulary The *vocabulary* provides an inventory of semantic entities (concepts) that form the building blocks of the annotations and the relations (links) that may exist between them (e.g. constituent or dependency relations, coreference, and others). The CLARIN Data Concept Registry[5] (formerly ISOcat) is an example of a vocabulary for linguistic annotations.

Schema A *schema* provides an abstract specification (as opposed to a concrete realization) of the structure of annotation information, by identifying the allowable relations among entities from the vocabulary that may be expressed in an annotation. A schema is often expressed using a diagrammatic representation such as a UML diagram or entity-relationship model, in which entities label nodes in the diagram and relations label the edges between them. Note that the vocabulary and the schema that uses it are often defined together, thus blurring the distinction between them, as for example, in the LAPPS Web Service Exchange Vocabulary (see Section 3) or any UIMA CAS type system.

Serialization A serialization of the annotations is used for storage and exchange. Annotations following a given schema can be serialized in a variety of formats such as (basic) XML, database (column-based) formats, compact binary formats, JSON, ISO LAF/GrAF (Ide and Suderman, 2014; ISO, 2012), etc.

3 A Simple Example

In the following sections, we will walk through a simple English example with multiple layers of linguistic annotations. Figure 1 shows a rendering of our running example in a compact, graphical visualization commonly used in academic writing. However, even for this simple sentence, we will point out some hidden complexity and information left implicit at this informal level of representation.

For example, there are mutual dependencies among the various layers of annotation: parts of speech and lemmatization both encode aspects of

---

[5]`https://openskos.meertens.knaw.nl/ccr/browser/`

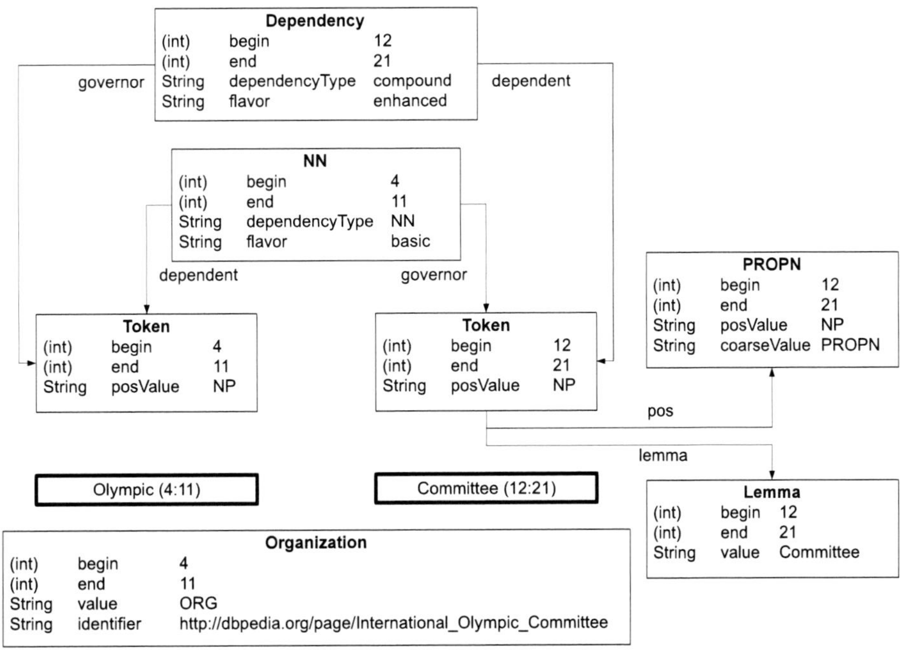

Figure 2: DKPro Core Zoom

token-level morphological analysis; syntactic dependencies, in turn, are plausibly interpreted as building on top of the morphological information; finally, also the semantic dependencies, will typically be based on some or maybe all layers of morpho-syntactic analysis. In practice, on the other hand, various layers of annotation are often computed by separate tools, which may or may not take into account information from 'lower' analysis layers. In this respect, the visualization in Figure 1 gives the impression of a single, 'holistic' representation, even though it need not always hold that all analysis layers have been computed to be mutually consistent with each other. In Section 4 below, we will observe that a desire to make explicit the *provenance* of separate annotation layers can provide an important design constraint.

DKPro Core Type System The DKPro Core Type System extends the type system that is built into the UIMA[6] framework (Ferrucci and Lally, 2004). It provides types for many layers of linguistic analysis, such as segmentation, morphology, syntax, discourse, semantics, etc. Additionally, there are several types that carry metadata about

the document being processed, about tagsets, etc.

UIMA represents data using the Common Analysis System (CAS) (Götz and Suhre, 2004). The CAS consists of typed feature structures organized in a type system that supports single inheritance. There are various serialization formats for the CAS. The most prominent is based on the XML Metadata Interchange specification (XMI) (OMG, 2002). However, there are also e.g. various binary serializations of the CAS with specific advantages, e.g. built-in compression for efficient network transfer.

The built-in types of UIMA are basic ones, such as *TOP* (a generic feature structure), *Annotation* (a feature structure anchored on text via start/end offsets), or *SofA* (short for 'subject of analysis', the signal that annotations are anchored on). A single CAS can accommodate multiple *SofA*s which is useful in many cases: holding multiple translations of a document; holding a markup and a plaintext version; holding an audio signal and its transcription; etc. *Annotation* and all types inheriting from it are always anchored on a single *SofA*, but they may refer to annotations anchored on a different *SofA*, e.g. to model word alignment between translated texts. The CAS also allows for feature structures inheriting from *TOP* that are not anchored to a particular *SofA*.

---

[6]When talking about UIMA, we refer to the Apache UIMA implementation: `http://uima.apache.org`.

Figure 2 shows a zoom on the sub-string *Olympic Committee* from Figure 1. All of the shown annotations are anchored on the text using offsets. The *Token*, PoS (*PROPN*), and *Lemma* annotations are anchored each on a single word. The named entity (*Organization*) annotation spans two words. The *Dependency* relation annotations anchored by convention on the span of the dependent *Token*. Syntactic and semantic dependencies are distinguished via the *flavor* feature. All annotations (except *Token*) have a feature which contains the original output(s) of the annotation tool (*value, posValue, coarseValue, dependencyType*). The possible values for these original outputs are not specified in the DKPro Core type system. However, for the convenience of the user, DKPro Core supports so-called *elevated types* which are part of the type system and function as universal tags. Using mappings, the elevated type is derived from the original tool output. The Penn Treebank tag NNP, for example. is mapped to the type PROPN. For example, for PoS tags DKPro Core uses the Universal Dependency PoS categories.

Lap eXchange Format (LXF) Closely following the ISO LAF guidelines (Ide and Suderman, 2014), LXF represents annotations as a directed graph that references pieces of text; elements comprising the annotation graph and the base segmentation of the text are explicitly represented in LXF with a set of *node*, *edge*, and *region* elements. Regions describe text segmentation in terms of character offsets, while nodes contain (sets of) annotations (and optionally direct *links* to regions). Edges record relations between nodes and are optionally annotated with (non-linguistic) structural information. Nodes in LXF are typed, ranging for example over *sentence, token, morphology, chunk,* or *dependency* types. There are some technical properties common to all nodes (e.g. a unique identifier, sequential index, as well as its *rank* and *receipt*, as discussed below), and each node further provides a feature structure with linguistic annotations, where the particular range of features is determined by the node type.

Consider the example of Figure 1. Assuming sentence segmentation prior to word tokenization, the corresponding LXF graph comprises ten regions, one for the full sentence and one for each of the tokens. Figure 3 pictures the LXF version of Figure 2 described in the previous section. For sentence segmentation, LXF includes one node of type *sentence*, which contains links (represented as dashed edges in Figure 3) to the corresponding regions; similarly, *token*-typed nodes also directly link to their respective region, effectively treating sentence segmentation and word tokenization equally. If these two annotation types are obtained sequentially as part of an annotation *workflow* (i.e. the word tokenizer segments one sentence at a time), the LXF graph includes one directed edge from each token node to its sentence node, thus ensuring that the *provenance* of the annotation is explicitly modeled in the output representation.

Moving upwards to parts of speech, LXF for the example sentence includes one node (of type *morphology*) per PoS, paired with one edge pointing to the token node it annotates. Similarly to the sentence–token relationship, separate *morphology* nodes report the result of lemmatization, with direct edges to PoS nodes when lemmatization requires tagged input (or to *token* nodes otherwise). In general, running a new tool results in new LXF (nodes and) edges linking incoming nodes to the highest (i.e. topologically farthest from segmentation) annotation consumed. This holds true also for the nodes of type *dependency* in Figure 3; here each dependency arc from Figure 1 is 'reified' as a full LXF node, with an incoming and outgoing edge each recording the directionality of the head–dependent relation. The named entity, in turn, is represented as a node of type *chunk*, with edges pointing to nodes for PoS tags, reflecting that the named entity recognizer operated on tokenized and tagged input.

LXF graph elements (including the annotated media and regions) are in principle serialization-agnostic, and currently implemented in LAP as a multitude of individual, atomic records in a NoSQL database. A specific annotation (sub-)graph, i.e. a collection of interconnected nodes and edges, in this approach is identified by a so-called *receipt*, essentially a mechanism for group formation. Each step in a LAP workflow consumes one or more receipts as input and returns a new receipt comprising additional annotations. Thus, each receipt uniquely identifies the set of annotations contributed by one tool, as reflected in the receipt properties on the nodes of Figure 3. LAP imposes a strict principle of monotonicity, meaning that existing annotations are never modified by later processing, but rather each tool adds its own, new layer of annotations (which could in principle 'overlay' or 'shadow'

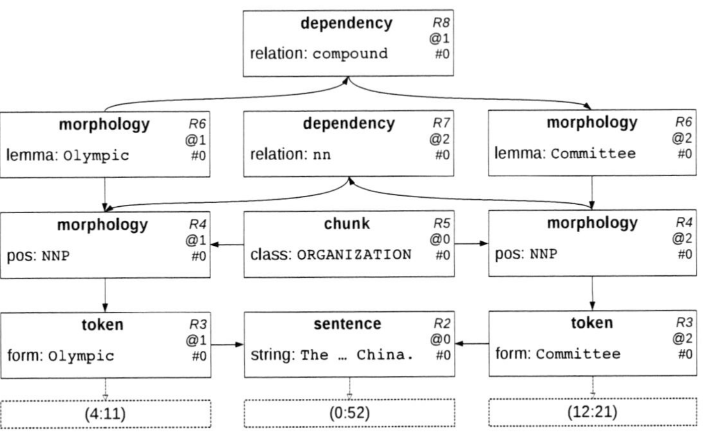

Figure 3: Excerpt from the LXF graph for the running example in Figure 1, zooming in on *Olympic Committee*. Segmentation regions are shown as dashed boxes, with character offsets for the two tokens and the full sentence, respectively. Nodes display their type (e.g. *morphology*), part of the feature structure containing the linguistic annotation (e.g. the part of speech), and their receipt, index, and rank properties ('R4', '@1' and '#0', respectively).

information from other layers). Therefore, for example, parallel runs of the same (type of) tool can output graph elements that co-exist in the same LXF graph but can be addressed each by their own receipt (see Section 4 below).

LAPPS Interchange Format (LIF) The LAPPS Grid exchanges annotations across web services using LIF (Verhagen et al., 2016), an instantiation of JSON-LD (JavaScript Object Notation for Linked Data), a format for transporting Linked Data using JSON, a lightweight, text-based, language-independent data interchange format for the portable representation of structured data. Because it is based on the W3C Resource Definition Framework (RDF), JSON-LD is trivially mappable to and from other graph-based formats such as ISO LAF and UIMA CAS, as well as a growing number of formats implementing the same data model. JSON-LD extends JSON by enabling references to annotation categories and definitions in semantic-web vocabularies and ontologies, or any suitably defined concept identified by a URI. This allows for referencing linguistic terms in annotations and their definitions at a readily accessible canonical web location, and helps ensure consistent term usage across projects and applications. For this purpose, the LAPPS Grid project provides a Web Service Exchange Vocabulary (WSEV; Ide et al. (2014b)), which defines a schema comprising an inventory of web-addressable entities and relations.[7]

Figure 4 shows the LIF equivalent of Figures 2 and 3 in the previous sections. Annotations in LIF are organized into *views*, each of which provides information about the annotations types it contains and what tool created the annotations. Views are similar to annotation 'layers' or 'tasks' as defined by several mainstream annotation tools and frameworks. For the full example in Figure 1, a view could be created for each annotation type in the order it was produced, yielding six consecutive views containing sentence boundaries, tokens, parts of speech and lemmas, named entities, syntactic dependencies, and semantic dependencies.[8] In Figure 4, a slightly simplified graph is shown with only three views and where token and part of speech information is bundled in one view and where lemmas and semantic relations are ignored. A view

---

[7] The WSEV links terms in the inventory to equivalent or similar terms defined elsewhere on the web.

[8] The last three views could be in a different order, depending on the sequence in which the corresponding tools were applied.

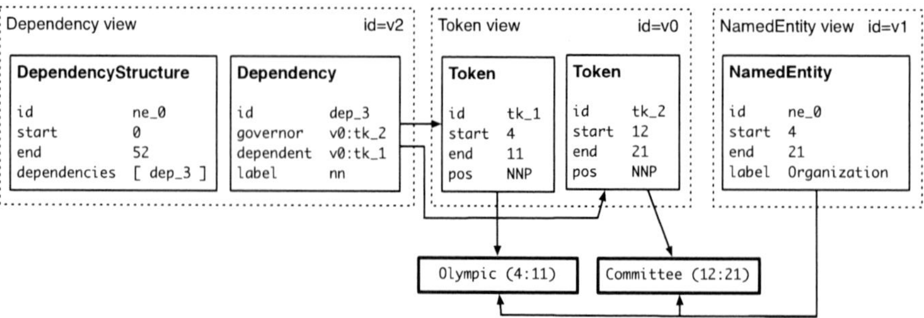

Figure 4: Excerpt from the LIF graph for the running example in Figure 1, zooming in on *Olympic Committee*. Views are shown as dashed boxes and annotations as regular boxes with annotation types in bold and with other attributes as appropriate for the type. Arrows follow references to other annotations or to the source data.

is typically created by one processing component and will often contain all information added by that component. All annotations are in standoff form; an annotation may therefore reference a span (region) in the primary data, using character offsets, or it may refer to annotations in another view by providing the relevant ID or IDs. In the example, a named entity annotation in the Named Entity view refers to character offsets in the primary data and the dependency annotation in the Dependency view refers to tokens in the Token view, using Token view ID and the annotation IDs as defined in the Token view.[9]

Preliminary Observations Each of the three representations has been created based on a different background and with a different focus. For example, LIF is coupled with JSON-LD as its serialization format and uses *views* to carry along the full analysis history of a document including per-view provenance data. LXF uses explicit relations between annotations to model provenance and has strong support for multiple concurrent annotations and for managing annotation data persisted in a database. The DKPro Core is optimized for ease of use and processing efficiency within analysis workflows and has rather limited support for concurrent annotations, provenance, and stable IDs.

Some technical differences between the three designs actually remain hidden in the abbreviated, diagrammatic representations of Figures 2 to 4. Abstractly, all three are directed graphs, but the relations between nodes in DKPro Core and LIF

are established by having the identifier or reference of the target node as a feature value on a source node, whereas LXF (in a faithful rendering of the ISO LAF standard) actually realizes each edge as a separate, structured object. In principle, separate edge objects afford added flexibility in that they could bear annotations of their own—for example, it would be possible to represent a binary syntactic or semantic dependency as just one edge (instead of reifying the dependency as a separate node, connected to other nodes by two additional edges). However, Ide and Suderman (2014) recommend to restrict edge annotations to non-linguistic information, and LXF in its current development status at least heeds that advice. Hence, the DKPro Core and LIF representations are arguably more compact (in the number of objects involved).

A broad view of the three approaches shows that at what we may regard as the 'micro-level', that is, the representation of individual annotations, differences are irrelevant in terms of the *schema* applied, which are trivially mappable based on a common underlying (graph-based) model. At a higher level, however, different goals have led to divergences in the content and organization of the information that is sent from one tool to another in a workflow chain. In the following section, we consider these differences.

4 Pushing a Little Farther

While our above side-by-side discussion of 'basic' layers of morpho-syntactic annotations may seem to highlight more abstract similarity than divergence, in the following we will discuss a few more

---

[9]Note that multiple Token views can co-exist in the annotation set.

intricate aspects of specific annotation design. We expect that further study of such 'corner cases' may shed more light on inherent degrees of flexibility in a particular design, as well as on its scalability in annotation complexity.

Media–Tokenization Mismatches Tokenizers may apply transformations to the original input text that introduce character offset mismatches with the normalized output. For example, some Penn Treebank–compliant tokenizers normalize different conventions for quotation marks (which may be rendered as straight 'typewriter' quotes or in multi-character LaTeX-style encodings, e.g. " or ``) into opening (left) and closing (right) Unicode glyphs (Dridan and Oepen, 2012). To make such normalization accessible to downstream processing, it is insufficient to represent tokens as only a region (sub-string) of the underlying linguistic signal.

In LXF, the string output of tokenizers is recorded in the annotations encapsulated with each *token* node, which is in turn linked to a region recording its character offsets in the original media. LIF (which is largely inspired by ISO LAF, much like LXF) also records the token string and its character offsets in the original medium. LIF supports this via the *word* property on tokens. DKPro Core has also recently started introducing a *TokenForm* annotation optionally attached to *Token* feature structures to support this.

Tokenizers may also return more than one token for the same region. Consider the Italian word *del*, which combines the preposition *di* and the definite article *il*. With both tokens anchored to the same character offsets, systems require more than reasoning over sub-string character spans to represent the linear order of tokens. LXF and LIF encode the ordering of annotations in an index property on nodes, trivializing this kind of annotation. DKPro Core presently does not support this.

Alternative Annotations and Ambiguity While relatively uncommon in the manual construction of annotated corpora, it may be desirable in a complex workflow to allow multiple annotation layers of the same type, or to record in the annotation graph more than the one-best hypothesis from a particular tool. Annotating text with different segmenters, for example, may result in diverging base units, effectively yielding parallel sets of segments. In our running example, the contraction *don't* is conventionally tokenized as ⟨do,n't⟩, but a linguistically less informed tokenization regime might also lead to the three-token sequence ⟨don,',t⟩ or just the full contraction as a single token.

In LXF, diverging segmentations originating from different annotators co-exist in the same annotation graph. The same is true for LIF, where the output of each tokenizer (if more than one is applied) exists in its own view with unique IDs on each token, which can be referenced by annotations in views added later. Correspondingly, alternative annotations (i.e. annotations of the same type produced by different tools) are represented with their own set of nodes and edges in LXF and their own views in LIF. The DKPro Core type system does not link tokens explicitly to the sentence but relies on span offsets to infer the relation. Hence, it is not possible to represent multiple segmentations on a single *SofA*. However, it is possible to have multiple *SofA*s with the same text and different segmentations within a single CAS.

A set of alternative annotations may also be produced by a single tool, for instance in the form of an n-best list of annotations with different confidence scores. In LXF, this kind of ambiguous analyses translates to a set of graph elements sharing the same receipt identifier, with increasing values of the *rank* property for each alternative interpretation. Again, the DKPro Core type system largely relies on span offsets to relate annotations to tokens (e.g. named entities). Some layers, such as dependency relations also point directly to tokens. However, it is still not possible to maintain multiple sets of dependency relations in DKPro Core because each relation exists on its own and there is presently nothing that ties them together. The views in LIF are the output produced by any single run of a given tool over the data; therefore, in this case all the variants would be contained in a single view, and the alternatives would appear in a list of values associated with the corresponding feature (e.g. a list of PoS–confidence score pairs). Additionally, LIF provides a *DependencyStructure* which can bind multiple dependency relations together and thus supports multiple parallel dependency structures even within a single LIF view.

Parallel Annotation At times it is necessary to have multiple versions of a text or multiple parallel texts during processing, e.g. when correcting mistakes, removing markup, or aligning translations. DKPro Core inherits from the UIMA CAS the ability to maintain multiple *SofA*s in parallel. This features of UIMA is for example used in the DKPro Core normalization framework where *SofaChangeAnnotations* can be created on one view, stating that text should be inserted, removed, or replaced. These annotations can then be *applied* to the text using a dedicated component which creates a new *SofA* that contains the modified text. Further processing can then happen on the modified text without any need for the DKPro Core type system or DKPro Core components to be aware of the fact that they operate on a derived text. The alignment information between the original text and the derived text is maintained such that the annotations created on the derived text can be transferred back to the original text.

The LXF and LIF designs support multiple layers or views with annotations, but both assume a single base text. In these frameworks, text-level edits or normalizations would have to be represented as 'overlay' annotations, largely analogous to the discussion of token-level normalization above.

Provenance Metadata describing the software used to produce annotations, as well as the rules and/or annotation scheme—e.g. tokenization rules, part-of-speech tagset—may be included with the annotation output. This information can be used to validate the compatibility of input/output requirements for tool sequences in a pipeline or workflow.

LIF provides all of this information in metadata appearing at the beginning of each view, consisting of URI pointing to the producing software, tagset, or scheme used, and accompanying rules for identifying the annotation objects (where applicable).

The LXF principle of monotonicity in accumulating annotation layers is key to its approach to provenance. For our running example in Section 3 above, we assume that PoS tagging and lemmatization were applied as separate steps; hence, there are separate nodes for these (all of type *morphology*) and two distinct receipts. Conversely, if a combined tagger–lemmatizer had been used, its output would be recorded as a single layer of *morphology* nodes—yielding a different (albeit equivalent in linguistic content) graph structure.

The provenance support in DKPro Core is presently rather limited but also distinctly different from LXF or LIF. Presently, for a given type of annotation, e.g. PoS tags, the name of one creator component can be stored. This assumes that every type of annotation is produced by at most

by one component. Additionally, whenever possible, DKPro Core extracts tagsets from the models provided with taggers, parsers, and similar components and stores these along with the model language, version, and name in a *TagsetDescription*. This even lists tags not output by the component.

5   Conclusions & Outlook

We have surveyed the differences and commonalities among three workflow analysis systems in order to move toward identifying the needs to achieve greater interoperability among workflow systems for NLP. This preliminary analysis shows that while some basic elements have common models and are therefore easily usable by other systems, the handling of *alternative* annotations and representation of provenance are among the primary differences in approach. This suggests that future work aimed at interoperability needs to address this level of representation, as we attempt to move toward means to represent linguistically annotated data and achieve universal interoperability and accessibility.

In ongoing work, we will seek to overcome remaining limitations through (a) incremental refinement (working across the developer communities involved) that seeks to eliminate unnecessary, superficial differences (e.g. in vocabulary naming choices) and (b) further exploring the relationships between distinct designs via the implementation of a bidirectional converter suite. Information-preserving round-trip conversion, on this view, would be a strong indicator of abstract design equivalence, whereas conversion errors or information loss in round-trip conversion might either point to contentful divergences or room for improvement in the converter suite.

Acknowledgments

This work was funded in parts from the European Union's Horizon 2020 research and innovation programme (H2020-EINFRA-2014-2) under grant agreement No. 654021. It reflects only the author's views and the EU is not liable for any use that may be made of the information contained therein. It was further supported in parts by the German Federal Ministry of Education and Research (BMBF) under the promotional reference 01UG1416B (CEDIFOR) and by the U.S. National Science Foundation grants NSF-ACI 1147944 and NSF-ACI 1147912. LAP development is supported by the Norwegian Research Council through the national CLARINO initiative, as well as by the Norwegian national computing and storage e-infrastructures, and the Department of Informatics at the University of Oslo. We are grateful to everyone involved, in particular all taxpayers.

References

Rebecca Dridan and Stephan Oepen. 2012. Tokenization. Returning to a long solved problem. A survey, contrastive experiment, recommendations, and toolkit. In *Proceedings of the 50th Meeting of the Association for Computational Linguistics*, page 378 – 382, Jeju, Republic of Korea, July.

Richard Eckart de Castilho and Iryna Gurevych. 2014. A broad-coverage collection of portable NLP components for building shareable analysis pipelines. In *Proceedings of the Workshop on Open Infrastructures and Analysis Frameworks for HLT*, page 1 – 11, Dublin, Ireland.

Francis Ferraro, Max Thomas, Matthew R Gormley, Travis Wolfe, Craig Harman, and Benjamin Van Durme. 2014. Concretely annotated corpora. In *Proceedings of the AKBC Workshop at NIPS 2014*, Montreal, Canada, December.

David Ferrucci and Adam Lally. 2004. UIMA. An architectural approach to unstructured information processing in the corporate research environment. *Natural Language Engineering*, 10(3-4):327 – 348, September.

Maarten van Gompel and Martin Reynaert. 2013. FoLiA. A practical XML format for linguistic annotation. A descriptive and comparative study. *Computational Linguistics in the Netherlands Journal*, 3:63 – 81.

Thilo Götz and Oliver Suhre. 2004. Design and implementation of the UIMA Common Analysis System. *IBM Systems Journal*, 43(3):476 – 489.

Ulrich Heid, Helmut Schmid, Kerstin Eckart, and Erhard W. Hinrichs. 2010. A corpus representation format for linguistic web services. The D-SPIN Text Corpus Format and its relationship with ISO standards. In *Proceedings of the 7th International Conference on Language Resources and Evaluation*, page 494 – 499, Valletta, Malta.

Nancy Ide and Keith Suderman. 2014. The Linguistic Annotation Framework. A standard for annotation interchange and merging. *Language Resources and Evaluation*, 48(3):395 – 418.

Nancy Ide, James Pustejovsky, Christopher Cieri, Eric Nyberg, Denise DiPersio, Chunqi Shi, Keith Suderman, Marc Verhagen, Di Wang, and Jonathan Wright. 2014a. The Language Application Grid. In *Proceedings of the 9th International Conference on Language Resources and Evaluation*, Reykjavik, Iceland.

Nancy Ide, James Pustejovsky, Keith Suderman, and Marc Verhagen. 2014b. The Language Application Grid Web Service Exchange Vocabulary. In *Proceedings of the Workshop on Open Infrastructures and Analysis Frameworks for HLT*, Dublin, Ireland.

ISO. 2012. Language Resource Management. Linguistic Annotation Framework. ISO 24612.

Emanuele Lapponi, Erik Velldal, Stephan Oepen, and Rune Lain Knudsen. 2014. Off-road LAF: Encoding and processing annotations in NLP workflows. In *Proceedings of the 9th International Conference on Language Resources and Evaluation*, page 4578 – 4583, Reykjavik, Iceland.

OMG. 2002. OMG XML metadata interchange (XMI) specification. Technical report, Object Management Group, Inc., January.

Marc Verhagen, Keith Suderman, Di Wang, Nancy Ide, Chunqi Shi, Jonathan Wright, and James Pustejovsky. 2016. The LAPPS Interchange Format. In *Revised Selected Papers of the Second International Workshop on Worldwide Language Service Infrastructure - Volume 9442*, WLSI 2015, pages 33–47, New York, NY, USA. Springer-Verlag New York, Inc.

TDB 1.1: Extensions on Turkish Discourse Bank

Deniz Zeyrek
Middle East Technical University
Ankara, Turkey
dezeyrek@metu.edu.tr

Murathan Kurfalı
Middle East Technical University
Ankara, Turkey
kurfali@metu.edu.tr

Abstract

In this paper we present the recent developments on Turkish Discourse Bank (TDB). We first summarize the resource and present an evaluation. Then, we describe TDB 1.1, i.e. enrichments on 10% of the corpus (namely, added senses for explicit discourse connectives and new annotations for implicit relations, entity relations and alternative lexicalizations). We explain the method of annotation and evaulate the data.

1 Introduction

The annotation of linguistic corpora has recently extended its scope from morphological or syntactic tagging to discourse-level annotation. Discourse annotation, however, is known to be highly challenging due to the multiple factors that make up texts (anaphors, discourse relations, topics, etc.). The challenge may become even more heightened depending on the type of text to be annotated, e.g. spoken vs written, or texts belonging to different genres. Yet, discourse-level information is highly important for language technology and it is more so for languages such as Turkish that are relatively less resource-rich when compared to European languages.

Given that systematically and consistently annotated corpora would help advance state-of-the-art discourse-level annotation, this paper aims to describe the methodology of enriching Turkish Discourse Bank, a multi-genre, 400.000-word corpus of written texts containing annotations for discourse relations in the PDTB style. Thus, the motivation of this paper is to contribute to the empirical analysis of Turkish at the level of discourse relations and enable further LT applications on the corpus. The corpus can also be used by linguists, applied linguists and translators interested in Turkish or Turkic languages in general.

The rest of the paper proceeds as follows. §2 provides an overview of Turkish Discourse Bank, summarizes the linguistic decisions underlying the corpus and presents an evaluation of the corpus. §3 introduces TDB 1.1, explains the added annotations and how the data are evaluated. §4 shows the distribution of discourse relation types and presents a preliminary cross-linguistic comparison with similarly annotated corpora. Finally, §5 summarizes the study and draws some conclusions.

2 An Overview of Turkish Discourse Bank (TDB)

The current release of Turkish Discourse Bank, or TDB 1.0 annotates discourse relations, i.e. semantic relations that hold between text segments (expansion, contrast, contingency, etc.). Discourse relations (DRs) may be expressed by explicit devices or may be conveyed implicitly. Explicit discourse connecting devices (*but, because, however*) make a DR explicit. These will be referred to as discourse connectives in this paper. Even when a DR lacks an explicit connective, the sense can be inferred. In these cases, native speakers can add an explicit discourse connective to the text to support their inference. These have been known as implicit (discourse) relations. However, TDB 1.0 only annotates DRs with an explicit connective.

While sharing the goals and annotation principles of PDTB[1], TDB takes the linguistic characteristics of Turkish into account. Here we briefly review some of these characteristics, which have an impact on the annotation decisions (see §2.1 for more principles that guide the annotation procedure).

Turkish belongs to the Altaic language family with the SOV as the dominant word order, though it exhibits all other possible word orders. It is an agglutinating language with rich morphology.

---

[1] https://www.seas.upenn.edu/ pdtb/

Proceedings of the 11th Linguistic Annotation Workshop, pages 76–81,
Valencia, Spain, April 3, 2017. ©2017 Association for Computational Linguistics

Two of its characteristics are particularly relevant for this paper. Firstly, it is characterized (a) by clause-final function words, such as postpositions that select a verb with nominalization and/or case suffixes; (b) by simple suffixes attached to the verb stem (termed as converbs). These are referred to as complex and simplex subordinators, respectively (Zeyrek and Webber, 2008). Both types of subordinators largely correspond to subordinating conjunctions in English (see Ex.1 for a complex subordinator *için* 'for/in order to' and the accompanying suffixes on the verb, and Ex.2 for a converb, *-yunca* 'when', underlined). Only the independent part of the complex subordinators have been annotated so far.

(1) Gör-<u>me-si</u>   için Ankara'ya gel-dik.
     see-NOM-ACC <u>to</u>   to-Ankara came-we

     <u>For</u> him <u>to</u> see her, we came to Ankara.

(2) Kuru-<u>yunca</u> fırçala-yacağ-ım.
     dry-<u>when</u>   brush-will-I

     I will brush it <u>when</u> it dries.

Secondly, Turkish is a null-subject language; the subject of a tensed clause is null as long as the text continues to talk about the same topic (Ex.3).

(3) Ali her gün koşar. Sağlıklı yiyecekler yer.
     Ali jogs everyday.   (He) maintains a healthy diet.

We take postpositions (and converbs) as potential explicit discourse connectives and consider the null subject property of the language as a signal for possible entity relations.

TDB adopts PDTB's lexical approach to discourse as an annotation principle, which means that all discourse relations are grounded on a lexical element (Prasad et al., 2014). The lexically grounded approach applies not only to explicitly marked discourse relations but also to implicit ones; i.e., it necessitates annotating implicit DRs by supplying an explicit connective that would make the sense of the DR explicit, as in Ex.4.

(4) ... bu çocuğun sınırsız bir düş gücü var.
     [IMP=bu yüzden] Sen bunu okulundan mahrum etme.

     ... the child has a vivid imagination. [IMP=for this reason] Don't stop him from going to school.

2.1 Principles that Guide Annotation

In TDB 1.0, explicit discourse connectives (DCs) are selected from three major lexical classes. This is motivated by the need to start from well-defined syntactic classes known to function as discourse connectives: (a) complex subordinators (postpositions, e.g. *rağmen* 'despite', and similar clause final elements, such as *yerine* 'instead of'), (b) coordinating conjunctions (*ve* 'and', *ama* 'but'), and (c) adverbials (*ayrıca* 'in addition'). TDB 1.0 also annotates phrasal expressions; these are devices that contain a postposition or a similar clause final element taking a deictic item as an argument, e.g. *buna rağmen* 'despite this', as in Ex.5 below. This group of connectives are morphologically and syntactically well-formed but not lexically frozen. Moreover, due to the presence of the deictic element in their composition, they are processed anaphorically. Because of these reasons, phrasal expressions, which are annotated separately in TDB 1.0, are merged with alternative lexicalizations in TDB 1.1 (see §3).

It is important to note that connectives may have a DC use as well as a non-DC use. The criterion to distinguish the DC/non-DC use is Asher's (2012) notion of abstract objects (AO) (events, activities, states, etc.). We take a lexical signal as a DC to the extent it relates text segments with an AO interpretation. The DC is referred to as the head of a DR, the text segments it relates are termed as the arguments. We also adhere to the minimality principle of PDTB (MP), a principle that applies to the length of text spans related by a DC. It means that annotators are required to choose an argument span that is minimally necessary for the sense of the relation (Prasad et al., 2014).

With the MP and the AO criterion in mind, the annotators went through the whole corpus searching for predetermined connectives one by one in each file, determining and annotating their DC use, leaving the non-DC use unannotated. Here, to annotate means that (explicit) DCs and phrasal expressions are tagged mainly for their predicate-argument structure; i.e. for their head (Conn) and two arguments (Arg1, Arg2) as well as the material that supplements them (Supp1, Supp2)[2].

---

[2]Following the PDTB principles, Arg2 is taken as the text segment that syntactically hosts the discourse connective; the other text segment is Arg1. The clause order of sentences with complex subordinators is Arg2-Arg1 while the other relations have the Arg1-Arg2 order. Supp1 and Supp2 stand for text segments that support the interpretation of an argument.

In the examples in the rest of the paper, Arg2 is shown in bold, Arg1 is rendered in italics; the DC itself is underlined. Any null subjects are shown by parenthesized pronouns in the glosses.

(5) *Çalışması gerekiyordu.* **Buna rağmen, üniversiteyi bırakmadı.**

(She) had to work. Despite this, **(she) did not quit university.**

Conn. Syn. Type	DC	Non-DC	Arg1	Arg2
Coord.	3609	6947	0.78	0.83
Subord. [3]	3439	5154	0.75	0.80
Disc. Adv.	698	223	0.74	0.83
Subtotal [4]	7746	12324	0.76	0.82
IAA not avl.	737	903	-	-
TOTAL	8483	13227		

Table 1: DC/Non-DC counts of connective types in TDB 1.0 (coordinators, complex subordinators, adverbials) and Fleiss' Kappa IAA results for argument spans (Sevdik-Çallı, 2015)

2.2 Evaluation of TDB 1.0

TDB 1.0 has a total of 8483 annotations on 77 Conn types and 147 tokens including coordinating conjunctions, complex subordinators, and discourse adverbials. However, it does not contain sense annotations; it does not annotate implicit DRs or entity relations; neither does it annotate alternative lexicalizations as conceived by the PDTB. The addition of these relations and their senses would enhance the quality of the corpus. Thus, this study describes an effort that involves the addition of new annotations to TDB 1.0, part of which involves sense-tagging of pre-annotated explicit DCs.

Before explaining the details about the enrichment of the corpus, we provide an evaluation of TDB 1.0. In earlier work, we reported the annotation procedure and the annotation scheme (Zeyrek et al., 2010) and provided inter-annotator agreement for complex subordinators and phrasal expressions (Zeyrek et al., 2013), but a complete evaluation of the corpus has not been provided. Table 1 presents inter-annotator agreement (IAA) of the connectives by syntactic type. We measured IAA by Fleiss' Kappa (Fleiss, 1971) using words as the boundaries of the text spans selected by the annotators, as explained in Zeyrek et al. (2013).

The agreement statistics for argument spans are important because they show how much the annotators agreed on the AO interpretation of a text span. Table 1 shows that overall, IAA of both arguments is $\geqslant 0.7$. Although this is below the commonly accepted threshold of 0.8, we take it satisfactory for discourse-level annotation, which is highly challenging due to the ambiguity of coherence relations (Spooren and Degand, 2010).

---

[3] Some phrasal expressions are retrieved by the same search token as subordinators; thus, 'Subord' indicates IAA for subordinators and phrasal expressions calculated jointly.

[4] 'Subtotal' represents the total of connectives for which IAA could be calculated; 'IAA not avl.' (available) means IAA could not be calculated.

3 Creating TDB 1.1

Due to lack of resources, we built TDB 1.1 on 10% of TDB (40.000 words). We used PDTB 2.0 annotation guidelines and the sense hierarchy therein (see fn 1).

Four part-time working graduate students annotated the corpus in pairs. We trained them by going over the PDTB guidelines and the linguistic principles provided in §2.1. Each pair annotated 50% of the corpus using an annotation tool developed by Aktaş et al. (2010). The annotation task took approximately three months, including adjudication meetings where we discussed the annotations, revised and/or corrected them where necessary.

3.1 Annotation Procedure

The PDTB sense hierarchy is based on four top level (or level-1) senses (TEMPORAL, CONTINGENCY, COMPARISON, EXPANSION) and their second and third level senses. The annotation procedure involved two rounds. First, we asked the annotators to add senses to the pre-annotated explicit DCs and phrasal expressions. The annotators implemented this task by going through each file. In this way, they fully familiarized themselves with the predicate-argument structure of DCs in TDB 1.0, as well as the PDTB 2.0 sense hierarchy.

In the second round, the annotators first tagged alternative lexicalizations (AltLexs) independently of all other DRs in each file. Given that phrasal expressions could be considered as a subset of PDTB-style AltLexs, this step ensured that TDB 1.1 not only includes phrasal expressions but various subtypes of Altlexs as well. Finally, the annotators identified and annotated implicit DRs and entity relations (EntRels) simultaneously in each file by searching them within paragraphs and between adjacent sentences delimited by a full stop, a colon, a semicolon or a question mark.

Alternative Lexicalizations: This refers to cases which could be taken as evidence for the lexicalization of a relation. The evidence may be a phrasal expression (Ex. 5), or a verb phrase, as in Ex. 6:

(6) *... genç Marx, Paris'de Avrupa'nın en devrimci işçi sınıfı ile tanışır.* **Bu, onun düşüncesinin oluşmasında** en önemli kilometre taşlarından birini teşkil eder.
... in Paris, young Marx meets Europe's the most revolutionary working class. **This** constitutes one of the most important milestones **that shapes his thoughts.**

Entity Relations: In entity relations, the inferred relation between two text segments is based on an entity, where Arg1 mentions an entity and Arg2 describes it further. As mentioned in §2, a null subject in Arg2 (or in both Arg1 and Arg2) is often a sign of an EntRel (Ex. 7).

(7) *Kerem ter içindeydi.* **"Kurtulamamışım demek," diye mırıldandı.**
Kerem was all sweaty. "So I was not set free" (he) muttered.

Implicit DRs: For the annotation of implicit DRs, we provided the annotators with an example explicit DC or a phrasal expression (in Turkish) for each level of the PDTB 2.0 sense hierarchy. We told the annotators to insert the example connective (or another connective of their choice if needed) between two sentences where they infered an implicit DR (Ex. 5 above). While EntRels were only annotated for their arguments, Altlexs and implicit DRs required senses as well. While annotating the senses, the annotators were free to chose multiple senses where necessary.

3.2 Additional Sense Tags

To capture some senses we came across in Turkish, we added three level-2 senses to the top-level senses, COMPARISON and EXPANSION.

COMPARISON: Degree. This sense tag captures the cases where one eventuality is compared to the other in terms of the degree it is similar to or different from the other eventuality. The label seemed necessary particularly to capture the sense conveyed by the complex subordinator *kadar*, which can be translated to English as, 'as ADJ/ADV as' or 'so AJD/ADV that'. When *kadar* is used to compare two eventualities in terms of

how they differ, Arg2 is a negative clause (Ex. 8). So far, this label has only been used to annotate explicit DRs.

(8) **Tanınmayacak** kadar *değişmişti.*
(He) changed so much **that (he) could not be recognized.**

EXPANSION: Manner. This tag indicates the manner by which an eventuality takes place.[5] It was particularly needed to capture the sense of the pre-annotated complex subordinator *gibi* 'as', and the simplex subordinator *-erek* 'by', which we aim to annotate. So far, the Manner tag has only been used to annotate explicit DRs.

(9) **Dediği** gibi *yaptı.*
(S/he) did as **(S/he) said (s/he) would**

EXPANSION: Correction. The Correction tag is meant to capture the relations where an incorrect judgement or opinion gets corrected or rectified in the other clause. So far, the majority of Correction relations in TDB 1.1 are implicit. There are polysemous tokens (Ex. 10), as well as single-sense tokens (Ex. 11). These do not convey the PDTB chosen alternative sense (the sense where one of the alternatives replaces the other). For example, to insert *onun yerine* 'instead of this' in Ex. 11 would be odd (though this connective would fit Ex. 10). Although further research is needed, we predict that Correction relations are characterized by the negative marker of nominal constituents, *değil* (underlined) in Arg1.

(10) *Ben yere bakmazdım.* (IMP=*ama* 'but') **Gözüne bakardım insanların.** (Chosen alternative; Correction)
I wouldn't look down. **(I) would look into peoples eyes.**

(11) *O olayları yaşayan ben değilim.* (IMP=*bilakis* 'to the contrary') **Benim yaşamım bambaşka.** (Correction)
I am not the one who went through those events. **My life is completely different.**

---

[5]PDTB-3 sense hierarchy (Webber et al., 2016) introduces Expansion:Manner and Comparison:Similarity, among other sense tags. The PDTB Manner label conveys the same sense we wanted to capture. On the other hand, the PDTB label 'Similarity' is similar to Degree only to the extent it conveys how two eventualities are similar. To the best of our knowledge, the Similarity label does not indicate comparison on the basis of how two things differ. Finally, we became aware of the revised PDTB sense hierarchy after we have started our annotation effort. We decided to continue with PDTB 2.0 labels (plus our new labels) for consistency.

3.3 Annotation Evaluation

TDB 1.1 was doubly-annotated by annotators who were blind to each other's annotations. To determine the disagreements, we calculated IAA regularly by the exact match method (Miltsakaki et al., 2004). At regular adjudication meetings involving all the annotators and the project leader, we discussed the disagreements and created an agreed set of annotations with a unanimous decision.

We measured two types of IAA: type agreement (the extent at which annotators agree over a certain DR type), and sense agreement (agreement/disagreement on sense identity for each token). For the senses added to the pre-annotated explicit DCs and phrasal expressions, we only calculated sense agreement. For the new relations, we measured both type agreement and sense agreement. This was done in two steps. Following Forbes-Riley et al. (2016), in the first step, we measured type agreement. Type agreement is defined as the number of common DRs over the number of unique relations, where all discourse relations are of the same type. For example, assume annotator1 produced 12 implicit discourse relations for a certain text whereas annotator2 produced 13, where the total number of unique discourse relations were 15 and the common annotations 11. In this case, type agreement is 73.3%. Then, we calculated sense agreement among the common annotations using the exact match method [6] (see Table 2 and Table 3 below).

Relation Type	Agreement
Implicit	33.4%
AltLex	72.6%
EntRel	79.5%

Table 2: IAA results for type agreement in TDB 1.1

Sense	Explicit	Implicit	AltLex
Level-1	88.4%	85.7%	93.9%
Level-2	79.8%	78.8%	79.5%
Level-3	75.9%	73.1%	73.4%

Table 3: IAA results for sense agreement in TDB 1.1

According to Table 2, the type agreement for AltLexs and EntRels is satisfactory ($\geqslant 0.7$) but implicit DRs display too low a type agreement. Due to this low score, we evaluated the reliability of the gold standard implicit relations: one year after TDB 1.1 was created, we asked one of our

Type	TDB 1.1	PDTB 2.0	Hindi DRB
Explicit	800 (43.1%)	18459 (45.4%)	189 (31.4%)
Implicit	407 (21.9%)	16224 (39.9%)	185 (30.7%)
Altlex	108 (5.8%)	624 (1.5%)	37 (6.15%)
Entrel	541 (29.1%)	5210 (12.8%)	140 (23.2%)
NoRel	-	254 (0.6%)	51 (8.4%)
TOTAL	1,856	40,600	602

Table 4: Cross linguistic comparison of DR types. The numbers within the parenthesis indicate the ratio of DR tokens.

four annotators to annotate the implicit DRs (both for type and sense) by going through 50% of the corpus he had not annotated before. He searched and annotated implicit DRs between adjacent sentences within paragraphs, skipping other kinds of relations. This procedure is different from the earlier one where we asked the annotators to annotate EntRels and implicit DRs simultaneously in each file. We also told the annotator to pay attention to the easily confused implicit EXPANSION:Restatement:specification relations and EntRels. (We stressed that in the former, one should detect an eventuality being further talked about rather than an entity as in the latter.)

Then, we assessed intra-rater agreement between the annotator's annotations and the gold standard data. In this way, we reached the score of 72.9% for type agreement on implicit DRs.[7] This result shows that implicit DRs have been consistently detected in the corpus; in addition, it suggests that annotating implicit DRs independently of EntRels is a helpful annotation procedure.

Table 3 shows that for explicit DCs, the IAA results for all the sense levels is $\geqslant 0.7$, indicating that the senses were detected consistently. Similarly, the sense agreement results for implicit DRs and AltLexs for all the sense levels are $\geqslant 0.7$, corroborating the reliability of the guidelines.

4 Distribution of Discourse Relation Types

This section offers a preliminary cross-linguistic comparison. It presents the distribution of discourse relation types in TDB 1.1 and compares them with PDTB 2.0 (Prasad et al., 2014) and Hindi Discourse Relation Bank (Oza et al., 2009), which also follows the PDTB principles (Table 4).

---

[6]Since no sense tag is assigned to Entrels, for them only type agreement is calculated.

[7]Intra-rater agreement between the implicit relation sense annotations of the annotator and the gold standard data is also satisfactory, i.e. $\geqslant 0.7$ for all sense levels (Level-1: 87.5%, Level-2: 79.3%, Level-3: 74.6%). We calculated sense agreement in the same way explained thoroughout the current section.

It is known that implicit relations abound in texts; thus, it is important to reveal the extent of implicitation in discourse-annotated corpora. Table 4 indicates that in TDB 1.1, explicit DRs are highest in number, followed by EntRels and implicit DRs. The ratio of explicit DRs to implicit DRs is 1.96. This ratio is 1.13 for PDTB 2.0, and 1.02 for Hindi DRB. That is, among the corpora represented in the table, TDB displays the largest difference in terms of the explicit-implicit split. However, it is not possible at this stage to generalize the results of this cross-linguistic comparison to tendencies at the discourse level. TDB 1.1 does not annotate simplex subordinators and leaves implicit VP conjunctions out of scope. Thus, when these are annotated, the ratio of explicit DRs to implicit DRs would change. Issues related to the distribution of explicit and implicit relations across genres are also necessary to reveal. We leave these matters for further research.

5   Conclusion

We presented an annotation effort on 10% of Turkish Discourse Bank 1.0 resulting in an enriched corpus called TDB 1.1. We described how PDTB principles were implemented or adapted, and presented a complete evaluation of TDB 1.1 as well as TDB 1.0, which has not been provided before. The evaluation procedure of TDB 1.1 involved measuring inter-annotator agreement for all relations and assessing intra-annotator agreement for implicit relations. The agreement statistics are overall satisfactory. While inter-annotator agreement measurements show reliability of annotations (and hence the re-usability of the annotation guidelines), intra-rater agreement results indicate the reproducibility of gold standard annotations by an experienced annotator. Using the same methodology, we aim to annotate a larger part of the TDB including attribution and no relations in the future.

Acknowledgements   We would like to thank our anonymous reviewers for their useful comments. We also thank METU Project Funds (BAP-07-04-2015-004) for their support.

References

Berfin Aktaş, Cem Bozsahin, and Deniz Zeyrek. 2010. Discourse relation configurations in Turkish and an annotation environment. In *Proc. of the 4th Linguistic Annotation Workshop*, pages 202–206. ACL.

Nicholas Asher. 2012. *Reference to abstract objects in discourse*, volume 50. Springer Science & Business Media.

Joseph L Fleiss. 1971. Measuring nominal scale agreement among many raters. *Psychological bulletin*, 76(5):378.

Kate Forbes-Riley, Fan Zhang, and Diane Litman. 2016. Extracting PDTB discourse relations from student essays. In *Proc. of the SIGDIAL*, pages 117–127.

Eleni Miltsakaki, Rashmi Prasad, Aravind K Joshi, and Bonnie L Webber. 2004. The Penn Discourse Treebank. In *LREC*.

Umangi Oza, Rashmi Prasad, Sudheer Kolachina, Dipti Misra Sharma, and Aravind Joshi. 2009. The Hindi Discourse Relation Bank. In *Proc. of the 3rd Linguistic Annotation Workshop*, pages 158–161. Association for Computational Linguistics.

Rashmi Prasad, Bonnie Webber, and Aravind Joshi. 2014. Reflections on the Penn Discourse Treebank, comparable corpora, and complementary annotation. *Computational Linguistics*.

Ayışığı Sevdik-Çallı. 2015. *Assessment of the Turkish Discourse Bank and a Cascaded Model to Automatically Identify Discursive Phrasal Expressions in Turkish*. Ph.D. thesis, Middle East Technical University.

Wilbert Spooren and Liesbeth Degand. 2010. Coding coherence relations: Reliability and validity. *Corpus Linguistics and Linguistic Theory*, 6(2):241–266.

Bonnie Webber, Rashmi Prasad, Alan Lee, and Aravind Joshi. 2016. A discourse-annotated corpus of conjoined VPs. In *Proc. of the 10th Linguistics Annotation Workshop*, pages 22–31.

Deniz Zeyrek and Bonnie L Webber. 2008. A discourse resource for Turkish: Annotating discourse connectives in the METU corpus. In *IJCNLP*, pages 65–72.

Deniz Zeyrek, Işın Demirşahin, Ayışığı Sevdik-Çallı, Hale Ögel Balaban, İhsan Yalçinkaya, and Ümit Deniz Turan. 2010. The annotation scheme of the Turkish Discourse Bank and an evaluation of inconsistent annotations. In *Proc. of the 4th Linguistics Annotation Workshop*, pages 282–289. Association for Computational Linguistics.

Deniz Zeyrek, Işın Demirşahin, Ayışığı Sevdik-Çallı, and Ruket Çakıcı. 2013. Turkish Discourse Bank: Porting a discourse annotation style to a morphologically rich language. *Dialogue and Discourse*, 4(2):174–184.

Two Layers of Annotation for Representing
Event Mentions in News Stories

Maria Pia di Buono[1]   **Martin Tutek**[1]   **Jan Šnajder**[1]   **Goran Glavaš**[2]
Bojana Dalbelo Bašić[1]   **Nataša Milić-Frayling**[3]

[1] TakeLab, Faculty of Electrical Engineering and Computing, University of Zagreb, Croatia
`firstname.lastname@fer.hr`
[2] Data and Web Science Group, University of Mannheim, Germany
`goran@informatik.uni-mannheim.de`
[3] School of Computer Science, University of Nottingham, United Kingdom
`natasa.milic-frayling@nottingham.ac.uk`

Abstract

In this paper, we describe our preliminary study of methods for annotating event mentions as part of our research on high-precision models for event extraction from news. We propose a two-layer annotation scheme, designed to capture the functional and the conceptual aspects of event mentions separately. We hypothesize that the precision can be improved by modeling and extracting the different aspects of news events separately, and then combining the extracted information by leveraging the complementarities of the models. We carry out a preliminary annotation using the proposed scheme and analyze the annotation quality in terms of inter-annotator agreement.

1 Introduction

The task of representing events in news stories and the way in which they are formalized, namely their linguistic expressions (event mentions), is interesting from both a theoretical and practical perspective. Event mentions can be analyzed from various aspects; two aspects that emerge as particularly interesting are the linguistic aspect and the more practical information extraction (IE) aspect.

As far as the linguistic aspect is concerned, news reporting is characterized by specific mechanisms and requires a specific descriptive structure. Generally speaking, such mechanisms convey non-linear temporal information that complies with news values rather than narrative norms (Setzer and Gaizauskas, 2000). In fact, unlike traditional story telling, news writing follows the "in-verted pyramid" mechanism that consists of introducing the main information at the beginning of an article and pushing other elements to the margin, as shown in Figure 1 (Ingram and Henshall, 2008). Besides, news texts use a mechanism of gradual specification of event-related information, entailing a widespread use of coreference relations among the textual elements.

On the other hand, the IE aspect is concerned with the information that can be automatically acquired from news story texts, to allow for more efficient processing, retrieval, and analysis of massive news data nowadays available in digital form.

In this paper, we describe our preliminary study on annotating event mention representations in news stories. Our work rests on two main assumptions. The first assumption is that event in news substantially differ from events in other texts, which warrants the use of a specific annotation scheme for news events. The second assumption is that, because news events can be analyzed from different aspects, it makes sense also to use different annotation layers for the different aspects. To this end, in this paper we propose a two-layer annotation scheme, designed to capture the functional and the conceptual aspects of event mentions separately. In addition, we carry out a preliminary annotation using the proposed scheme and analyze the annotation quality in terms of inter-annotator agreement.

The study presented in this paper is part of our research on high-precision models for event extraction from news. We hypothesize that the precision can be improved by modeling and extracting the different aspects of news events separately, and then combining the extracted information by leveraging the complementarities of the models. As a

Proceedings of the 11th Linguistic Annotation Workshop, pages 82–90,
Valencia, Spain, April 3, 2017. ©2017 Association for Computational Linguistics

Narrative	News
When electricians wired the home of Mrs Mary Ume in Hohola, Port Moresby, some years ago they neglected to install sufficient insulation at a point in the laundry where a number of wires crossed. A short-circuit occurred early this morning. Contact between the wires is thought to have created a spark, which ignited the walls of the house. The flames quickly spread through the entire house. Mrs Ume, her daughter Peni (aged ten) and her son Jonah (aged five months) were asleep in a rear bedroom. They had no way of escape and all perished.	A Port Moresby woman and her two children died in a house fire in Hohola today. Mrs Mary Ume, her ten-year-old daughter Peni and baby son Jonah were trapped in a rear bedroom as flames swept through the house. The fire started in the laundry, where it is believed faulty electrical wiring caused a short-circuit. The family were asleep at the time. The flames quickly spread and soon the entire house was blazing.

Table 1: An example of narrative and news styles (Ingram and Henshall, 2008).

first step towards that goal, in this paper we carry out a preliminary comparative analysis of the proposed annotation layers.

The rest of the paper is structured as follows. In the next section we briefly describe the related work on representing and annotating events. In Section 3 we present the annotation methodology. In Section 4 we describe the annotation task, while in Section 5 we discuss the results. In Section 6 we describe the comparative analysis. Section 7 concludes the paper.

2 Related Work

Several definitions of events have been proposed in the literature, including that from the Topic Detection and Tracking (TDT) community: "a TDT event is defined as a particular thing that happens at a specific time and place, along with all necessary preconditions and unavoidable consequences" (TDT, 2004). On the other hand, the ISO TimeML Working Group (Pustejovsky et al., 2003) defines an event as "something that can be said to obtain or hold true, to happen or to occur."

On the basis of such definitions, different approaches have been developed to represent and extract events and those aspects considered representative of event factuality.

In recent years, several communities proposed different shared tasks aiming at evaluating event annotation systems, mainly devoted to recognize event factuality or specific aspects related to factuality representation (e.g., temporal annotation), or tasks devoted to annotate events in specific language, e.g., Event Factuality Annotation Task presented at EVALITA 2016, the first evaluation exercise for factuality profiling of events in Italian (Minard et al., 2016b).

Among the communities working in this field, the TimeML community provides a rich specification language for event and temporal expressions aiming to capture different phenomena in event descriptions, namely "aspectual predication, modal subordination, and an initial treatment of lexical and constructional causation in text" (Pustejovsky et al., 2003).

Besides the work at these shared tasks, several authors proposed different schemes for event annotation, considering both the linguistic level and the conceptual one. The NewsReader Project (Vossen et al., 2016; Rospocher et al., 2016; Agerri and Rigau, 2016) is an initiative focused on extracting information about what happened to whom, when, and where, processing a large volume of financial and economic data. Within this project, in addition to description schemes (e.g., ECB+. (Cybulska and Vossen, 2014a)) and multilingual semantically annotated corpus of Wikinews articles (Minard et al., 2016a), van Son et al. (2016) propose a framework for annotating perspectives in texts using four different layers, i.e., events, attribution, factuality, and opinion. In the NewsReader Project the annotation is based on the guidelines to detect and annotate markables and relations among markables (Speranza and Minard, 2014). In the detection and annotation of markables, the authors distinguish among entities and entity mention in order to "handle both the annotation of single mentions and of the coreference chains that link several mentions to the same entity in a text" (Lösch and Nikitina, 2009). Entities and entity mention are then connected by the REFER TO link.

Another strand of research are the conceptual schemes, rooted in formal ontologies. Several upper ontologies for annotating events have been developed, e.g., the EVENT Model F (Scherp et al.,

2009). This ontology represents events solving two *competency questions*[1] about the participants in the events and the previous events that caused the event in question. EVENT Model F is based on the foundational ontology DOLCE+DnS Ultra-lite (DUL) (Gangemi et al., 2002) and it focuses on the participants involved in the event and on mereological, causal, and correlative relationships between events.

Most of the proposed ontologies are tailored for financial or economic domains. A case in point is The newsEvent Ontology, a conceptual scheme for describing events in business events (Lösch and Nikitina, 2009).

3 Methodology

Our methodology arises from the idea that events in news call for a representation that is different from event representations in other texts. We believe that a coherent and consistent description and, subsequently, extraction of event mentions in news stories should be dealt with conveying temporal information (When), but also distinguishing other information related to the action (What), the participants (Who), the location (Where), the motivation (Why) and the manner in which the event happened (How). This means that a meaningful news/event description should cover the proverbial 5Ws and one H, regarded basic in information gathering, providing a factual answer for all these aspects.

The above assumption implies that events cannot be considered black boxes or monolithic blocks describable merely by means of the temporal chain description. Instead, it is necessary to capture the *functional* and *conceptual* aspects of event mentions. Indeed, as previously claimed, language used in news stories is characterized by mechanisms that differ from the narrative one. Such differences may manifest themselves in both the syntactic structures and the patterns of discursive features that effect the sentence structure.

In line with the above, our approach aims at accomplishing a fine-grained description of event mentions in news stories applying a two-layer annotation scheme. The first layer conveys the different syntactic structures of sentences, accounting the functional aspects and the components in

events on the basis of their role. As noted by Papafragou (2015), "information about individual event components (e.g., the person being affected by an action) or relationships between event components that determine whether an event is coherent can be extracted rapidly by human viewers". On the other hand, the second layer is suitable also to recognize the general topic or theme that underlies a news story, due to the fact that this layer concerns conceptual aspects. This theme can be described as a "semantic macro-proposition", namely a proposition composed by the sequences of propositions retrievable in the text (Van Dijk, 1991). Thus, the conceptual scheme makes it possible to recognize these structures reducing the complexity of the information and guaranteeing a summarization process that is closer to users' representation.

3.1 Functional Layer

Following the previously-mentioned broad definition of an event in news as something that happens or occurs, in the functional annotation layer we focus on the lower level representation of events, closer to the linguistic level.

We represent each event with an event action and a variable number of arguments of different (sub)categories. The event action is most commonly the verb associated with the event (e.g., "destroyed", "awarded"), however it can also be other parts of speech (e.g., "explosion") or a multiword expression (e.g., "give up"). The action defines the focus of the event and answers the "What happened" question, and is the main part of an event mention.

Along with the event action, we define four main categories of event arguments to be annotated, which are then split into fine-grained subcategories, as shown in Table 2. We subcategorize the standard Participant category into the AGENT, PATIENT, and OTHERPARTICIPANT subcategories. We further divide each of the aforementioned subcategory into HUMAN and NON-HUMAN subcategories. The AGENT subcategory pertains to the entities that perform an action either deliberately (usually in the case of human agents) or mindlessly (natural causes, such as earthquakes or hurricanes). The PATIENT is the entity that undergoes the action and, as a result of the action, changes its state. The TIME and LOCATION categories serve to further specify the event.

Category	Subcategory	
PARTICIPANT	AGENT	HUMAN
		NONHUMAN
	PATIENT	HUMAN
		NONHUMAN
	OTHERPARTICIPANT	HUMAN
		NONHUMAN
LOCATION	GEOLOCATION	
	OTHER	
TIME		
OTHERARGUMENT		

Table 2: Functional categories and subcategories.

Finally, the OTHERARGUMENT category covers themes and instruments (Baker, 1997; Jackendoff, 1985) of an action. Table 3 gives an example of sentence "Barcelona defeated Real Madrid yesterday at Camp Nou" annotated using the functional layer.

The action's arguments focus on the specifics of the event that occurred. We depart from the standard arguments that can be found in schemes like ECB+ (Cybulska and Vossen, 2014a) or TimeML (Pustejovsky et al., 2003) in that we included the Other_argument category. Furthermore, in TimeML, predicates related to states or circumstances are considered as events, while in the scope of this work, sentences describing a state, e.g., "They live in Maine", are not annotated. In fact, we argue that they do not represent the focus in news, but merely describe the situation surrounding the event.

Our functional annotation differs from Prop-Bank (Palmer et al., 2005) definitions of semantic roles as we do not delineate our functional roles through a verb-by-verb analysis. More concretely, PropBank adds predicate-argument relations to the syntactic trees of the Penn Treebank, representing these relations as *framesets*, which describe the different sets of roles required for the different meanings of the verb. In contrast, our analysis aims to describe the focus of an event mention by means of identifying *actions*, which can involve also other lexical elements in addition to the verb. This is easily demonstrated through the example "fire broke out" from Figure 2a, where we annotate "fire broke out" as an action, since it fully specifies the nature of the event defining in a less general way the action.

Text span	Label
Barcelona	AGENT
defeated	ACTION
Real Madrid	PATIENT
yesterday	TIME
at Camp Nou	GEOLOCATION

Table 3: Sample of functional event annotation.

Entity	Property	
PERSON	IDENTITY	MOVEMENT
ORGANIZATION	ASSOCIATION	LOCATION
ANIMAL	PARTICIPATION	CAUSE
OBJECT	OCCURRENCE	PERFORMANCE
PLACE	ATTRIBUTION	INFLUENCE
TIME	CONSTRUCTION	SUPPORT
MANIFESTATION	CREATION	PURPOSE
	MODIFICATION	CLASSIFICATION
	DECLARATION	DEATH

Table 4: Main entity classes and properties.

3.2 Conceptual Layer

In order to represent semantically meaningful event mentions and, consequently, to develop an ontology of the considered domain, we define also a second layer of annotation, namely a conceptual model for news stories. This model, putting forward a classification of the main concepts retrievable in news stories, defines seven entity classes, six entity subclasses, and eighteen properties (Table 4).

Entities and properties. Entity classes are defined in order to represent a set of different individuals, sharing common characteristics. Thus, being representative of concepts in the domain, entities may be identified by noun phrases. On the other hand, properties describe the relations that link entity classes to each other and can be represented by the verb phrase. For this reason, each property is associated with some association rules that specify the constraints related to both its syntactic behaviors and the pertinence and the intension of the property itself. In other words, these association rules contribute to the description of the way in which entity classes can be combined through properties in sentence contexts. To formalize such rules in the form of a set of axioms, we take in consideration the possibility of combining semantic and lexical behaviors, suitable for identifying specific event patterns. Thus, for instance, the property MOVEMENT may connect the entity class PERSON and the entity classes PLACE and TIME, but the same property cannot be used to describe the relation between MANIFESTATION and PLACE. The definition of these rules, and the corresponding axioms, relies on word combination principles that may occur in a language, derived from an analysis of work of Harris (1988), and conceptual considerations related to the domain.

Factuality. To represent the factuality in event descriptions, we specify three attributes for each property: polarity, speculation, and passive markers. The polarity refers to the presence of an explicit negation of the verb phrase or the property itself. The speculation attribute for the property identifies something that is characterized by speculation or uncertainty. Such an attribute is associated with the presence of some verbal aspects (e.g., the passive applied to specific verbs as in they were thought to be), some specific constructions/verbs (e.g., to suggest, to suppose, to hypothesize, to propose) or modality verbs. According to Hodge and Kress (1988), the "modality refers to the status, authority and reliability of a message, to its ontological status, or to its value as truth or fact". Finally, we use an attribute for a passive marker due to the fact that passive voice is used mainly to indicate a process and can be applied to infer factual information. Note that, although the time marker is typically considered to be indicative of factuality, we prefer to avoid annotating time markers in our schema. Thus, we infer the temporal chain in event mentions by means of both temporal references in the sentence, e.g., the presence of adverbs of time, and the syntactic tense of the verb.

Coreference. To account for the coreference phenomenon among entities, we introduce a symmetric-transitive relation taking two entity classes as arguments. This allows for annotation of two types of coreference, identity and apposition, and can be used at inter-sentence level to annotate single or multiple mentions of the same entity; an example is shown in Table 5.

Complex events. In the description of event mentions in news stories we often encounter sentence structures expressing complex events, i.e., events characterized by the presence of more than one binary relation among their elements. Due to

Text span	Label
Blasts	MANMADEEVENT*
which	MANMADEEVENT*
killed	DEATH
38	COLLECTIVE
by stadium	PLACE
claimed by	DECLARATION (passive)
TAK	ORGANIZATION

Table 5: Sample of coreference and attribute annotation (* denotes coreferring elements).

the fact that properties generally express binary relationships between two entity classes, we introduce N-ary relations, namely reified relations, in order to describe these complex structures. The reified relations allow for the description of complex events composed by more than two entities and one property. According to the recommendation of the W3C,[2] these additional elements, which contribute to constitute complex events, can be formalized as a value of the property or as other arguments (entity classes) occurring in the sentence. In our scheme, we decide to deal with some of these reified relations creating three additional entity classes – MANNER, SCOPE, and INSTRUMENT – which may hold heterogeneous elements. Nevertheless, these elements present a shared intensive property defined by the main property they refer to.

4   Annotation Task

To calibrate the two annotation schemes, we performed two rounds of annotation on a set of news stories in English. We hired four annotators to work on each layer separately, to avoid interference between the layers.

We set up the annotation task as follows. First, we collected a corpus of news documents. Secondly, we gave each of four annotators per schema the same document set to annotate, along with the guidelines for that schema. We then examined the inter-annotator agreement for the documents, and discussed the major disagreements in person with the annotators. After the discussion, we revised the guidelines and again gave the annotators the

---

[2]We refer to W3C protocols for representing these structures to warrant the compliance of our schema with Semantic Web languages. More information can be found here: https://www.w3.org/TR/swbp-n-aryRelations/.

same set of documents. For the annotation tool, we used Brat (Stenetorp et al., 2012).

We collected the documents by compiling a list of recent events, then querying the web to find news articles about those events from various sources. We collected the articles from various sources to be invariant of the writing style of specific news sites. We aimed for approximately the same length of articles to keep the scale of agreement errors comparable. For this annotator calibration step, we used a set of five news documents, approximately 20 sentences in length each.

We computed the inter-annotator agreement between the documents on sentence level in order to determine the sources of annotator disagreement. We then organized discussion meetings with all of the annotators for each schema to determine whether the disagreement stems from the ambiguity of the source text or from the incomprehensiveness of the annotation schema.

After the meetings, we revised and refined the guidelines in a process which mostly included smaller changes such as adding explanatory samples of annotation for borderline cases as well as rephrasing and clarifying the text of the guidelines. However, we also made a couple of more substantial revisions such as adding label classes and determining what should or should not be included in the text spans for particular labels.

5 Inter-Annotator Agreement

We use two different metrics for calculating the inter-annotator agreement (IAA), namely Cohen's kappa coefficient (Cohen, 1960) and the F1-score (van Rijsbergen, 1979). The former has been used in prior work on event annotations, e.g., in (Cybulska and Vossen, 2014b). On the other hand, F1-score is routinely used for evaluating annotations that involve variable-length text spans, e.g., named entity annotations (Tjong Kim Sang and De Meulder, 2003) used in named entity recognition (NER) tasks. In line with NER evaluations, we consider two F1-score calculations: strict F1-score (both the labels and the text spans have to match perfectly) and lenient F1-score (labels have to match, but text spans may only partially overlap). In both cases, we calculate the macro F1-score by averaging the F1-scores computed for each label.

The motivation for using the F1-score along with Cohen's kappa coefficient lies in the fact that Cohen's kappa treats the untagged tokens as true

	Kappa	F1-strict	F1-lenient
Functional layer			
Round 1	0.428 ± 0.08	0.383 ± 0.04	0.671 ± 0.10
Round 2	0.409 ± 0.07	0.424 ± 0.04	0.621 ± 0.07
Conceptual layer			
Round 1	0.280 ± 0.08	0.350 ± 0.06	0.680 ± 0.15
Round 2	0.476 ± 0.07	0.475 ± 0.03	0.778 ± 0.06

Table 6: Inter-annotator agreement scores for the two annotation layers and two annotation rounds, averaged across annotator pairs and documents.

negatives. If the majority of tokens is untagged, the agreement values will be inflated, as demonstrated by Cybulska and Vossen (2014b). In contrast, the F1-score disregards the untagged tokens, and is therefore a more suitable measure for sequence labeling tasks. In our case, the ratio of untagged vs. tagged tokens was less skewed (6:4 and 1:2 for the functional and conceptual layer, respectively), i.e., for both annotation layers a fair portion of text is covered by annotated text spans, which means that the discrepancy between kappa values and F1-scores is expected to be lower.

We compute the IAA across all annotator pairs working on the same document, separately for the same round of annotation, and separately for each annotation layer. We then calculate the IAA averaged across the five documents, along with standard deviations. Table 6 shows the IAA scores.

For the functional layer, the Cohen's kappa coefficient is above 0.4, which, according to Landis and Koch (1977), is considered a borderline between fail and moderate agreement. Interestingly enough, the kappa agreement dropped between the first and the second round. We attribute this to the fact that the set of labels was refined (extended) between the two rounds, based on the discussion we had with the annotators after the first round of annotations. Apparently, the refinement made the annotation task more difficult, or we failed to cater for it in the guidelines. Conversely, for the conceptual layer, the agreement in first round was lower, but increased to a moderate level in the second round. The same observations hold for the F1-strict and F1-lenient measures. Furthermore, the IAA scores for the second round for the conceptual layer are higher than for the functional layer. A number of factors could be at play here: the annotators working on the conceptual layer were perhaps more skilled, the guidelines were more comprehensive, or the task is inherently less difficult or perhaps more intuitive.

While the IAA scores may seem moderate at first, one has to bear in mind the total number of different labels, which is 17 and 28 for the functional and conceptual layer, respectively. In view of this, and considering also the fact that this is a preliminary study, we consider the moderate agreement scores to be very satisfactory. Nonetheless, we believe the scores could be improved even further with additional calibration rounds.

6 Comparative analysis

In this section, we provide examples of a couple of sentences annotated in both layers, along with a brief discussion on why we believe that each layer compensates the shortcomings of the other.

Fig. 1 provides an example of a sentence annotated in the functional and conceptual layer. We observe that the last part of the sentence, "reading: Bye all!!!", is not annotated in the functional layer (Fig. 1a). This is due to the fact that the last part is a modifier of the patient, and not the action. Even though we could argue that in this case the information provided by the modifier is unimportant for the event, we could conceive of a content of the note that would indeed be important. Along with that, any modifier of the event arguments that is not directly linked to the arguments is not annotated in the functional layer, leading to information loss. We argue that in such cases the conceptual layer (Fig. 1b) is more suited towards gathering the full picture of the event along with all the descriptions.

Fig. 2a exemplifies the case where, in the functional layer, the action is a noun phrase. Such cases are intentionally meant to be labeled as actions as they change the meaning of the verb itself. In the conceptual case (Fig. 2b), as the occurrence we label "broke out", a phrase that, although clear, gives no indication of the true nature of the event, and the conceptual layer relies on the "natural event" argument for the full understanding of the event. We argue that having a noun phrase as an action, such as in the functional layer, is a more natural representation of an event as it fully answers the "What" question. We also argue that making a distinction between "fire broke out" and "broke out" as actions is beneficial for the training of the event extraction model as it emphasizes the distinction between a verb and an action.

7 Conclusions

We have presented a two-layered scheme for the annotation of event mentions in news, conveying different information aspects: the functional aspect and the conceptual aspect. The first one deals with a more general analysis of sentence structures in news and the lexical elements involved in events. The conceptual layer aims at describing event mentions in news focusing on the "semantic macro-propositions", which compose the theme of the news story.

Our approach to event mentions in news is a part of a research project on high-precision news event extraction models. The main hypothesis, leading the development of our system, is that the precision of models can be improved by modeling and extracting separately the different aspects of news events, and then combining the extracted information by leveraging the complementarities of the models. As part of this examination, we have presented also a preliminary analysis of the inter-annotator agreement.

Acknowledgments

This work has been funded by the Unity Through Knowledge Fund of the Croatian Science Foundation, under the grant 19/15: "EVEnt Retrieval Based on semantically Enriched Structures for Interactive user Tasks (EVERBEST)".

References

Rodrigo Agerri and German Rigau. 2016. Robust multilingual named entity recognition with shallow semi-supervised features. *Artificial Intelligence*, 238:63–82.

Mark C. Baker. 1997. Thematic roles and syntactic structure. In *Elements of grammar*, pages 73–137. Springer.

Jacob Cohen. 1960. A coefficient of agreement for nominal scales. *Educational and psychological measurement*, 20(1):37–46.

Agata Cybulska and Piek Vossen. 2014a. Guidelines for ECB+ annotation of events and their coreference. Technical report, Technical report, Technical Report NWR-2014-1, VU University Amsterdam.

Agata Cybulska and Piek Vossen. 2014b. Using a sledgehammer to crack a nut? lexical diversity and event coreference resolution. In *LREC*, pages 4545–4552.

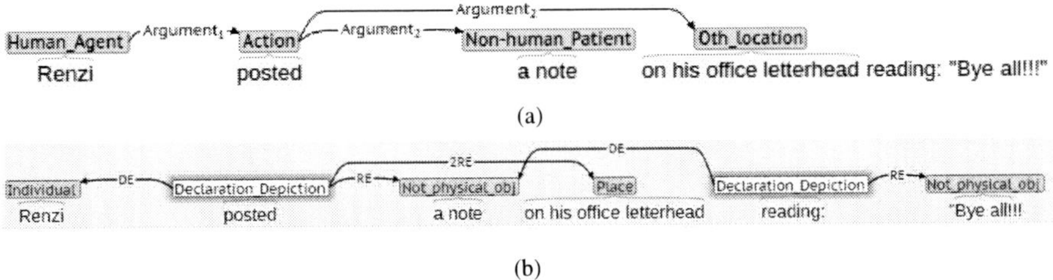

(a)

(b)

Figure 1: Example of sentence annotated in the (a) functional and the (b) conceptual layer.

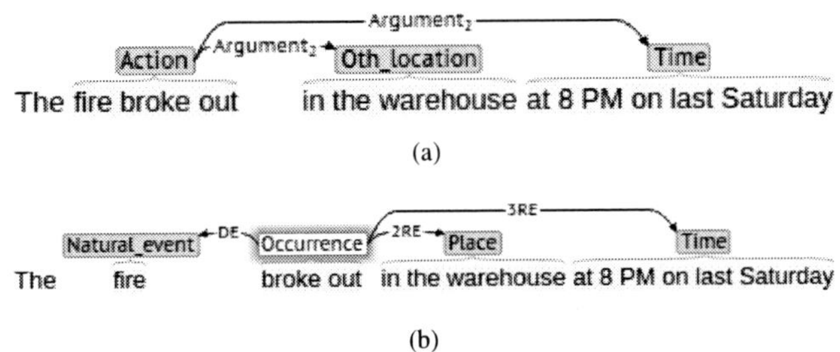

(a)

(b)

Figure 2: Example of sentence annotated in the (a) functional and the (b) conceptual layer.

Aldo Gangemi, Nicola Guarino, Claudio Masolo, Alessandro Oltramari, and Luc Schneider. 2002. Sweetening ontologies with dolce. In *International Conference on Knowledge Engineering and Knowledge Management*, pages 166–181. Springer.

Zellig Harris. 1988. *Language and information.* Columbia University Press.

Robert Hodge and Gunther R. Kress. 1988. *Social semiotics.* Cornell University Press.

D. Ingram and P. Henshall. 2008. The news manual.

Ray Jackendoff. 1985. Semantic structure and conceptual structure. *Semantics and Cognition*, pages 3–22.

J. Richard Landis and Gary G. Koch. 1977. The measurement of observer agreement for categorical data. *biometrics*, pages 159–174.

Uta Lösch and Nadejda Nikitina. 2009. The newsevents ontology: an ontology for describing business events. In *Proceedings of the 2009 International Conference on Ontology Patterns-Volume 516*, pages 187–193. CEUR-WS. org.

A-L Minard, Manuela Speranza, Ruben Urizar, Begona Altuna, MGJ van Erp, AM Schoen, CM van Son, et al. 2016a. MEANTIME, the NewsReader multilingual event and time corpus.

Anne-Lyse Minard, Manuela Speranza, Tommaso Caselli, and Fondazione Bruno Kessler. 2016b. The EVALITA 2016 event factuality annotation task (FactA). In *Proceedings of Third Italian Conference on Computational Linguistics (CLiC-it 2016) & Fifth Evaluation Campaign of Natural Language Processing and Speech Tools for Italian. Final Workshop (EVALITA 2016).*

Martha Palmer, Daniel Gildea, and Paul Kingsbury. 2005. The proposition bank: An annotated corpus of semantic roles. *Computational linguistics*, 31(1):71–106.

Anna Papafragou. 2015. The representation of events in language and cognition. *The conceptual mind: New directions in the study of concepts*, page 327.

James Pustejovsky, José M Castano, Robert Ingria, Roser Sauri, Robert J Gaizauskas, Andrea Setzer, Graham Katz, and Dragomir R. Radev. 2003. TimeML: Robust specification of event and temporal expressions in text. *New directions in question answering*, 3:28–34.

Marco Rospocher, Marieke van Erp, Piek Vossen, Antske Fokkens, Itziar Aldabe, German Rigau, Aitor Soroa, Thomas Ploeger, and Tessel Bogaard. 2016. Building event-centric knowledge graphs from news. *Web Semantics: Science, Services and Agents on the World Wide Web*, 37:132–151.

Ansgar Scherp, Thomas Franz, Carsten Saathoff, and Steffen Staab. 2009. F – a model of events based on the foundational ontology DOLCE+DnS ultralite. In *Proceedings of the fifth international conference on Knowledge capture*, pages 137–144. ACM.

Andrea Setzer and Robert J. Gaizauskas. 2000. Annotating events and temporal information in newswire texts. In *LREC*, volume 2000, pages 1287–1294.

Manuela Speranza and Anne-Lyse Minard. 2014. NewsReader guidelines for cross-document annotation NWR-2014-9.

Pontus Stenetorp, Sampo Pyysalo, Goran Topić, Tomoko Ohta, Sophia Ananiadou, and Jun'ichi Tsujii. 2012. BRAT: a web-based tool for NLP-assisted text annotation. In *Proceedings of the Demonstrations at the 13th Conference of the European Chapter of the Association for Computational Linguistics*, pages 102–107. Association for Computational Linguistics.

Tdt TDT. 2004. Annotation manual version 1.2. *From knowledge accumulation to accommodation: cycles of collective cognition in work groups*.

Erik F Tjong Kim Sang and Fien De Meulder. 2003. Introduction to the CoNLL-2003 shared task: Language-independent named entity recognition. In *Proceedings of the seventh conference on Natural language learning at HLT-NAACL 2003-Volume 4*, pages 142–147. Association for Computational Linguistics.

Mike Uschold and Michael Gruninger. 1996. Ontologies: Principles, methods and applications. *The knowledge engineering review*, 11(02):93–136.

Teun A. Van Dijk. 1991. Media contents: the interdisciplinary study of news as discourse, a handbook of qualitative methodologies for mass communication research.

C.J. van Rijsbergen. 1979. *Information Retreival*. Butterworths.

Chantal van Son, Tommaso Caselli, Antske Fokkens, Isa Maks, Roser Morante, Lora Aroyo, and Piek Vossen. 2016. Grasp: A multilayered annotation scheme for perspectives. In *Proceedings of the 10th Edition of the Language Resources and Evaluation Conference (LREC)*.

Piek Vossen, Rodrigo Agerri, Itziar Aldabe, Agata Cybulska, Marieke van Erp, Antske Fokkens, Egoitz Laparra, Anne-Lyse Minard, Alessio Palmero Aprosio, German Rigau, et al. 2016. NewsReader: Using knowledge resources in a cross-lingual reading machine to generate more knowledge from massive streams of news. *Knowledge-Based Systems*, 110:60–85.

Word Similarity Datasets for Indian Languages:
Annotation and Baseline Systems

Syed S. Akhtar   Arihant Gupta   Avijit Vajpayee   Arjit Srivastava   M. Shrivastava

International Institute of Information Technology

Hyderabad, Telangana, India

{syed.akhtar, arihant.gupta, arjit.srivastava}@research.iiit.ac.in,

avijit.vajpayee@students.iiit.ac.in,

manish.shrivastava@iiit.ac.in

Abstract

With the advent of word representations, word similarity tasks are becoming increasing popular as an evaluation metric for the quality of the representations. In this paper, we present manually annotated monolingual word similarity datasets of six Indian languages – Urdu, Telugu, Marathi, Punjabi, Tamil and Gujarati. These languages are most spoken Indian languages worldwide after Hindi and Bengali. For the construction of these datasets, our approach relies on translation and re-annotation of word similarity datasets of English. We also present baseline scores for word representation models using state-of-the-art techniques for Urdu, Telugu and Marathi by evaluating them on newly created word similarity datasets.

1   Introduction

Word representations are being increasingly popular in various areas of natural language processing like dependency parsing (Bansal et al., 2014), named entity recognition (Miller et al., 2004) and parsing (Socher et al., 2013). Word similarity task is one of the most popular benchmark for the evaluation of word representations. Applications of word similarity range from Word Sense Disambiguation (Patwardhan et al., 2005), Machine Translation Evaluation (Lavie and Denkowski, 2009), Question Answering (Mohler et al., 2011), and Lexical Substitution (Diana and Navigli, 2009).

Word Similarity task is a computationally efficient method to evaluate the quality of word vectors. It relies on finding correlation between human assigned semantic similarity (between words) and corresponding word vectors. We have used Spearman's Rho for calculating correlation. Unfortunately, most of the word similarity tasks have been majorly limited to English language because of availability of well annotated different word similarity test datasets and large corpora for learning good word representations, where as for Indian languages like Marathi, Punjabi, Telugu etc. – which even though are widely spoken by significant number of people, are still computationally resource poor languages. Even if there are models trained for these languages, word similarity datasets to test reliability of corresponding learned word representations do not exist.

Hence, primary motivation for creation of these six word similarity datasets has been to provide necessary evaluation resources for all the current and future work in field of word representations on these six Indian languages – all ranked in top 25 most spoken languages in the world, since no prior word similarity datasets have been publicly made available.

The main contribution of this paper is the set of newly created word similarity datasets which would allow for fast and efficient comparison between. Word similarity is one of the most important evaluation metric for word representations and hence as an evaluation metric, these datasets would promote development of better techniques that employ word representations for these languages. We also present baseline scores using state-of-the-art techniques which were evaluated using these datasets.

The paper is structured as follows. We first discuss the corpus and techniques used for training our models in section 2 which are later used for evaluation. We then talk about relevant related work that has been done with respect to word similarity datasets in section 3. We then move on to explain how these datasets have been created in section 4 followed by our evaluation criteria and

91

Proceedings of the 11th Linguistic Annotation Workshop, pages 91–94,
Valencia, Spain, April 3, 2017. ©2017 Association for Computational Linguistics

experimental results of various models evaluated on these datasets in section 5. Finally, we analyze and explain the results in section 6 and finish this paper with how we plan to extend our work in section 7.

2 Datasets

For all the models trained in this paper, we have used the Skip-gram, CBOW (Mikolov et al., 2013a) and FastText (Bojanowski et al., 2016) algorithms. The dimensionality has been fixed at 300 with a minimum count of 5 along with negative sampling.

As training set of Marathi, we use the monolingual corpus created by IIT-Bombay. This data contains 27 million tokens. For Urdu, we use the untagged corpus released by Jawaid et. al. (2014) containing 95 million tokens. For Telugu, we use Telugu wikidump available at `https://archive.org/details/tewiki-20150305` having 11 million tokens.

For testing, we use the newly created datasets. The word similarity datatsets for Urdu, Marathi, Telugu, Punjabi, Gujarati and Tamil contain 100, 104, 111, 143, 163 and 97 word pairs respectively.

For rest of the paper, we have calculated the Spearman ρ (multiplied by 100) between human assigned similarity and cosine similarity of our word embeddings for the word-pairs. For any word which was is not found, we assign it a zero vector.

In order to learn initial representations of the words, we train word embeddings (word2vec) using the parameters described above on the training set.

3 Related Work

Multitude of word similarity datasets have been created for English, like WordSim-353 (Finkelstein et al., 2002), MC-30 (Miller and Charles, 1991), Simlex-999 (Hill et al., 2016), RG-65 (Rubenstein and Goodenough, 2006) etc. RG-65 is one of the oldest and most popular datasets, being used as a standard benchmark for measuring reliability of word representations.

RG-65 has also acted as base for various other word similarity datasets created in different languages: French (Joubarne and Inkpen, 2011), German (Zesch and Gurevyc, 2006), Portuguese (Granada et al., 2014), Spanish and Farsi (Camacho-Collados et al., 2015). While German and Portuguese reported IAA (Inter Annotator Agreement) of 0.81 and 0.71 respectively, no IAA was calculated for French. For Spanish and Farsi, inter annotator agreement of 0.83 and 0.88 respectively was reported. Our datasets were created using RG-65 and WordSim-353 as base, and their respective IAA(s) are mentioned later in the paper.

4 Construction of Monolingual Word Similarity datasets

4.1 Translation

English RG-65 and WordSim-353 were used as base for creating all of our six different word similarity datasets. Translation of English data set to target language (one of the six languages) was manually done by a set of three annotators who are native speakers of the target language and are fluent in English. Initially, translations are provided by two of them, and in case of disparity, third annotator was used as a tie breaker.

Finally, all three annotators reached a final set of translated word pairs in target language, ensuring that there were no repeated word pairs. This approach was followed by Camacho-Callados et al. (2015) where they created word similarity datasets for Spanish and Farsi in a similar manner.

4.2 Scoring

For each of the six languages, 8 native speakers were asked to manually evaluate each word similarity data set individually. They were instructed to indicate, for each pair, their opinion of how similar in meaning the two words are on a scale of 0-10, with 10 for words that mean the same thing, and 0 for words that mean completely different things. The guidelines provided to the annotators were based on the SemEval task on Cross-Level Semantic Similarity (Jurgens et al., 2014), which provides clear indications in order to distinguish similarity and relatedness.

The results were averaged over the 8 responses for each word similarity data set, and each data set saw good agreement amongst the evaluators, except for Tamil, which saw relatively weaker agreement with respect to other languages (see table 1).

5 Evaluation

5.1 Inter Annotator Agreement (IAA)

The meaning of a sentence and its words can be interpreted in different ways by different readers. This subjectivity can also reflect in annotation of sentences of a language despite the annotation guidelines being well defined. Therefore, inter-annotator agreement is calculated to give a measure of how well the annotators can make the same annotation decision for a certain category.

Language	Inter Annotator Agreement
Urdu	0.887
Punjabi	0.821
Marathi	0.808
Tamil	0.756
Telugu	0.866
Gujarati	0.867

Table 1: Inter Annotator Agreement (Fleiss Kappa) scores for word similarity datasets created for six languages.

5.1.1 Fleiss' Kappa

Fleiss' kappa is a statistical measure for assessing the reliability of agreement between a fixed number of raters when assigning categorical ratings to a number of items or classifying items. This contrasts with other kappas such as Cohen's kappa, which only work when assessing the agreement between not more than two raters or the interrater reliability for one appraiser versus himself. The measure calculates the degree of agreement in classification over that which would be expected by chance (Wikipedia contributors, 2017).

We have calculated Fleiss' Kappa for all our word similarity datasets (see table 1).

6 Result and Analysis

System	Score	OOV	Vocab
CBOW	28.30	19	130K
SG	34.40	19	130K
FastText	34.61	19	130K
FastText w/ OOV	45.47	14	-

Table 2: Results for **Urdu**

We present baseline scores using state of the art techniques – CBOW and Skipgram (Mikolov et al., 2013a) and FastText-SG (Bojanowski et al., 2016), evaluated using our word similarity datasets in tables 2, 3 and 4. As we can see the models trained encountered unseen word pairs when evaluated on their corresponding word similarity datasets. This goes on to show that all word

System	Score	OOV	Vocab
CBOW	36.16	3	194K
SG	41.22	3	194K
FastText	33.68	3	194K
FastText w/ OOV	38.66	0	-

Table 3: Results for **Marathi**

System	Score	OOV	Vocab
CBOW	26.01	14	174K
SG	27.04	14	174K
FastText	34.29	14	174K
FastText w/ OOV	46.02	0	-

Table 4: Results for **Telugu**

pairs in our word similarity sets are not too common, and contain word pairs with some rarity.

We see that FastText w/ OOV (Out of Vocabulary) performed better than FastText in all the experiments, because character based models perform better than rest of the models since they are able to handle unseen words by generating word embeddings for missing words via character model.

7 Future Work

There are a lot of Indian languages that are still computationally resource poor even though they are widely spoken by significant number of people. Our work is a small step towards generating resources to further the research involving word representations on Indian languages.

To further extend our work, we will create rare-word word similarity datasets for six languages we worked on in this paper, and creating word similarity datasets for other major Indian languages as well.

We will also work on improving word representations for the languages we worked on, hence improve the baseline scores that we present here. This will require us to build new corpus to train our models for three languages that we couldn't provide baseline scores for – Punjabi, Tamil and Gujarati and build more corpus for Urdu, Telugu and Marathi to train better word embeddings.

References

Alon Lavie, and Michael J. Denkowski. 2009. *The METEOR metric for automatic evaluation of ma-*

chine translation. Machine translation 23, no. 2-3 (2009): 105-115.

Piotr Bojanowski, Edouard Grave, Armand Joulin, and Tomas Mikolov 2016. *Enriching word vectors with subword information*. arXiv preprint arXiv:1607.04606 (2016).

Bushra Jawaid, Amir Kamran, and Ondrej Bojar. 2014. *A Tagged Corpus and a Tagger for Urdu*. LREC 2014.

Camacho-Collados, Jos, Mohammad Taher Pilehvar, and Roberto Navigli. 2015. *A Framework for the Construction of Monolingual and Cross-lingual Word Similarity Datasets*. In ACL (2) (pp. 1-7).

Colette Joubarne and Diana Inkpen. 2011. *Comparison of semantic similarity for different languages using the Google n-gram corpus and second-order co-occurrence measures*. In Advances in Artificial Intelligence – 24th Canadian Conference on Artificial Intelligence, pages 216-221.

David Jurgens, Mohammad Taher Pilehvar, and Roberto Navigli. 2014. *Semeval-2014 task 3: Cross-level semantic similarity*. Proceedings of the 8th International Workshop on Semantic Evaluation (SemEval 2014), in conjunction with COLING. 2014.

Diana McCarthy, and Roberto Navigli. 2009. *The English lexical substitution task*. Language resources and evaluation 43, no. 2 (2009): 139-159.

Felix Hill, Roi Reichart, and Anna Korhonen. 2016. *Simlex-999: Evaluating semantic models with (genuine) similarity estimation*. Computational Linguistics.

George A. Miller, and Walter G. Charles. 1991. *Contextual correlates of semantic similarity*. Language and cognitive processes 6.1 (1991): 1-28.

Herbert Rubenstein and John B. Goodenough. 2006. *Contextual correlates of synonym*. Communications of the ACM, volume 8, number 10, pages 627-633.

Lev Finkelstein, Evgeniy Gabrilovich, Yossi Matias, Ehud Rivlin, Zach Solan, Gadi Wolfman and Eytan Ruppin. 2002. *Placing search in context: The concept revisited*. Proceedings of the 10th international conference on World Wide Web, pages 406-414.

Michael Mohler, Razvan Bunescu, and Rada Mihalcea.. 2011. *Learning to grade short answer questions using semantic similarity measures and dependency graph alignments*. In Proceedings of the 49th Annual Meeting of the Association for Computational Linguistics: Human Language Technologies-Volume 1 (pp. 752-762). Association for Computational Linguistics.

Mohit Bansal, Kevin Gimpel, and Karen Livescu. 2014. *Tailoring continuous word representations for dependency parsing*. In Proceedings of the 52nd Annual Meeting of the Association for Computational Linguistics, ACL 2014, June 22-27, Baltimore, MD, USA, Volume 2: Short Papers, pages 809815.

Richard Socher, John Bauer, Christopher D. Manning, and Andrew Y. Ng. 2013. *Parsing With Compositional Vector Grammars*. In ACL, pages 455-465.

Roger Granada, Cassia Trojahn, and Renata Vieira. 2014. *Comparing semantic relatedness between word pairs in Portuguese using Wikipedia*. International Conference on Computational Processing of the Portuguese Language. Springer International Publishing, 2014.

Scott Miller, Jethran Guinness, and Alex Zamanian. 2004. *Name tagging with word clusters and discriminative training*. In Proceedings of HLT-NAACL, volume 4, pages 337-342.

Siddharth Patwardhan, Satanjeev Banerjee, and Ted Pedersen 2005. *SenseRelate:: TargetWord: a generalized framework for word sense disambiguation*. Proceedings of the ACL 2005 on Interactive poster and demonstration sessions (pp. 73-76). Association for Computational Linguistics.

Tomas Mikolov, Kai Chen, Greg Corrado, and Jeff Dean. 2006. *Efficient estimation of word representations in vector space*. In In arXiv preprint arXiv:1301.3781

Tomas Mikolov, Wen-tau Yih, and Geoffrey Zweig. 2013. *Linguistic regularities in continuous space word representations*. In Proceedings of HLT-NAACL, volume 13, pages 746-751.

Tomas Mikolov, Quoc V. Le, and lya Sutskever. 2013. *Exploiting similarities among languages for machine translation*. arXiv preprint arXiv:1309.4168 (2013).

Torsten Zesch and Iryna Gurevyc. 2006. *Automatically creating datasets for measures of semantic relatedness*. In Proceedings of the Workshop on Linguistic Distances, pages 16-24.

Wikipedia contributors. 2017. *"Fleiss' kappa." Wikipedia, The Free Encyclopedia.*. Wikipedia, The Free Encyclopedia, 6 Feb. 2017. Web. 16 Feb. 2017.

The BECauSE Corpus 2.0: Annotating Causality and Overlapping Relations

Jesse Dunietz
Computer Science Department
Carnegie Mellon University
Pittsburgh, PA 15213, USA
`jdunietz@cs.cmu.edu`

Lori Levin and **Jaime Carbonell**
Language Technologies Institute
Carnegie Mellon University
Pittsburgh, PA 15213, USA
`{lsl, jgc}@cs.cmu.edu`

Abstract

Language of cause and effect captures an essential component of the semantics of a text. However, causal language is also intertwined with other semantic relations, such as temporal precedence and correlation. This makes it difficult to determine when causation is the primary intended meaning. This paper presents BECauSE 2.0, a new version of the BECauSE corpus with exhaustively annotated expressions of causal language, but also seven semantic relations that are frequently co-present with causation. The new corpus shows high inter-annotator agreement, and yields insights both about the linguistic expressions of causation and about the process of annotating co-present semantic relations.

1 Introduction

We understand our world in terms of causal networks – phenomena causing, enabling, or preventing others. Accordingly, the language we use is full of references to cause and effect. In the Penn Discourse Treebank (PDTB; Prasad et al., 2008), for example, over 12% of explicit discourse connectives are marked as causal, as are nearly 26% of implicit discourse relationships. Recognizing causal assertions is thus invaluable for semantics-oriented applications, particularly in domains such as finance and biology where interpreting these assertions can help drive decision-making.

In addition to being ubiquitous, causation is often co-present with related meanings such as temporal order (cause precedes effect) and hypotheticals (the *if* causes the *then*). This paper presents the Bank of Effects and Causes Stated Explicitly (BECauSE) 2.0, which offers insight into these overlaps. As in BECauSE 1.0 (Dunietz et al., 2015, in press), the corpus contains annotations for causal language. It also includes annotations for seven commonly co-present meanings when they are expressed using constructions shared with causality.

To deal with the wide variation in linguistic expressions of causation (see Neeleman and Van de Koot, 2012; Dunietz et al., 2015), BECauSE draws on the principles of Construction Grammar (CxG; Fillmore et al., 1988; Goldberg, 1995). CxG posits that the fundamental units of language are *constructions* – pairings of meanings with arbitrarily simple or complex linguistic forms, from morphemes to structured lexico-syntactic patterns.

Accordingly, BECauSE admits arbitrary constructions as the bearers of causal relationships. As long as there is at least one fixed word, any conventionalized expression of causation can be annotated. By focusing on causal *language* – conventionalized expressions of causation – rather than real-world causation, BECauSE largely sidesteps the philosophical question of what is truly causal. It is not concerned, for instance, with whether there is a real-world causal relationship within *flu virus* (virus causes flu) or *delicious bacon pizza* (bacon causes deliciousness); neither is annotated.

Nonetheless, some of the same overlaps and ambiguities that make real-world causation so hard to circumscribe seep into the linguistic domain, as well. Consider the following examples (with **causal constructions** in bold, CAUSES in small caps, and *effects* in italics):

(1) **After** I DRANK SOME WATER, *I felt much better.*
(2) **As** VOTERS GET TO KNOW MR. ROMNEY BETTER, *his poll numbers will rise.*
(3) **THE MORE** HE COMPLAINED, ***the less** his captors fed him.*
(4) THE RUN ON BEAR STERNS **created** *a crisis.*
(5) THE IRAQI GOVERNMENT will **let** *Represen-*

Proceedings of the 11th Linguistic Annotation Workshop, pages 95–104,
Valencia, Spain, April 3, 2017. ©2017 Association for Computational Linguistics

Each sentence conveys a causal relation, but piggybacks it on a related relation type. (1) uses a temporal relationship to suggest causality. (3) employs a correlative construction, and (2) contains elements of both time and correlation in addition to causation. (4), meanwhile, is framed as bringing something into existence, and (5) suggests both permission and enablement.

Most semantic annotation schemes have required that each token be assigned just one meaning. BECauSE 1.0 followed this policy, as well, but this resulted in inconsistent handling of cases like those above. For example, the meaning of *let* varies from "allow to happen" (clearly causal) to "verbalize permission" (not causal) to shades of both. These overlaps made it difficult for annotators to decide when to annotate such cases as causal.

The contributions of this paper are threefold. First, we present a new version of the BECauSE corpus, which offers several improvements over the original. Most importantly, the updated corpus includes annotations for seven different relation types that overlap with causality: temporal, correlation, hypothetical, obligation/permission, creation/termination, extremity/sufficiency, and context. Overlapping relations are tagged for any construction that can also be used to express a causal relationship. The improved scheme yields high inter-annotator agreement. Second, using the new corpus, we derive intriguing evidence about how meanings compete for linguistic machinery. Finally, we discuss the issues that the annotation approach does and does not solve. Our observations suggest lessons for future annotation projects in semantic domains with fuzzy boundaries between categories.

2 Related Work

Several annotation schemes have addressed elements of causal language. Verb resources such as VerbNet (Schuler, 2005) and PropBank (Palmer et al., 2005) include verbs of causation. Likewise, preposition schemes (e.g., Schneider et al., 2015, 2016) include some purpose- and explanation-related senses. None of these, however, unifies all linguistic realizations of causation into one framework; they are concerned with specific classes of words, rather than the semantics of causality.

FrameNet (Ruppenhofer et al., 2016) is closer in spirit to BECauSE, in that it starts from meanings

and catalogs/annotates a wide variety of lexical items that can express those meanings. Our work differs in several ways. First, FrameNet represents causal relationships through a variety of unrelated frames (e.g., CAUSATION and THWARTING) and frame roles (e.g., PURPOSE and EXPLANATION). As with other schemes, this makes it difficult to treat causality in a uniform way. (The ASFALDA French FrameNet project recently proposed a reorganized frame hierarchy for causality, along with more complete coverage of French causal lexical units [Vieu et al., 2016]. Merging their framework into mainline FrameNet would mitigate this issue.) Second, FrameNet does not allow a lexical unit to evoke more than one frame at a time (although SALSA [Burchardt et al., 2006], the German FrameNet, does allow this).

The Penn Discourse Treebank includes causality under its hierarchy of contingency relations. Notably, PDTB does allow annotators to mark discourse relations as both causal and something else. However, it is restricted to discourse relations; it excludes other realizations of causal relationships (e.g., verbs and many prepositions), as well as PURPOSE relations, which are not expressed as discourse connectives. BECauSE 2.0 can be thought of as an adaptation of PDTB's multiple-annotation approach. Instead of focusing on a particular type of construction (discourse relations) and annotating all the meanings it can convey, we start from a particular meaning (causality), find all constructions that express it, and annotate each instance in the text with all the meanings it expresses.

Other projects have attempted to address causality more narrowly. For example, a small corpus of event pairs conjoined with *and* has been tagged as causal or not causal (Bethard et al., 2008). The CaTeRS annotation scheme (Mostafazadeh et al., 2016), based on TimeML, also includes causal relations, but from a commonsense reasoning standpoint rather than a linguistic one. Similarly, Richer Event Description (O'Gorman et al., 2016) integrates real-world temporal and causal relations between events into a unified framework. A broader-coverage linguistic approach was taken by Mirza and Tonelli (2014), who enriched TimeML to include causal links and their lexical triggers. Their work differs from ours in that it requires arguments to be TimeML events; it requires causal connectives to be contiguous; and its guidelines define causality less precisely, relying on intuitive notions of causing, preventing, and enabling.

2.1 BECauSE 1.0

Our work is of course most closely based on BE-CauSE 1.0. Its underlying philosophy is to annotate any form of *causal language* – conventionalized linguistic mechanisms used to appeal to cause and effect. Thus, the scheme is not concerned with what real-world causal relationships hold, but rather with what relationships are presented in the text. It defines causal language as "any construction which presents one event, state, action, or entity as promoting or hindering another, and which includes at least one lexical trigger." Each annotation consists of a **cause** span; an **effect** span; and a **causal connective**, the possibly discontinuous lexical items that express the causal relationship (e.g., *because of* or *opens the way for*).

3 Extensions and Refactored Guidelines in BECauSE 2.0

This update to BECauSE improves on the original in several ways. Most importantly, as mentioned above, the original scheme precluded multiple co-present relations. Tagging a connective as causal was taken to mean that it was primarily expressing causation, and not temporal sequence or permission. (In fact, temporal expressions that were intended to suggest causation were explicitly excluded.) Based on the new annotations, there were 210 instances in the original corpus where multiple relations were present and annotators had to make an arbitrary decision.[1] The new scheme extends the previous one to include these overlapping relations.

Second, although the first version neatly handled many different kinds of connectives, adjectives and nouns were treated in a less general way. Verbs, adverbs, conjunctions, prepositions, and complex constructions typically have two natural slots in the construction. For example, the *because* construction can be schematized as ⟨effect⟩ *because* ⟨cause⟩, and the causative construction present in *so loud it hurt* as ⟨so cause⟩ (that) ⟨effect⟩.

Adjective and noun connectives, however, do not offer such natural positions for ⟨cause⟩ and ⟨effect⟩. In the following example, BECauSE 1.0 would annotate the connective as marked in bold: *the*

*cause of her illness **was** dehydration*. But this is an unparsimonious account of the causal construction: the copula and preposition do not contribute to the causal meaning, and other language could be used to tie the connective to the arguments. For instance, it would be equally valid to say *her illness' cause was dehydration*, or even *the chart listed her illness' cause as dehydration*. The new corpus addresses this by annotating just the noun or adjective as the connective (e.g., *cause*), and letting the remaining argument realization language vary. A number of connectives were similarly refactored to make them simpler and more consistent.

Finally, version 1.0 struggled with the distinction between the causing event and the causing agent. For example, in *I caused a commotion by shattering a glass*, either the agent (*I*) or the agent's action (*shattering a glass*) could plausibly be annotated as the cause. The guidelines for version 1.0 suggested that the true cause is the action, so the agent should be annotated as the cause only when no action is described. (In such cases, the agent would be considered metonymic for the action.) However, given the scheme's focus on constructions, it seems odd to say that the arguments to the construction change when a *by* clause is added.

The new scheme solves this by labeling the agent as the cause in both cases, but adding a MEANS argument for cases where both an agent and their action are specified.[2]

4 BECauSE 2.0 Annotation Scheme

4.1 Basic Features of Annotations

The second version of the BECauSE corpus retains the philosophy and most of the provisions of the first, with the aforementioned changes.

To circumscribe the scope of the annotations, we follow BECauSE 1.0 in excluding causal relationships with no lexical trigger (e.g., *He left. He wasn't feeling well.*); connectives that lexicalize the means or result of the causation (e.g., *kill* or *convince*); and connectives that underspecify the nature of the causal relationship (e.g., *linked to*).

---

[1]This is the total number, in the new corpus, of instances that are annotated with both causal and overlapping relations and which would have been ambiguous under the 1.0 guidelines – i.e., the guidelines did not either explictly exclude them or deem them always causal.

[2]Another possibility would have been to divvy up causes into CAUSE and AGENT arguments. Although FrameNet follows this route in some of its frames, we found that this distinction was difficult to make in practice. For example, a non-agentive cause might still be presented with a separate means clause, as in *inflammation triggers depression by altering immune responses*. In contrast, MEANS are relatively easy to identify when present, and tend to exhibit more consistent behavior with respect to what constructions introduce them.

As in BECauSE 1.0, the centerpiece of each instance of causal language is the **causal connective**. The connective is not synonymous with the causal construction; rather, it is a lexical proxy indicating the presence of the construction. It consists of all words present in every use of the construction. For example, the bolded words in ***enough** money **for us to get by*** would be marked as the connective. Annotators' choices of what to include as connectives were guided by a *constructicon*, a catalog of constructions specified to a human-interpretable level of precision (but not precise enough to be machine-interpretable). The constructicon was updated as needed throughout the annotation process.

In addition to the connective, each instance includes **cause** and **effect** spans. (Either the cause or the effect may be absent, as in a passive or infinitive.) BECauSE 2.0 also introduces the **means** argument, as mentioned above. Means arguments are annotated when an agent is given as the cause, but the action taken by that agent is also explicitly described, or would be but for a passive or infinitive. They are marked only when expressed as a *by* or *via* clause, a dependent clause (e.g., *Singing loudly, she caused winces all down the street*), or a handful of other conventional devices. If any of an instance's arguments consists of a bare pronoun, including a relativizing pronoun such as *that*, a coreference link is added back to its antecedent (assuming there is one in the same sentence).

The new scheme distinguishes three types of causation, each of which has slightly different semantics: CONSEQUENCE, in which the cause naturally leads to the effect; MOTIVATION, in which some agent perceives the cause, and therefore consciously thinks, feels, or chooses something; and PURPOSE, in which an agent chooses the effect because they desire to make the cause true. Unlike BECauSE 1.0, the new scheme does not include evidentiary uses of causal language, such as *She met him previously, because she recognized him yesterday*. These were formerly tagged as INFERENCE. We eliminated them because unlike other categories of causation, they are not strictly causal, and unlike other overlapping relations, they never also express true causation; they constitute a different sense of *because*.

The scheme also distinguishes positive causation (FACILITATE) from inhibitory causation (INHIBIT); see Dunietz et al. (2015) for full details.

Examples demonstrating all of these categories are shown in Table 1.

4.2 Annotating Overlapping Relations

The constructions used to express causation overlap with many other semantic domains. For example, the *if/then* language of hypotheticals and the *so ⟨adjective⟩* construction of extremity have become conventionalized ways of expressing causation, usually in addition to their other meanings. In this corpus, we annotate the presence of these overlapping relations, as well.

A connective is annotated an instance of either causal language or a non-causal overlapping relation whenever it is used in a sense and construction that *can* carry causal meaning. The operational test for this is whether the word sense and linguistic structure allow it to be coerced into a causal interpretation, and the meaning is either causal or one of the relation types below.

Consider, for example, the connective *without*. It is annotated in cases like *without your support, the campaign will fail*. However, annotators ignored uses like *we left without saying goodbye*, because in this linguistic context, *without* cannot be coerced into a causal meaning. Likewise, we include *if* as a HYPOTHETICAL connective, but not *suppose that*, because the latter cannot indicate causality.

All overlapping relations are understood to hold between an ARGC and an ARGE. When annotating a causal instance, ARGC and ARGE refer to the cause and effect, respectively. When annotating a non-causal instance, ARGC and ARGE refer to the arguments that would be cause and effect if the instance were causal. For example, in a TEMPORAL relation, ARGC would be the earlier argument and ARGE would be the later one.

The following overlapping relation types are annotated:

- TEMPORAL: when the causal construction explicitly foregrounds a temporal order between two arguments (e.g., *once*, *after*) or simultaneity (e.g., *as*, *during*).

- CORRELATION: when the core meaning of the causal construction is that ARGC and ARGE vary together (e.g., *as, the more… the more…*).

- HYPOTHETICAL: when the causal construction explicitly imagines that a questionable premise is true, then establishes what would hold in the world where it is (e.g., *if… then…*).

- OBLIGATION/PERMISSION: when ARGE (effect) is an agent's action, and ARGC (cause)

	FACILITATE	INHIBIT
CONSEQUENCE	*We are in serious economic trouble* **because of** INADEQUATE REGULATION.	THE NEW REGULATIONS should **prevent** *future crises.*
MOTIVATION	WE DON'T HAVE MUCH TIME, **so** *let's move quickly.*	THE COLD **kept** *me* **from** *going outside.*
PURPOSE	*Coach them in handling complaints* **so that** THEY CAN RESOLVE PROBLEMS IMMEDIATELY.	(Not possible)

Table 1: Examples of every allowed combination of the three types of causal language and the two degrees of causation (with **connectives** in bold, CAUSES in small caps, and *effects* in italics).

is presented as some norm, rule, or entity with power that is requiring, permitting, or forbidding ARGE to be performed (e.g., *require* in the legal sense, *permit*).

- CREATION/TERMINATION: when the construction frames the relationship as an entity or circumstance being brought into existence or terminated (e.g., *generate, eliminate*).

- EXTREMITY/SUFFICIENCY: when the causal construction also expresses an extreme or sufficient/insufficient position of some value on a scale (e.g., *so... that... , sufficient... to...*).

- CONTEXT: when the construction clarifies the conditions under which the effect occurs (e.g,. *with, without, when* in non-temporal uses). For instance, *With supplies running low, we didn't even make a fire that night.*

All relation types present in the instance are marked. For example, *so offensive that I left* would be annotated as both causal (MOTIVATION) and EXTREMITY/SUFFICIENCY. When causality is not present in a use of a sometimes-causal construction, the instance is annotated as NON-CAUSAL, and the overlapping relations present are marked.

It can be difficult to determine when language that expresses one of these relationships was also intended to convey a causal relationship. Annotators used a variety of questions to assess an ambiguous instance, largely based on Grivaz (2010):

- **The "why" test:** After reading the sentence, could a reader reasonably be expected to answer a "why" question about the potential effect argument? If not, it is not causal.

- **The temporal order test:** Is the cause asserted to precede the effect? If not, it is not causal.

- **The counterfactuality test:** Would the effect have been just as probable to occur or not occur had the cause not happened? If so, it is not causal.

- **The ontological asymmetry test:** Could you

just as easily claim the cause and effect are reversed? If so, it is not causal.

- **The linguistic test:** Can the sentence be rephrased as "It is because (of) X that Y" or "X causes Y?" If so, it is likely to be causal.

Figure 1 showcases several fully-annotated sentences that highlight the key features of the new BECauSE scheme, including examples of overlapping relations.

5 BECauSE 2.0 Corpus

5.1 Data

The BECauSE 2.0 corpus[3] is an expanded version of the dataset from BECauSE 1.0. It consists of:

- 59 randomly selected articles from the year 2007 in the Washington section of the New York Times corpus (Sandhaus, 2008)

- 47 documents randomly selected[4] from sections 2-23 of the Penn Treebank (Marcus et al., 1994)

- 679 sentences[5] transcribed from Congress' Dodd-Frank hearings, taken from the NLP Unshared Task in PoliInformatics 2014 (Smith et al., 2014)

- 10 newspaper documents (Wall Street Journal and New York Times articles, totalling 547 sentences) and 2 journal documents (82 sentences) from the Manually Annotated Sub-Corpus (MASC; Ide et al., 2010)

The first three sets of documents are the same dataset that was annotated for BECauSE 1.0.

5.2 Inter-Annotator Agreement

Inter-annotator agreement was calculated between the two primary annotators on a sample of 260

---

[3] Publicly available, along with the constructicon, at `https://github.com/duncanka/BECauSE`.

[4] We excluded WSJ documents that were either earnings reports or corporate leadership/structure announcements, as both tended to be merely short lists of names/numbers.

[5] The remainder of the document was not annotated due to constraints on available annotation effort.

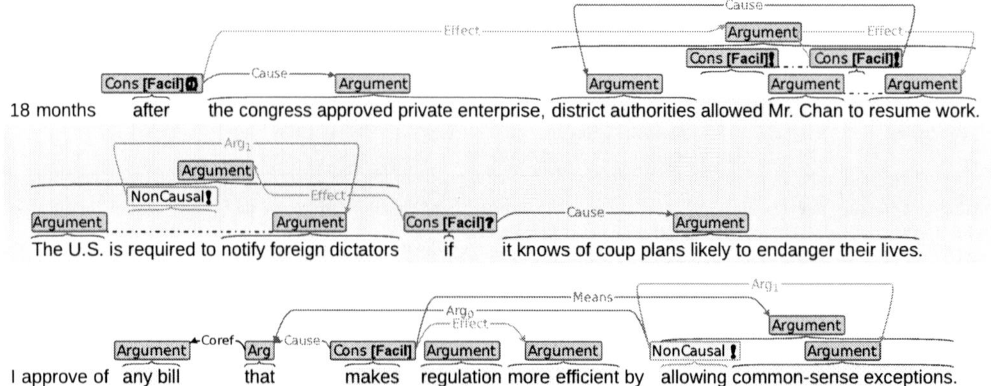

Figure 1: Several example sentences annotated in BRAT (Stenetorp et al., 2012). The question mark indicates a hypothetical, the clock symbol indicates a temporal relation, and the thick exclamation point indicates obligation/permission.

	Causal	Overlapping
Connective spans (F_1)	0.77	0.89
Relation types (κ)	0.70	0.91
Degrees (κ)	0.92	(n/a)
Cause/ARGC spans (%)	0.89	0.96
Cause/ARGC spans (J)	0.92	0.97
Cause/ARGC heads (%)	0.92	0.96
Effect/ARGE spans (%)	0.86	0.84
Effect/ARGE spans (J)	0.93	0.92
Effect/ARGE heads (%)	0.95	0.89

Table 2: Inter-annotator agreement for the new version of BECauSE. κ indicates Cohen's kappa; J indicates the average Jaccard index, a measure of span overlap; and % indicates percent agreement of exact matches. Each κ and argument score was calculated only for instances with matching connectives.

An argument's head was determined automatically by parsing the sentence with version 3.5.2 of the Stanford Parser (Klein and Manning, 2003) and taking the highest dependency node in the argument span.

Means arguments were not included in this evaluation, as they are quite rare – there were only two in the IAA dataset, one of which was missed by one annotator and the other of which was missed by both. Both annotators agreed with these two means arguments once they were pointed out.

sentences, containing 98 causal instances and 82 instances of overlapping relations (per the first author's annotations). Statistics appear in Table 2.

Overall, the results show substantially improved connective agreement. F_1 for causal connectives is up to 0.77, compared to 0.70 in BECauSE 1.0. (The documents were drawn from similar sources and containing connectives of largely similar complexity as the previous IAA set.) The improvement suggests that the clearer guidelines and the overlapping relations made decisions less ambiguous, although some of the difference may be due to chance differences in the IAA datasets. Agreement on causal relation types is somewhat lower than in version $1.0 - 0.7$ instead of 0.8 (possibly because more instances are annotated in the new scheme, which tends to reduce κ) – but it is still high. Unsurprisingly, most of the disagreements are between CONSEQUENCE and MOTIVATION. Degrees are close to full agreement; the only disagreement appears to have been a careless error. Agreement on argument spans is likewise quite good.

For overlapping relations, only agreement on ARGEs is lower than for causal relations; all other metrics are significantly higher. The connective F_1 score of 0.89 is especially promising, given the apparent difficulty of deciding which uses of connectives like *with* or *when* could plausibly be coerced to a causal meaning.

5.3 Corpus Statistics and Analysis

The corpus contains a total of 5380 sentences, among which are 1803 labeled instances of causal language. 1634 of these, or 90.7%, include both cause and effect arguments. 587 – about a third – involve overlapping relations. The corpus also includes 583 non-causal overlapping relation annotations. The frequency of both causal and overlapping relation types is shown in Table 3.

A few caveats about these statistics: first, PURPOSE annotations do not overlap with any of the categories we analyzed. However, this should not be interpreted as evidence that they have no overlaps. Rather, they seem to inhabit a different part of the semantic space. PURPOSE does share some language with origin/destination relationships (e.g., *toward the goal of*, ***in order to*** *achieve my goals*), both diachronically and synchronically; see §7.

	Consequence	Motivation	Purpose	All causal	Non-causal	**Total**
None	625	319	272	1216	-	1216
Temporal	120	135	-	255	463	718
Correlation	9	3	-	12	5	17
Hypothetical	73	48	-	121	24	145
Obligation/permission	67	5	-	72	27	99
Creation/termination	37	4	-	41	43	84
Extremity/sufficiency	53	9	-	62	-	62
Context	17	15	-	32	25	57
Total	994	537	272	1803	583	2386

Table 3: Statistics of various combinations of relation types. Note that there are 9 instances of Temporal+Correlation and 3 instances of Temporal+Context. This makes the bottom totals less than the sum of the rows.

Second, the numbers do not reflect all constructions that express, e.g., temporal or correlative relationships – only those that can be used to express causality. Thus, it would be improper to conclude that over a third of temporals are causal; many kinds of temporal language simply were not included. Similarly, the fact that all annotated Extremity/sufficiency instances are causal is an artifact of only annotating uses with a complement clause, such as *so loud I felt it*; *so loud* on its own could never be coerced to a causal interpretation.

Several conclusions and hypotheses do emerge from the relation statistics. Most notably, causality has thoroughly seeped into the temporal and hypothetical domains. Over 14% of causal expressions are piggybacked on temporal relations, and nearly 7% are expressed as hypotheticals. This is consistent with the close semantic ties between these domains: temporal order is a precondition for a causal relationship, and often hypotheticals are interesting specifically because of the consequences of the hypothesized condition. The extent of these overlaps speaks to the importance of capturing overlapping relations for causality and other domains with blurry boundaries.

Another takeaway is that most hypotheticals that are expressed as conditionals are causal. Not all hypotheticals are included in BECauSE (e.g., *suppose that* is not), but all conditional hypotheticals are[6]: any conditional could express a causal relationship in addition to a hypothetical one. In principle, non-causal hypotheticals could be more common, such as *if he comes, he'll bring his wife* or *if we must cry, let them be tears of laughter*. It appears, however, that the majority of conditional hypotheticals

(84%) in fact carry causal meaning.

Finally, the data exhibit a surprisingly strong preference for framing causal relations in terms of agents' motivations: nearly 45% of causal instances are expressed as Motivation or Purpose. Of course, the data could be biased towards events involving human agents; many of the documents are about politics and economics. Still, it is intriguing that many of the explicit causal relationships are not just about, say, politicians' economic decisions having consequences, but about why the agents made the choices they did. It is worth investigating further to determine whether there really is a preference for appeals to motivation even when they are not strictly necessary.

6 Lessons Learned

Our experience suggests several lessons about annotating multiple overlapping relations. First, it clearly indicates that a secondary meaning can be evoked without losing any of the original meaning. In terms of the model of prototypes and radial categories (Lewandowska-Tomaszczyk, 2007), the conventional model for blurriness between categories, an instance can simultaneously be prototypical for one type of relation and radial for another. For instance, *the ruling **allows** the police **to enter** your home* is a prototypical example a permission relationship. However, it is also a radial example of enablement (a form of causation): prototypical enablement involves a physical barrier being removed, whereas *allow* indicates the removal of a normative barrier.

A second lesson: even when including overlapping semantic domains in an annotation project, it may still be necessary to declare some overlapping domains out of scope. In particular, some adjacent domains will have their own overlaps with meanings that are far afield from the target domain. It

---

[6]We did not annotate *even if* as a hypothetical, since it seems to be a specialized concessive form of the construction. However, this choice does not substantially change the conclusion: even including instances of *even if*, 77% of conditional hypotheticals would still be causal.

would be impractical to simply pull all of these second-order domains into the annotation scheme; the project would quickly grow to encompass the entire language. If possible, the best solution is to dissect the overlapping domain into a more detailed typology, and only include the parts that directly overlap with the target domain. If this is not doable, the domain may need to be excluded altogether.

For example, we attempted to introduce a TOPIC relation type to cover cases like *The President is fuming **over** recent media reports* or *They're angry **about** the equipment we broke* (both clearly causal). Unfortunately, opening up the entire domain of topic relations turned out to be too broad and confusing. For example, it is hard to tell which of the following are even describing the same kind of topic relationship, never mind which ones can also be causal: *fought **over** his bad behavior* (behavior caused fighting); *fought **over** a teddy bear* (fought for physical control); *worried **about** being late*; *worried **that** I might be late*; *I'm skeptical **regarding** the code's robustness*. We ultimately determined that teasing apart this domain would have to be out of scope for this work.

7 Contributions and Lingering Difficulties

Our approach leaves open several questions about how to annotate causal relations and other semantically blurry relations.

First, it does not eliminate the need for binary choices about whether a given relation is present; our annotators must still mark each instance as either indicating causation or not. Likewise for each of the overlapping relations. Yet some cases suggest overtones of causality or correlation, but are not prototypically causal or correlative. These cases still necessitate making a semi-abitrary call.

The ideal solution would somehow acknowledge the continuous nature of meaning – that an expression can indicate a relationship that is not causal, entirely causal, slightly causal, or anywhere in between. But it is hard to imagine how such a continuous representation would be annotated in practice.

Second, some edge cases remain a challenge for our new scheme. Most notably, we did not examine every semantic domain sharing some overlap with causality. Relations we did not address include:

- Origin/destination (as mentioned in §5.3; e.g., *the sparks **from** the fire, **toward** that goal*)
- Topic (see §6)

- Componential relationships (e.g., ***As part of** the building's liquidation, other major tenants will also vacate the premises*)
- Evidentiary basis (e.g., *We went to war **based on** bad intelligence*)
- Having a role (e.g., ***As** an American citizen, I do not want to see the President fail*)
- Placing in a position (e.g., *This move **puts** the American people **at** risk*)

These relations were omitted due to the time and effort it would have taken to determine whether and when to classify them as causal. We leave untangling their complexities for future work.

Other cases proved difficult because they seem to imply a causal relationship in each direction. The class of constructions indicating necessary preconditions was particularly troublesome. These constructions are typified by the sentence *(**For us**) to succeed, we all **have to** cooperate*. (Other variants use different language to express the modality of obligation, such as *require* or *necessary*.) On the one hand, the sentence indicates that cooperation enables success. On the other hand, it also suggests that the desire for success necessitates the cooperation.[7] We generally take the enablement relationship to be the primary meaning, but this is not an entirely satisfying account of the semantics.

Despite the need for further investigation of these issues, our attempt at extending causal language annotations to adjacent semantic domains was largely a success. We have demonstrated that it is practical and sometimes helpful to annotate all linguistic expressions of a semantic relationship, even when they overlap with other semantic relations. We were able to achieve high inter-annotator agreement and to extract insights about how different meanings compete for constructions. We hope that the new corpus, our annotation methodology and the lessons it provides, and the observations about linguistic competition will all prove useful to the research community.

---

[7]Necessary precondition constructions are thus similar to constructions of PURPOSE, such as *in order to*. As spelled out in Dunietz et al. (2015), a PURPOSE connective contains a similar duality of causations in opposing directions: it indicates that a desire for an outcome causes an agent to act, and hints that the action may in fact produce the desired outcome. However, in PURPOSE instances, it is clearer which relationship is primary: the desired outcome may not obtain, whereas the agent is centainly acting on their motivation. In precondition constructions, however, both the precondition and the result are imagined, making it harder to tell which of the two causal relationships is primary.

References

Steven Bethard, William J Corvey, Sara Klingenstein, and James H. Martin. 2008. Building a corpus of temporal-causal structure. In *Proceedings of LREC 2008*, pages 908–915.

Aljoscha Burchardt, Katrin Erk, Anette Frank, Andrea Kowalski, Sebastian Padó, and Manfred Pinkal. 2006. The SALSA corpus: a German corpus resource for lexical semantics. In *Proceedings of the 5th International Conference on Language Resources and Evaluation (LREC-2006)*. Association for Computational Linguistics.

Jesse Dunietz, Lori Levin, and Jaime Carbonell. 2015. Annotating causal language using corpus lexicography of constructions. In *The 9th Linguistic Annotation Workshop held in conjunction with NAACL 2015*, pages 188–196.

Jesse Dunietz, Lori Levin, and Jaime Carbonell. in press. Automatically tagging constructions of causation and their slot-fillers. *Transactions of the Association for Computational Linguistics*.

Charles J. Fillmore, Paul Kay, and Mary Catherine O'Connor. 1988. Regularity and idiomaticity in grammatical constructions: The case of let alone. *Language*, 64(3):501–538.

Adele Goldberg. 1995. *Constructions: A Construction Grammar Approach to Argument Structure*. Chicago University Press.

Cécile Grivaz. 2010. Human judgements on causation in French texts. In *Proceedings of LREC 2010*. European Languages Resources Association (ELRA).

Nancy Ide, Christiane Fellbaum, Collin Baker, and Rebecca Passonneau. 2010. The manually annotated sub-corpus: A community resource for and by the people. In *Proceedings of the 48th Annual Meeting of the Association for Computational Linguistics*, pages 68–73. Association for Computational Linguistics.

Dan Klein and Christopher D. Manning. 2003. Accurate unlexicalized parsing. In *Proceedings of the 41st Annual Meeting on Association for Computational Linguistics-Volume 1*, pages 423–430. Association for Computational Linguistics.

Barbara Lewandowska-Tomaszczyk. 2007. Polysemy, prototypes, and radial categories. *The Oxford handbook of cognitive linguistics*, pages 139–169.

Mitchell Marcus, Grace Kim, Mary Ann Marcinkiewicz, Robert MacIntyre, Ann Bies, Mark Ferguson, Karen Katz, and Britta Schasberger. 1994. The Penn Treebank: Annotating predicate argument structure. In *Proceedings of the Workshop on Human Language Technology*, HLT '94, pages 114–119. Association for Computational Linguistics, Stroudsburg, PA, USA.

Paramita Mirza and Sara Tonelli. 2014. An analysis of causality between events and its relation to temporal information. In *Proceedings of COLING*, pages 2097–2106.

Nasrin Mostafazadeh, Alyson Grealish, Nathanael Chambers, James Allen, and Lucy Vanderwende. 2016. CaTeRS: Causal and temporal relation scheme for semantic annotation of event structures. In *Proceedings of the 4th Workshop on Events: Definition, Detection, Coreference, and Representation*, pages 51–61. Association for Computational Linguistics.

Ad Neeleman and Hans Van de Koot. 2012. *The Theta System: Argument Structure at the Interface*, chapter The Linguistic Expression of Causation, pages 20–51. Oxford University Press.

Tim O'Gorman, Kristin Wright-Bettner, and Martha Palmer. 2016. Richer Event Description: Integrating event coreference with temporal, causal and bridging annotation. *Computing News Storylines*, page 47.

Martha Palmer, Daniel Gildea, and Paul Kingsbury. 2005. The Proposition Bank: An annotated corpus of semantic roles. *Computational Linguistics*, 31(1):71–106.

Rashmi Prasad, Nikhil Dinesh, Alan Lee, Eleni Miltsakaki, Livio Robaldo, Aravind Joshi, and Bonnie Webber. 2008. The Penn Discourse TreeBank 2.0. In Nicoletta Calzolari, Khalid Choukri, Bente Maegaard, Joseph Mariani, Jan Odijk, Stelios Piperidis, and Daniel Tapias, editors, *Proceedings of LREC 2008*. European Language Resources Association (ELRA), Marrakech, Morocco.

Josef Ruppenhofer, Michael Ellsworth, Miriam RL Petruck, Christopher R. Johnson, Jan Scheffczyk, and Collin F. Baker. 2016. FrameNet II: Extended theory and practice.

Evan Sandhaus. 2008. The New York Times annotated corpus. *Linguistic Data Consortium, Philadelphia*.

Nathan Schneider, Jena D. Hwang, Vivek Srikumar, Meredith Green, Abhijit Suresh, Kathryn Conger, Tim O'Gorman, and Martha Palmer. 2016. A corpus of preposition supersenses. In *Proceedings of the 10th Linguistic Annotation Workshop held in conjunction with ACL 2016 (LAW-X 2016)*, pages 99–109. Association for Computational Linguistics.

Nathan Schneider, Vivek Srikumar, Jena D. Hwang, and Martha Palmer. 2015. A hierarchy with, of, and for preposition supersenses. In *Proceedings of The 9th Linguistic Annotation Workshop*, pages 112–123. Association for Computational Linguistics, Denver, Colorado, USA.

Karin K. Schuler. 2005. *VerbNet: A Broad-Coverage, Comprehensive Verb Lexicon*. Ph.D. thesis, University of Pennsylvania, Philadelphia, PA. AAI3179808.

Noah A. Smith, Claire Cardie, Anne L. Washington, and John Wilkerson. 2014. Overview of the 2014 NLP unshared task in poliinformatics. In *Proceedings of the ACL 2014 Workshop on Language Technologies and Computational Social Science*.

Pontus Stenetorp, Sampo Pyysalo, Goran Topić, Tomoko Ohta, Sophia Ananiadou, and Jun'ichi Tsujii. 2012. BRAT: a web-based tool for NLP-assisted text annotation. In *Proceedings of the Demonstrations at the 13th Conference of the European Chapter of the Association for Computational Linguistics*, pages 102–107. Association for Computational Linguistics.

Laure Vieu, Philippe Muller, Marie Candito, and Marianne Djemaa. 2016. A general framework for the annotation of causality based on FrameNet. In Nicoletta Calzolari (Conference Chair), Khalid Choukri, Thierry Declerck, Sara Goggi, Marko Grobelnik, Bente Maegaard, Joseph Mariani, Helene Mazo, Asuncion Moreno, Jan Odijk, and Stelios Piperidis, editors, *Proceedings of LREC 2016*. European Language Resources Association (ELRA), Paris, France.

Catching the Common Cause: Extraction and Annotation of Causal Relations and their Participants

Ines Rehbein   **Josef Ruppenhofer**
IDS Mannheim/University of Heidelberg, Germany
Leibniz Science Campus "Empirical Linguistics and Computational Language Modeling"
{rehbein, ruppenhofer}@cl.uni-heidelberg.de

Abstract

In this paper, we present a simple, yet effective method for the automatic identification and extraction of causal relations from text, based on a large English-German parallel corpus. The goal of this effort is to create a lexical resource for German causal relations. The resource will consist of a lexicon that describes constructions that trigger causality as well as the participants of the causal event, and will be augmented by a corpus with annotated instances for each entry, that can be used as training data to develop a system for automatic classification of causal relations. Focusing on verbs, our method harvested a set of 100 different lexical triggers of causality, including support verb constructions. At the moment, our corpus includes over 1,000 annotated instances. The lexicon and the annotated data will be made available to the research community.

1 Introduction

Causality is an important concept that helps us to make sense of the world around us. This is exemplified by the *Causality-by-default* hypothesis (Sanders, 2005) that has shown that humans, when presented with two consecutive sentences expressing a relation that is ambiguous between a causal and an additive reading, commonly interpret the relation as causal.

Despite, or maybe because of, its pervasive nature, causality is a concept that has proven to be notoriously difficult to define. Proposals have been made that describe causality from a philosophical point of view, such as the Counterfactual Theory of causation (Lewis, 1973), theories of probabilistic causation (Suppes, 1970; Pearl, 1988), and production theories like the Dynamic Force Model (Talmy, 1988).

Counterfactual Theory tries to explain causality between two events C and E in terms of conditionals such as "If C had not occurred, E would not have occurred". However, psychological studies have shown that this not always coincides with how humans understand and draw causal inferences (Byrne, 2005). *Probabilistic theories*, on the other hand, try to explain causality based on the underlying probability of an event to take place in the world. The theory that has had the greatest impact on linguistic annotation of causality is probably Talmy's *Dynamic Force Model* which provides a framework that tries to distinguish weak and strong causal forces, and captures different types of causality such as "letting", "hindering", "helping" or "intending".

While each of these theories manages to explain some aspects of causality, none of them seems to provide a completely satisfying account of the phenomenon under consideration. The problem of capturing and specifying the concept of causality is also reflected in linguistic annotation efforts. Human annotators often show only a moderate or even poor agreement when annotating causal phenomena (Grivaz, 2010; Gastel et al., 2011). Some annotation efforts abstain altogether from reporting inter-annotator agreement at all.

A notable exception is Dunietz et al. (2015) who take a lexical approach and aim at building a *constructicon* for English causal language. By *constructicon* they mean "a list of English constructions that conventionally express causality" (Dunietz et al., 2015). They show that their approach dramatically increases agreement between the annotators and thus the quality of the annotations (for details see section 2). We adapt their approach of framing the annotation task as a lexicon creation process and present first steps towards build-

Proceedings of the 11th Linguistic Annotation Workshop, pages 105–114,
Valencia, Spain, April 3, 2017. ©2017 Association for Computational Linguistics

ing a causal constructicon for German. Our annotation scheme is based on the one of Dunietz et al. (2015), but with some crucial changes (section 3).

The resource under construction contains a lexicon component with entries for lexical units (individual words and multiword expressions) for different parts of speech, augmented with annotations for each entry that can be used to develop a system for the automatic identification of causal language.

The contributions of this paper are as follows.

1. We present a bootstrapping method to identify and extract causal relations and their participants from text, based on parallel corpora.

2. We present the first version of a German causal constructicon, containing 100 entries for causal verbal expressions.

3. We provide over 1,000 annotated causal instances (and growing) for the lexical triggers, augmented by a set of negative instances to be used as training data.

The remainder of the paper is structured as follows. First, we review related work on annotating causal language (section 2). In section 3, we describe our annotation scheme and the data we use in our experiments. Sections 4, 5 and 6 present our approach and the results, and we conclude and outline future work in section 7.

2 Related Work

Two strands of research are relevant to our work, a) work on automatic detection of causal relations in text, and b) annotation studies that discuss the description and disambiguation of causal phenomena in natural language. As we are still in the process of building our resource and collecting training data, we will for now set aside work on automatic classification of causality such as (Mirza and Tonelli, 2014; Dunietz et al., In press) as well as the rich literature on shallow discourse parsing, and focus on annotation and identification of causal phenomena.

Early work on identification and extraction of causal relations from text heavily relied on knowledge bases (Kaplan and Berry-Rogghe, 1991; Girju, 2003). Girju (2003) identifies instances of noun-verb-noun causal relations in WordNet glosses, such as *starvation$_{N1}$ causes bonyness$_{N2}$*.

She then uses the extracted noun pairs to search a large corpus for verbs that link one of the noun pairs from the list, and collects these verbs. Many of the verbs are, however, ambiguous. Based on the extracted verb list, Girju selects sentences from a large corpus that contain such an ambiguous verb, and manually disambiguates the sentences to be included in a training set. She then uses the annotated data to train a decision tree classifier that can be used to classify new instances.

Our approach is similar to hers in that we also use the English verb *cause* as a seed to identify transitive causal verbs. In contrast to Girju's WordNet-based approach, we use parallel data and project the English tokens to their German counterparts.

Ours is not the first work that exploits parallel or comparable corpora for causality detection. Hidey and McKeown (2016) work with monolingual comparable corpora, English Wikipedia and simple Wikipedia. They use explicit discourse connectives from the PDTB (Prasad et al., 2008) as seed data and identify alternative lexicalizations for causal discourse relations. Versley (2010) classifies German explicit discourse relations without German training data, solely based on the English annotations projected to German via word-aligned parallel text. He also presents a bootstrapping approach for a connective dictionary that relies on distribution-based heuristics on word-aligned German-English text.

Like Versley (2010), most work on identifying causal language for German has been focusing on discourse connectives. Stede et al. (1998; 2002) have developed a lexicon of German discourse markers that has been augmented with semantic relations (Scheffler and Stede, 2016). Another resource for German is the TüBa-D/Z that includes annotations for selected discourse connectives, with a small number of causal connectives (Gastel et al., 2011). Bögel et al. (2014) present a rule-based system for identifying eight causal German connectors in spoken multilogs, and the causal relations REASON, RESULT expressed by them.

To the best of our knowledge, ours is the first effort to describe causality in German on a broader scale, not limited to discourse connectives.

3 Annotation Scheme

Our annotation aims at providing a description of causal events and their participants, similar to FrameNet-style annotations (Ruppenhofer et al., 2006), but at a more coarse-grained level. In FrameNet, we have a high number of different causal frames with detailed descriptions of the actors, agents and entities involved in the event.[1] For instance, FrameNet captures details such as the intentionality of the triggering force, to express whether or not the action was performed volitionally.

In contrast, we target a more generic representation that captures different types of causality, and that allows us to generalize over the different participants and thus makes it feasible to train an automatic system by abstracting away from individual lexical triggers. The advantage of such an approach is greater generalizability and thus higher coverage, the success however remains to be proven. Our annotation scheme includes the following four participant roles:

1. CAUSE – a force, process, event or action that produces an effect

2. EFFECT – the result of the process, event or action

3. ACTOR – an entity that, volitionally or not, triggers the effect

4. AFFECTED – an entity that is affected by the results of the cause

Our role set is different from Dunietz et al. (2015) who restrict the annotation of causal arguments to CAUSE and EFFECT. Our motivation for extending the label set is twofold. First, different verbal causal triggers show strong selectional preferences for specific participant roles. Compare, for instance, examples (1) and (2). The two argument slots for the verbal triggers *erzeugen* (produce) and *erleiden* (suffer) are filled with different roles. The subject slot for *erzeugen* expresses either CAUSE or ACTOR and the direct object encodes the EFFECT. For *erleiden*, on the other hand, the subject typically realises the role of the AFFECTED entity, and we often have the CAUSE or ACTOR encoded as the prepositional object of a *durch* (by) PP.

(1) **Elektromagnetische Felder**$_{Cause}$
Electromagnetic fields
können *Krebs*$_{Effect}$ erzeugen.
can cancer produce.
"Electromagnetic fields can cause cancer."

(2) *Länder wie Irland*$_{Affected}$ werden
Countries like Ireland will
durch **die Reform**$_{Cause}$ *massive*
by the reform massive
Nachteile$_{Effect}$ erleiden
disadvantages suffer.
"Countries like Ireland will sustain massive disadvantages because of the reform."

Given that there are systematic differences between prototypical properties of the participants (e.g. an ACTOR is usually animate and a sentient being), and also in the way how they combine and select their predicates, we would like to preserve this information and see if we can exploit it when training an automatic system.

In addition to the participants of a causal event, we follow Dunietz et al. (2015) and distinguish four different types of causation (CONSEQUENCE, MOTIVATION, PURPOSE, INFERENCE), and two degrees (FACILITATE, INHIBIT). The degree distinctions are inspired by Wolff et al. (2005) who see causality as a continuum from total prevention to total entailment, and describe this continuum with three categories, namely CAUSE, ENABLE and PREVENT. Dunietz et al. (2015) further reduce this inventory to a polar distinction between a positive causal relation (e.g. *cause*) and a negative one (e.g. *prevent*), as they observed that human coders were not able to reliably apply the more fine-grained inventories.[2] The examples below illustrate the different types of causation.

(3) **Cancer**$_{Cause}$ is second only to **accidents**$_{Cause}$ as a <u>cause</u> of *death*$_{Effect}$ in *children*$_{Affected}$ CONSEQUENCE

(4) *I would like to say a few words <u>in order to</u>* **highlight two points**   PURPOSE

(5) *She must be home*$_{Effect}$ <u>because</u> **the light is on**$_{Cause}$ INFERENCE

(6) **The decision is made**$_{Cause}$ <u>so</u> *let us leave the matter there*$_{Effect}$ MOTIVATION

Epistemic uses of causality are covered by the INFERENCE class while we annotate instances

---

[1] Also see Vieu et al. (2016) for a revised and improved treatment of causality in FrameNet.

[2] For the polar distinction, they report perfect agreement.

of speech-act causality (7) as MOTIVATION (see Sweetser (1990) for an in-depth discussion on that matter). This is also different from Dunietz et al. (2015) who only deal with *causal language*, not with *causality in the world*. We, instead, are also interested in relations that are interpreted as causal by humans, even if they are not strictly expressed as causal by a lexical marker, such as temporal relations or speech-act causality.

(7) And if you want to say no, *say no$_{Effect}$ 'Cause* **there's a million ways to go**$_{Cause}$ MOTIVATION

A final point that needs to be mentioned is that Dunietz et al. (2015) exclude items such as *kill* or *persuade* that incorporate the result (e.g. death) or means (e.g. talk) of causation as part of their meaning. Again, we follow Dunietz et al. and also exclude such cases from our lexicon.

In this work, we focus on verbal triggers of causality. Due to our extraction method (section 4), we are mostly dealing with verbal triggers that are instances of the type CONSEQUENCE. Therefore we cannot say much about the applicability of the different annotation types at this point but will leave this to future work.

4 Knowledge-lean extraction of causal relations and their participants

We now describe our method for automatically identifying new causal triggers from text, based on parallel corpora. Using English-German parallel data has the advantage that it allows us to use existing lexical resources for English such as WordNet (Miller, 1995) or FrameNet (Ruppenhofer et al., 2006) as seed data for extracting German causal relations. In this work, however, we focus on a knowledge-lean approach where we refrain from using preexisting resources and try to find out how far we can get if we rely on parallel text only. As a trigger, we use the English verb *to cause* that always has a causal meaning.

4.1 Data

The data we use in our experiments come from the English-German part of Europarl corpus (Koehn, 2005). The corpus is aligned on the sentence-level and contains more than 1,9 mio. English-German parallel sentences. We tokenised and parsed the text to obtain dependency trees, using the Stanford parser (Chen and Manning, 2014) for English

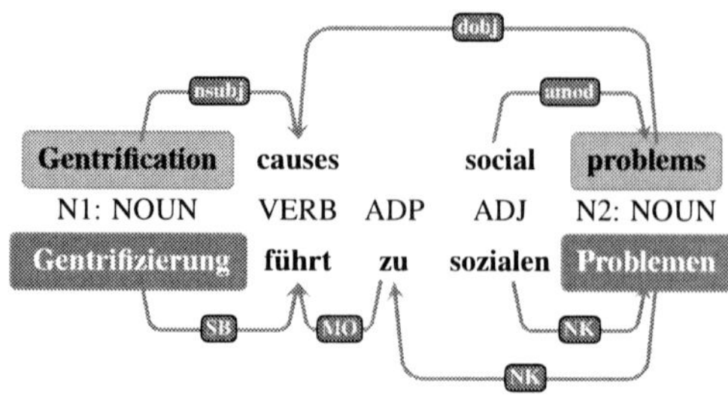

Figure 1: Parallel tree with English *cause* and aligned German noun pair

and the RBG parser (Lei et al., 2014) for German. We then applied the Berkeley Aligner (DeNero and Klein, 2007) to obtain word alignments for all aligned sentences. This allows us to map the dependency trees onto each other and to project (most of) the tokens from English to German and vice versa.[3]

4.2 Method

Step 1 First, we select all sentences in the corpus that contain a form of the English verb *cause*. We then restrict our set of candidates to instances of *cause* where both the subject and the direct object are realised as nouns, as illustrated in example (8).

(8) Alcohol$_{nsubj}$ causes 17 000 needless deaths$_{dobj}$ on the road a year.

Starting from these sentences, we filter our candidate set and only keep those sentences that also have German nouns aligned to the English subject and object position. Please note that we do not require that the grammatical function of the German counterparts are also subject and object, only that they are aligned to the English core arguments. We then extract the aligned German noun pairs and use them as seed data for step 2 of the extraction process.

For Figure 1, for example, we would first identify the English subject (*gentrification*) and direct object (*problems*), project them to their German nominal counterparts (*Gentrifizierung, Problemen*), the first one also filling the subject slot but the second one being realised as a prepositional object. We would thus extract the lemma forms for the German noun pair (*Gentrifizierung → Problem*) and use it for the extraction of causal triggers in step 2 (see Algorithm 1).

---

[3]Some tokens did not receive an alignment and are thus ignored in our experiments.

Data: Europarl (En-Ge)
Input: seed word: *cause* (En)
Output: list of causal triggers (Ge)
STEP 1: **if** *seed in sentence* **then**
    if *cause linked_to subj, dobj (En)* **then**
        if *subj, dobj == noun* **then**
            if *subj, dobj aligned with nouns (Ge)* **then**
                | extract noun pair (Ge);
            end
        end
    end
end
STEP 2: **for** *n1, n2 in noun pairs (Ge)* **do**
    if *n1, n2 in sentence* **then**
        if *common ancestor ca (n1, n2)* **then**
            if *dist(ca, n1) == 1 & dist(ca, n2) <= 3* **then**
                | extract ancestor as trigger;
            end
        end
    end
end

Algorithm 1: Extraction of causal triggers from parallel text (Step 1: extraction of noun pairs; Step 2: extraction of causal triggers)

Step 2 We now have a set of noun pairs that we use to search the monolingual German part of the data and extract all sentences that include one of these noun pairs. We test two settings, the first one being rather restrictive while the second one allows for more variation and thus will probably also extract more noise. We refer to the two settings as *strict* (setting 1) and *loose* (setting 2).

In setting 1, we require that the two nouns of each noun pair fill the subject and direct object slot of the same verb.[4] In the second setting, we extract all sentences that include one of the noun pairs, with the restriction that the two nouns have a common ancestor in the dependency tree that is a direct parent of the first noun[5] and not further away from the second noun than three steps up in the tree.

This means that the tree in Figure 1 would be ignored in the first setting, but not for setting 2.

---

[4]Please note that in this step of the extraction we do not condition the candidates on being aligned to an English sentence containing the English verb *cause*.

[5]As word order in German is more flexible than in English, the first noun is not defined by linear order but is the one that fills a subject slot in the parse tree.

Here we would extract the direct head of the first noun, which will give us the verb *führen* (lead), and extract up to three ancestors for the second noun. As the second noun, *Problem*, is attached to the preposition *zu* (to) (distance 1) which is in turn attached to the verb *führen* (distance 2), we would consider the example a true positive and extract the verb *führen* as linking our two nouns.

While the first setting is heavily biased towards transitive verbs that are causal triggers, setting 2 will also detect instances where the causal trigger is a noun, as in (9).

(9)   **Gentrifizierung**$_{Cause}$ ist die <u>Ursache</u>
    gentrification   is the reason
    von *sozialen Problemen*$_{Effect}$
    of social   problems.
    "Gentrification causes social problems."

In addition, we are also able to find support verb constructions that trigger causality, as in (10).

(10)   **Die gemeinsame Agrarpolitik**$_{Cause}$
    The common   agricultural policy
    <u>gibt</u> stets   <u>Anlass</u> <u>zu</u> *hitzigen*
    gives always rise   to heated
    Debatten$_{Effect}$
    debates
    "The common agricultural policy always gives rise to heated debates"

As both the word alignments and the dependency parses have been created automatically, we can expect a certain amount of noise in the data. Furthermore, we also have to deal with translation shifts, i.e. sentences that have a causal meaning in English but not in the German translation. A case in point is example (11) where the English *cause* has been translated into German by the non-causal *stattfinden* (take place) (12).

(11)   [...] that none of the upheaval$_{nsubj}$ would have been <u>caused</u> [...]

(12)   [...] dass diese Umwälzungen nicht
      that this upheaval   not
    stattgefunden hätten [...]
    take_place   had
    [...] that none of the upheaval would have taken place [...]

109

Using the approach outlined above, we want to identify new causal triggers to populate the lexicon. We also want to identify causal instances for these triggers for annotation, to be included in our resource. To pursue this goal and to minimize human annotation effort, we are interested in i) how many German causal verbs can be identified using this method, and ii) how many false positives are extracted, i.e. instances that cannot have a causal reading. Both questions have to be evaluated on the type level. In addition, we want to know iii) how many of the extracted candidate sentences are causal instances. This has to be decided on the token level, for each candidate sentence individually.

5 Results for extracting causal relations from parallel text

Step 1 Using the approach described in section 4.2, we extracted all German noun pairs from Europarl that were linked to two nouns in the English part of the corpus that filled the argument slots of the verb *cause*. Most of the noun pairs appeared only once, 12 pairs appeared twice, 3 pairs occured 3 times, and the noun pair *Hochwasser* (floodwater) − *Schaden* (damage) was the most frequent one with 6 occurrences. In total, we extracted 343 unique German noun pairs from Europarl that we used as seed data to indentify causal triggers in step 2.

We found 45 different verb types that linked these noun pairs, the most frequent one being, unsurprisingly, *verursachen* (cause) with 147 instances. Also frequent were other direct translations of *cause*, namely *hervorrufen* (induce) and *auslösen* (trigger), both with 31 instances, and *anrichten* (wreak) with 21 instances. We also found highly ambiguous translations like *bringen* (bring, 18 instances) and verbs that often appear in support verb constructions, like *haben* (have, 11 instances), as illustrated below (examples (13), (14)).

> (13) Fundamentalismus$_{N1}$ **bringt** in
> fundamentalism   brings in
> Gesellschaften gravierende Probleme$_{N2}$
> societies   serious   problems
> mit sich
> with itself
> "Fundamentalism causes many problems within societies"

> (14) Nun weiß man aber , daß die
> Now know one but , that the
> Müllverbrennung$_{N1}$ die Emission$_{N2}$
> incineration of waste the emission
> von Substanzen **zur**   **Folge hat**
> of   substances to the result has
> "It is well known that the incineration of waste causes emissions of substances"

Please note that at this point we do ignore the verbs and only keep the noun pairs, to be used as seed data for the extraction of causal triggers in step 2. From examples (13) and (14) above, we extract the following two noun pairs:

	N1		N2
1	Fundamentalismus	$\Rightarrow$	Problem
	fundamentalism	$\Rightarrow$	*problem*
2	Müllverbrennung	$\Rightarrow$	Emission
	incineration_of_waste	$\Rightarrow$	*emission*

Step 2 Using the 343 noun pairs extracted in step 1, we now search the monolingual part of the corpus and extract all sentences that include one of these noun pairs as arguments of the same verb. As a result, we get a list of verbal triggers that potentially have a causal reading. We now report results for the two different settings, *strict* and *loose*.

For **setting 1**, we harvest a list of 68 verb types. We manually filtered the list and removed instances that did not have a causal reading, amongst them most of the instances that occurred only once, such as *spielen* (play), *schweigen* (be silent), *zugeben* (admit), *nehmen* (take), *finden* (find).

Some of the false positives are in fact instances of causal particle verbs. In German, the verb particle can be separated from the verb stem. We did consider this for the extraction and contracted verb particles with their corresponding verb stem. However, sometimes the parser failed to assign the correct POS label to the verb particle, which is why we find instances e.g. of *richten* (rather than: *anrichten*, wreak), *stellen* (*darstellen*, pose), *treten* (*auftreten*, occur) in the list of false positives.

After manual filtering, we end up with a rather short list of 22 transitive German verbs with a causal reading for the first setting.

For **setting 2** we loosen the constraints for the extraction and obtain a much larger list of 406 unique trigger types. As expected, the list also includes more noise, but is still managable for doing a manual revision in a short period of time.

step1: noun pairs	343
step2: causal triggers	**types**
setting 1 (strict)	22
setting 2 (loose)	79
setting 3 (boost)	100

Table 1: No. of causal triggers extracted in different settings (Europarl, German-English)

example trigger	Cause/ Actor	Effect	Affected
verursachen (cause)	subj	dobj	for-PP
abhängen (depend)	iobj	subj	for-PP
zwingen (force)	subj	to-PP	dobj
zu Grunde liegen (be at the bottom of)	subj	iobj	
aus der Welt schaffen (to dispose of once and for all)	subj		dobj

Table 2: Examples for causal triggers and their roles

As shown in Table 1, after filtering we obtain a final list of 79 causal triggers, out of which 48 follow the transitive pattern $<N1_{subj}\ causes\ N2_{dobj}>$ where the subject expresses the cause and the direct object the effect. There seem to be no restrictions on what grammatical function can be expressed by what causal role but we find strong selectional preferences for the individual triggers, at least for the core arguments (Table 2). The verb *verursachen* (cause), for example, expresses CAUSE/ACTOR as the subject and EFFECT as the direct object while *abhängen* (depend) puts the EFFECT in the subject slot and realises the CAUSE as an indirect object. Often additional roles are expressed by a PP or a clausal complement. While many triggers accept either CAUSE or ACTOR to be expressed interchangeably by the same grammatical function, there also exist some triggers that are restricted to one of the roles. *Zu Grunde liegen* (be at the bottom of), for example, does not accept an ACTOR role as subject. These restrictions will be encoded in the lexicon, to support the annotation.

5.1 Annotation and inter-annotator agreement

From our extraction experiments based on parallel corpora (setting 2), we obtained a list of 79 causal triggers to be included in the lexicon. As we also want to have annotated training data to accompany the lexicon, we sampled the data and randomly selected $N = 50$ sentences for each trigger.[6]

We then started to manually annotate the data. The annotation process includes the following two subtasks:

1. Given a trigger in context, does it convey a causal meaning?

2. Given a causal sentence, which roles are expressed within the sentence?[7]

What remains to be done is the annotation of the causal type of the instance. As noted above, the reason for postponing this annotation step is that we first wanted to create the lexicon and be confident about the annotation scheme. A complete lexicon entry for each trigger specifying the type (or types and/or constraints) will crucially support the annotation and make it not only more consistent, but also much faster.

So far, we computed inter-annotator agreement on a subsample of our data with 427 instances (and 22 different triggers), to get a first idea of the feasibility of the annotation task. The two annotators are experts in linguistic annotation (the two authors of the paper), but could not use the lexicon to guide their decisions, as this was still under construction at the time of the annotation.

We report agreement for the following two subtasks. The first task concerns the decision whether or not a given trigger is causal. Here the two annotators obtained a percentage agreement of 94.4% and a Fleiss' κ of 0.78.

An error analysis reveals that the first annotator had a stricter interpretation of causality than annotator 2. Both annotators agreed on 352 instances being causal and 51 being non-causal. However, annotator 1 also judged 24 instances as non-causal that had been rated as causal by annotator 2. Many of the disagreements concerned the two verbs *bringen* (bring) and *bedeuten* (mean) and were systematic differences that could easily be resolved and documented in the lexicon and annotation guidelines, e.g. the frequent support verb construction in example (15).

---

[6]In this work we focused on verbal triggers, thus the unit of analysis is the clause. This will not be the case for triggers that evoke a discourse relation between two abstract objects, where an abstract object can be realized by one or more sentences, or only by a part of a sentence.

[7]We do not annotate causal participants across sentence borders even if that this is a plausible scenario. See, e.g., the annotation of implicit roles in SRL (Ruppenhofer et al., 2013).

		no.	% agr.	κ
task 1	**causal**	427	94.4	0.78
task 2	**N1**	352	94.9	0.74
	N2	352	99.1	0.95

Table 3: Annotation of causal transitive verbs: number of instances and IAA (percentage agreement and Fleiss' κ) for a subset of the data (427 sentences, 352 instances annotated as causal by both annotators)

(15) zum Ausdruck bringen
      to the expression bring
      "to express something"

For the second task, assigning role labels to the first (N1) and the second noun (N2), it became obvious that annotating the role of the first noun is markedly more difficult than for the second noun (Table 3). The reason for this is that the Actor-Cause distinction that is relevant to the first noun is not always a trivial one. Here we also observed systematic differences in the annotations that were easy to resolve, mostly concerning the question whether or not organisations such as the European Union, a member state or a comission are to be interpreted as an actor or rather than as a cause.

We think that our preliminary results are promising and confirm the findings of Dunietz et al. (2015), and expect an even higher agreement for the next round of the annotations, where we also can make use of the lexicon.

5.2 Discussion

Section 4 has shown the potential of our method for identifying and extracting causal relations from text. The advantage of our approach is that we do not depend on the existence of precompiled knowledge bases but rely on automatically preprocessed parallel text only. Our method is able to detect causal patterns across different parts of speech. Using a strong causal trigger and further constraints for the extraction, such as restricting the candidate set to sentences that have a subject and direct object NP that is linked to the target predicate, we are able to guide the extraction towards instances that, to a large degree, are in fact causal. In comparison, Girju reported a ratio of 0.32 causal sentences (2,101 out of 6,523 instances) while our method yields a ratio of 0.74 (787 causal instances out of 1069). Unfortunately, this also reduces the variation in trigger types and

Unsicherheit	uncertainty	cos
Verunsicherung	uncertainty	0.87
Unsicherheiten	insecurities	0.80
Unzufriedenheit	dissatisfaction	0.78
Frustration	frustration	0.78
Nervosität	nervousness	0.75
Ungewissheit	incertitude	0.74
Unruhe	concern	0.74
Ratlosigkeit	perplexity	0.74
Überforderung	excessive demands	0.73

Table 4: The 10 most similar nouns for *Unsicherheit* (insecurity), based on cosine similarity and word2vec embeddings.

is thus not a suitable method for creating a representative training set. We address this problem by loosening the constraints for the extraction, which allows us to detect a high variety of causal expressions, at a reasonable cost.

Our approach, using bilingual data, provides us with a natural environment for bootstrapping. We can now use the already known noun pairs as seed data, extract similar nouns to expand our seed set, and use the expanded set to find new causal expressions. We will explore this in our final experiment.

6 Bootstrapping causal relations

In this section, we want to generalise over the noun pairs that we extracted in the first step of the extraction process. For instance, given the noun pair {*smoking, cancer*}, we would also like to search for noun pairs expressing a similar relation, such as {*alcohol, health_problems*} or {*drugs, suffering*}. Accordingly, we call this third setting *boost*. Sticking to our knowledge-lean approach, we do not make use of resources such as WordNet or FrameNet, but instead use word embeddings to identify similar words.[8] For each noun pair in our list, we compute cosine similarity to all words in the embeddings and extract the 10 most similar words for each noun of the pair. We use a lemma dictionary extracted from the TüBa-D/Z treebank (release 10.0) (Telljohann et al., 2015) to look up the lemma forms for each word, and ignore all words that are not listed as a noun in our dictionary.

Table 4 shows the 10 words in the embedding file that have the highest similarity to the target noun *Unsicherheit* (uncertainty). To minimise noise, we also set a threshold of 0.75 and exclude

---

[8]We use the pre-trained word2vec embeddings provided by Reimers et al. (2014), with a dimension of 100.

all words with a cosine similarity below that score. Having expanded our list, we now create new noun pairs by combining noun N1 with all similar words for N2, and N2 with all similar words for N1.[9] We then proceed as usual and use the new, expanded noun pair list to extract new causal triggers the same way as in the loose setting. As we want to find new triggers that have not already been included in the lexicon, we discard all verb types that are already listed.

Using our expanded noun pair list for extracting causal triggers, we obtain 131 candidate instances for manual inspection. As before, we remove false positives due to translation shifts and to noise and are able to identify 21 new instances of causal triggers, resulting in a total number of *100 German verbal triggers* to be included in the lexicon (Table 1).

7 Conclusions and Future Work

We have presented a first effort to create a resource for describing German causal language, including a lexicon as well as an annotated training suite. We use a simple yet highly efficient method to detect new causal triggers, based on English-German parallel data. Our approach is knowledge-lean and succeeded in identifying and extracting 100 different types for causal verbal triggers, with only a small amount of human supervision.

Our approach offers several avenues for future work. One straightforward extension is to use other English causal triggers like nouns, prepositions, discourse connectives or causal multiword expressions, to detect German causal triggers with different parts of speech. We would also like to further exploit the bootstrapping setting, by projecting the German triggers back to English, extracting new noun pairs, and going back to German again. Another interesting setup is triangulation, where we would include a third language as a pivot to harvest new causal triggers. The intuition behind this approach is, that if a causal trigger in the source language is aligned to a word in the pivot language, and that again is aligned to a word in the target language, then it is likely that the aligned token in the target language is also causal. Such a setting gives us grounds for generalisations while, at the same time, offering the opportunity to formulate constraints and filter out noise.

---

[9]To avoid noise, we are conservative and do not combine the newly extracted nouns with each other.

Once we have a sufficient amount of training data, we plan to develop an automatic system for tagging causality in German texts. To prove the benefits of such a tool, we would like to apply our system in the context of argumentation mining.

Acknowledgments

This research has been conducted within the Leibniz Science Campus "Empirical Linguistics and Computational Modeling", funded by the Leibniz Association under grant no. SAS-2015-IDS-LWC and by the Ministry of Science, Research, and Art (MWK) of the state of Baden-Württemberg.

References

Tina Bögel, Annette Hautli-Janisz, Sebastian Sulger, and Miriam Butt. 2014. Automatic detection of causal relations in German multilogs. In *Proceedings of the EACL 2014 Workshop on Computational Approaches to Causality in Language*, CAtoCL, Gothenburg, Sweden.

Ruth M.J. Byrne. 2005. The rational imagination: How people create counterfactual alternatives to reality. *Behavioral and Brain Sciences*, 30:439–453.

Danqi Chen and Christopher Manning. 2014. A fast and accurate dependency parser using neural networks. In *Proceedings of the 2014 Conference on Empirical Methods in Natural Language Processing*, EMNLP, Doha, Qatar.

John DeNero and Dan Klein. 2007. Tailoring word alignments to syntactic machine translation. In *Proceedings of the 45th Annual Meeting of the Association of Computational Linguistics*, ACL'07, Prague, Czech Republic, June.

Jesse Dunietz, Lori Levin, and Jaime Carbonell. 2015. Annotating causal language using corpus lexicography of constructions. In *Proceedings of The 9th Linguistic Annotation Workshop*, LAW IX, Denver, Colorado, USA.

Jesse Dunietz, Lori Levin, and Jaime Carbonell. In press. Automatically tagging constructions of causation and their slot-fillers. In *Transactions of the Association for Computational Linguistics*.

Anna Gastel, Sabrina Schulze, Yannick Versley, and Erhard Hinrichs. 2011. Annotation of explicit and implicit discourse relations in the TüBa-D/Z treebank. In *Proceedings of the Conference of the German Society for Computational Linguistics and Language Technology*, GSCL'11, Hamburg, Germany.

Roxana Girju. 2003. Automatic detection of causal relations for question answering. In *Proceedings of the ACL 2003 Workshop on Multilingual Summarization and Question Answering*, Sapporo, Japan.

Cécile Grivaz. 2010. Human judgements on causation in french texts. In *Proceedings of the Seventh International Conference on Language Resources and Evaluation*, LREC'10, Valletta, Malta.

Christopher Hidey and Kathy McKeown. 2016. Identifying causal relations using parallel wikipedia articles. In *Proceedings of the 54th Annual Meeting of the Association for Computational Linguistics*, ACL'16, Berlin, Germany.

Randy M. Kaplan and Genevieve Berry-Rogghe. 1991. Knowledge-based acquisition of causal relationships in text. *Knowledge Acquisition*, 3(3):317–337.

Philipp Koehn. 2005. Europarl: A parallel corpus for statistical machine translation. In *Proceedings of the 10th Machine Translation Summit*, Phuket, Thailand.

Tao Lei, Yu Xin, Yuan Zhang, Regina Barzilay, and Tommi Jaakkola. 2014. Low-rank tensors for scoring dependency structures. In *Proceedings of the 52nd Annual Meeting of the Association for Computational Linguistics*, ACL'14, Baltimore, Maryland.

David K. Lewis. 1973. *Counterfactuals*. Blackwell.

George A. Miller. 1995. Wordnet: A lexical database for english. *Communications of the ACM*, 38(11):39–41.

Paramita Mirza and Sara Tonelli. 2014. An analysis of causality between events and its relation to temporal information. In *Proceedings of the 25th International Conference on Computational Linguistics*, COLING'14.

Judea Pearl. 1988. *Probabilistic Reasoning in Intelligent Systems*. San Francisco: Morgan Kaufman.

Rashmi Prasad, Nikhil Dinesh, Alan Lee, Eleni Miltsakaki, Livio Robaldo, Aravind K. Joshi, and Bonnie L. Webber. 2008. The Penn Discourse Tree-Bank 2.0. In *Language Resources and Evaluation*, LREC'08, Marrakech, Morocco.

Nils Reimers, Judith Eckle-Kohler, Carsten Schnober, Jungi Kim, and Iryna Gurevych. 2014. GermEval-2014: Nested Named Entity Recognition with neural networks. In *Workshop Proceedings of the 12th Edition of the KONVENS Conference*, Hildesheim, Germany.

Josef Ruppenhofer, Michael Ellsworth, Miriam R.L. Petruck, Christopher R. Johnson, and Jan Scheffczyk. 2006. *FrameNet II: Extended Theory and Practice*. International Computer Science Institute, Berkeley, California. Distributed with the FrameNet data.

Josef Ruppenhofer, Russell Lee-Goldman, Caroline Sporleder, and Roser Morante. 2013. Beyond sentence-level semantic role labeling: linking argument structures in discourse. *Language Resources and Evaluation*, 47(3):695–721.

Ted J.M. Sanders. 2005. Coherence, causality and cognitive complexity in discourse. In *First International Symposium on the Exploration and Modelling of Meaning*, SEM-05, Toulouse, France.

Tatjana Scheffler and Manfred Stede. 2016. Adding semantic relations to a large-coverage connective lexicon of German. In *Proceedings of the 10th International Conference on Language Resources and Evaluation*, LREC'16, Portorož, Slovenia.

Manfred Stede and Carla Umbach. 1998. DiMLex: A lexicon of discourse markers for text generation and understanding. In *The 17th International Conference on Computational Linguistics*, COLING'98.

Manfred Stede. 2002. DiMLex: A lexical approach to discourse markers. In *Exploring the Lexicon – Theory and Computation*. Alessandria (Italy): Edizioni dell'Orso.

Patrick Suppes. 1970. *A Probabilistic Theory of Causality*. Amsterdam: North-Holland Publishing Company.

Eve Sweetser. 1990. *From etymology to pragmatics: metaphorical and cultural aspects of semantic structure*. Cambridge; New York: Cambridge University Press.

Leonard Talmy. 1988. Force dynamics in language and cognition. *Cognitive Science*, 12(1):49–100.

Heike Telljohann, Erhard Hinrichs, Sandra Kübler, Heike Zinsmeister, and Katrin Beck. 2015. Stylebook for the Tübingen Treebank of Written German (TüBa-D/Z). Revised Version. Technical report, Seminar für Sprachwissenschaft, Universität Tübingen.

Yannick Versley. 2010. Discovery of ambiguous and unambiguous discourse connectives via annotation projection. In *Workshop on the Annotation and Exploitation of Parallel Corpora*, AEPC'10, Tartu, Estland.

Laure Vieu, Philippe Muller, Marie Candito, and Marianne Djemaa. 2016. A general framework for the annotation of causality based on FrameNet. In *Proceedings of the 10th International Conference on Language Resources and Evaluation*, LREC'16, Portorož, Slovenia.

Phillip Wolff, Bianca Klettke, Tatyana Ventura, and Grace Song. 2005. Expressing causation in English and other languages. In Woo kyoung Ahn, Robert Goldstone, Bradley C. Love, Arthur B. Markman, and Phillip Wolff, editors, *Categorization inside and outside the laboratory: Essays in honor of Douglas Medin*, pages 29–48. American Psychological Association, Washington, DC, US.

Assessing SRL Frameworks with Automatic Training Data Expansion

Silvana Hartmann[†‡]   Éva Mújdricza-Maydt[*‡]   Ilia Kuznetsov[†]
Iryna Gurevych[†‡]   Anette Frank[*‡]

[†]Ubiquitous Knowledge Processing Lab
Department of Computer Science
Technische Universität Darmstadt
[‡]Research Training School AIPHES
{hartmann,kuznetsov,gurevych}
@ukp.informatik.tu-darmstadt.de

[*]Department of
Computational Linguistics
Heidelberg University
[‡]Research Training School AIPHES
{mujdricza,frank}
@cl.uni-heidelberg.de

Abstract

We present the first experiment-based study that explicitly contrasts the three major semantic role labeling frameworks. As a prerequisite, we create a dataset labeled with parallel FrameNet-, PropBank-, and VerbNet-style labels for German. We train a state-of-the-art SRL tool for German for the different annotation styles and provide a comparative analysis across frameworks. We further explore the behavior of the frameworks with automatic training data generation. VerbNet provides larger semantic expressivity than PropBank, and we find that its generalization capacity approaches PropBank in SRL training, but it benefits less from training data expansion than the sparse-data affected FrameNet.

1   Introduction

We present the first study that explicitly contrasts the three popular theoretical frameworks for semantic role labeling (SRL) – FrameNet, PropBank, and VerbNet[1] in a comparative experimental setup, i.e., using the same training and test sets annotated with predicate and role labels from the different frameworks and applying the same conditions and criteria for training and testing.

Previous work comparing these frameworks either provides theoretical investigations, for instance for the pair PropBank–FrameNet (Ellsworth et al., 2004), or presents experimental investigations for the pair PropBank–VerbNet (Zapirain et al., 2008; Merlo and van der Plas, 2009). Theoretical analyses contrast the richness of the semantic model of FrameNet with efficient annotation of PropBank labels and their suitability for system training. Verb-

Net is considered to range between them on both scales: it fulfills the need for semantically meaningful role labels; also, since the role labels are shared across predicate senses, it is expected to generalize better to unseen predicates than FrameNet, which suffers from data sparsity due to a fine-grained sense-specific role inventory. Yet, unlike PropBank and FrameNet, VerbNet has been neglected in recent work on SRL, partially due to the lack of training and evaluation data, whereas PropBank and FrameNet were popularized in shared tasks. As a result, the three frameworks have not been compared under equal experimental conditions.

This motivates our contrastive analysis of *all three frameworks* for German. We harness existing datasets for German (Burchardt et al., 2006; Hajič et al., 2009; Mújdricza-Maydt et al., 2016) to create *SR3de (Semantic Role Triple Dataset for German)*, the first benchmark dataset labeled with FrameNet, VerbNet and PropBank roles in parallel.

Our motivation for working on German is that – as for many languages besides English – sufficient amounts of training data are not available. This clearly applies to our German dataset, which contains about 3,000 annotated predicates. In such a scenario, methods to extend training data automatically or making efficient use of generalization across predicates (i.e., being able to apply role labels to unseen predicates) are particularly desirable. We assume that SRL frameworks that generalize better across predicates gain more from automatic training data generation, and lend themselves better to cross-predicate SRL. System performance also needs to be correlated with the semantic expressiveness of frameworks: with the ever-growing expectations in semantic NLP applications, SRL frameworks also need to be judged with regard to their contribution to advanced applications where expressiveness may play a role, such as question answering or summarization.

---

[1]See Fillmore et al. (2003), Palmer et al. (2005) and Kipper-Schuler (2005), respectively.

115

Proceedings of the 11th Linguistic Annotation Workshop, pages 115–121,
Valencia, Spain, April 3, 2017. ©2017 Association for Computational Linguistics

Our work explores the generalization properties of three SRL frameworks in a contrastive setup, assessing SRL performance when training and evaluating on a dataset with parallel annotations for each framework in a uniform SRL system architecture. We also explore to what extent the frameworks benefit from training data generation via annotation projection (Fürstenau and Lapata, 2012).

Since all three frameworks have been applied to several languages,[2] we expect our findings for German to generalize to other languages as well.

Our contributions are (i) novel resources: parallel German datasets for the three frameworks, including automatically acquired training data; and (ii) empirical comparison of the labeling performance and generalization capabilities of the three frameworks, which we discuss in view of their respective semantic expressiveness.

2 Related Work

Overview on SRL frameworks *FrameNet* defines frame-specific roles that are shared among predicates evoking the same frame. Thus, generalization across predicates is possible for predicates that belong to the same *existing* frame, but labeling predicates for unseen frames is not possible. Given the high number of frames – FrameNet covers about 1,200 frames and 10K role labels – large training datasets are required for system training.

PropBank offers a small role inventory of five core roles (A0 to A4) for obligatory arguments and around 18 roles for optional ones. The core roles closely follow syntactic structures and receive a predicate-specific interpretation, except for the Agent-like A0 and Patient-like A1 that implement Dowty's proto-roles theory (Dowty, 1991).

VerbNet defines about 35 semantically defined *thematic* roles that are not specific to predicates or predicate senses. Predicates are labeled with Levin-type semantic classes (Levin, 1993). VerbNet is typically assumed to range between FrameNet with respect to its rich semantic representation and PropBank with its small, coarse-grained role inventory.

Comparison of SRL frameworks Previous experimental work compares VerbNet and PropBank: Zapirain et al. (2008) find that PropBank SRL is more robust than VerbNet SRL, generalizing better to unseen or rare predicates, and relying less on predicate sense. Still, they aspire to use more mean-

ingful VerbNet roles in NLP tasks and thus propose using automatic PropBank SRL for core role identification and then converting the PropBank roles into VerbNet roles heuristically to VerbNet, which appears more robust in cross-domain experiments compared to training on VerbNet data. Merlo and van der Plas (2009) also confirm that PropBank roles are easier to assign than VerbNet roles, while the latter provide better semantic generalization. To our knowledge, there is no experimental work that compares all three major SRL frameworks.

German SRL frameworks and data sets The SALSA project (Burchardt et al., 2006; Rehbein et al., 2012) created a corpus annotated with over 24,200 predicate argument structures, using English *FrameNet* frames as a basis, but creating new frames for German predicates where required.

About 18,500 of the manual SALSA annotations were converted semi-automatically to *PropBank*-style annotations for the CoNLL 2009 shared task on syntactic and semantic dependency labeling (Hajič et al., 2009). Thus, the CoNLL dataset shares a subset of the SALSA annotations. To create PropBank-style annotations, the predicate senses were numbered such that different frame annotations for a predicate lemma indicate different senses. The SALSA role labels were converted to PropBank-style roles using labels A0 and A1 for Agent- and Patient-like roles, and continuing up to A9 for other arguments. Instead of spans, arguments were defined by their dependency heads for CoNLL. The resulting dataset was used as a benchmark dataset in the CoNLL 2009 shared task.

For VerbNet, Mújdricza-Maydt et al. (2016) recently published a small subset of the CoNLL shared task corpus with *VerbNet*-style roles. It contains 3,500 predicate instances for 275 predicate lemma types. Since there is no taxonomy of verb classes for German corresponding to original VerbNet classes, they used GermaNet (Hamp and Feldweg, 1997) to label predicate senses. GermaNet provides a fine-grained sense inventory similar to the English WordNet (Fellbaum, 1998).

Automatic SRL systems for German State-of-the-art SRL systems for German are only available for PropBank labels: Björkelund et al. (2009) developed mate-tools; Roth and Woodsend (2014) and Roth and Lapata (2015) improved on mate-tools SRL with their mateplus system. We base our experiments on the *mateplus* system.

116

	Der Umsatz	*stieg*	*um 14 %*	*auf 1,9 Milliarden .*
	'Sales	rose	by 14%	to 1.9 billion'
PB	A1	**steigen.1**	A2	A3
VN	Patient	**steigen-3**	Extent	Goal
FN	Item	**Change_position _on_a_scale**	Difference	Final_value

Figure 1: Parallel annotation example from SR3de for predicate **steigen** ('rise, increase').

Corpus	train		dev		test	
	type	token	type	token	type	token
predicate	198	2196	121	250	152	520
	sense role	role	sense role	role	sense role	role
SR3de-PB	506 10	4,293	162 6	444	221 8	1,022
SR3de-VN	448 30	4,307	133 23	466	216 25	1,025
SR3de-FN	346 278	4,283	133 145	456	176 165	1,017

Table 1: Data statistics for SR3de (PB, VN, FN).

Training data generation   In this work, we use a corpus-based, monolingual approach to training data expansion. Fürstenau and Lapata (2012) propose monolingual annotation projection for lower-resourced languages: they create data labeled with FrameNet frames and roles based on a small set of labeled seed sentences in the target language. We apply their approach to the different SRL frameworks, and for the first time to VerbNet-style labels.

Other approaches apply cross-lingual projection (Akbik and Li, 2016) or paraphrasing, replacing FrameNet predicates (Pavlick et al., 2015) or Prop-Bank arguments (Woodsend and Lapata, 2014) in labeled texts. We do not employ these approaches, because they assume large role-labeled corpora.

3   Datasets and Data Expansion Method

SR3de: a German parallel SRL dataset   The VerbNet-style dataset by Mújdricza-Maydt et al. (2016) covers a subset of the PropBank-style CoNLL 2009 annotations, which are based on the German FrameNet-style SALSA corpus. This allowed us to create SR3de, the first corpus with parallel sense and role labels from SALSA, PropBank, and GermaNet/VerbNet, which we henceforth abbreviate as FN, PB, and VN respectively. Figure 1 displays an example with parallel annotations.

Data statistics in Table 1 shows that with almost 3,000 predicate instances, the corpus is fairly small. The distribution of role types across frameworks highlights their respective role granularity, ranging from 10 for PB to 30 for VN and 278 for FN. The corpus offers 2,196 training predicates and covers the CoNLL 2009 development and test sets; thus it is a suitable base for comparing the three frameworks. We use SR3de for the contrastive analysis of the different SRL frameworks below.

Training data expansion   To overcome the data scarcity of our corpus, we use *monolingual annotation projection* (Fürstenau and Lapata, 2012) to generate additional training data. Given a set of labeled *seed sentences* and a set of unlabeled *ex-*

pansion sentences, we select suitable expansions based on the predicate lemma and align dependency graphs of seeds and expansions based on lexical similarity of the graph nodes and syntactic similarity of the edges. The alignment is then used to map predicate and role labels from the seed sentences to the expansion sentences. For each seed instance, the k best-scoring expansions are selected. Given a seed set of size n and the maximal number of expansions per seed k, we get up to $n \cdot k$ additional training instances. Lexical and syntactic similarity are balanced using the weight parameter α.

Our adjusted re-implementation uses the mate-tools dependency parser (Bohnet, 2010) and word2vec embeddings (Mikolov et al., 2013) trained on deWAC (Baroni et al., 2009) for word similarity calculation. We tune the parameter α via intrinsic evaluation on the SR3de dev set. We project the seed set SR3de-train directly to SR3de-dev and compare the labels from the k=1 best seeds for a dev sentence to the gold label, measuring F1 for all projections. Then we use the best-scoring α value for each framework to project annotations from the SR3de training set to deWAC for predicate lemmas occurring at least 10 times. We vary the number of expansions k, selecting k from $\{1, 3, 5, 10, 20\}$. Using larger k values is justified because a) projecting to a huge corpus is likely to generate many high-quality expansions, and b) we expect a higher variance in the generated data when also selecting lower-scoring expansions.

Intrinsic evaluation on the dev set provides an estimate of the projection quality: we observe F1 score of 0.73 for PB and VN, and of 0.53 for FN. The lower scores for FN are due to data sparsity in the intrinsic setting and are expected to improve when projecting on a large corpus.

4   Experiments

Experiment setup   We perform extrinsic evaluation on SR3de with parallel annotations for the three frameworks, using the same SRL system for each framework, to a) compare the labeling performance of the learned models, and b) explore their behavior in response to expanded training data.

We employ the following settings (cf. Table 2):

#BL: *Baseline* We train on SR3de train, which is small, but comparable across frameworks.

#FB: *Full baseline* We train on the full CoNLL-training sections for PropBank and SALSA, to compare to state-of-the-art results and contrast the low-resource #BL to full resources.[3]

#EX: *Expanded* We train on data expanded via annotation projection.

We train mateplus using the reranker option and the default featureset for German[4] excluding word embedding features.[5] We explore the following role labeling tasks: predicate sense prediction (pd in mateplus), argument identification (ai) and role labeling (ac) for predicted predicate sense (pd+ai+ac) and oracle predicate sense (ai+ac). We report F1 scores for all three role labeling tasks.

We assure equivalent treatment of all three SRL frameworks in mateplus and train the systems only on the given training data without any framework-specific information. Specifically, we do not exploit constraints on predicate senses for PB in mateplus (i.e., selecting sense.1 as default sense), nor constraints for licensed roles (or role sets) for a given sense (i.e., encoding the FN lexicon). Thus, mateplus learns predicate senses and role sets only from training instances.

Experiment results for the different SRL frameworks are summarized in Table 2.[6] Below, we discuss the results for the different settings.

#BL: for role labeling with oracle senses (ai+ac), PB performs best, VN is around 5 percentage points (pp.) lower, and FN again 5 pp. lower. With predicate sense prediction (pd+ai+ac), performance only slightly decreases for VN and PB, while FN suffers strongly: F1 is 17 pp. lower than for VN, despite the fact that its predicate labeling F1 is similar to PB and higher than VN. This indicates that generalization across senses works much better for VN and PB roles. By contrast, FN, with its sense-dependent role labels, is lacking generalization capacity, and thus suffers from data sparsity.

[3]Both #FB training sets contain $\approx$ 17,000 predicate instances. There is no additional labeled training data for VN.

[4]https://github.com/microth/mateplus/tree/master/featuresets/ger

[5]Given only small differences in mateplus performance when using word embeddings, we report results without them.

[6]Significance is computed using approximation randomization, i.e., SIGF (Padó, 2006) two-tailed, 10k iterations.

no	train	sense (pd)	sense+role (pd+ai+ac)	role only (ai+ac)
	#BL: SR3de training corpora			
(1)	#BL-PB	58.84	73.70	74.76
(2)	#BL-VN	55.19	69.66	69.86
(3)	#BL-FN	58.26	52.76	64.72
\multicolumn	#FB: CoNLL training sections			
(4)	#FB-CoNLL	82.88	84.01	86.26
(5)	#FB-SALSA	84.03	78.03	84.34
\multicolumn	#EX: SR3de train with data expansion			
(1)	**#BL-PB**	58.84	73.70	74.76
(6)	#EX-k=1	58.65	75.09[*]	76.65[**]
(7)	#EX-k=3	58.65	75.43	77.71[**]
(8)	#EX-k=5	59.03	**76.30**[*]	**78.27**[**]
(9)	#EX-k=10	59.03	74.65	77.95[**]
(10)	#EX-k=20	**59.42**	74.36	78.15[**]
(2)	**#BL-VN**	55.19	69.66	69.86
(11)	#EX-k=1	55.00	68.75	68.86
(12)	#EX-k=3	55.19	**69.14**	**69.02**
(13)	#EX-k=5	55.19	68.49	68.57
(14)	#EX-k=10	55.19	66.34[**]	66.84[**]
(15)	#EX-k=20	**55.38**	65.70[**]	66.91[**]
(3)	**#BL-FN**	58.26	52.76	64.72
(16)	#EX-k=1	57.88	**55.47**[**]	69.18[**]
(17)	#EX-k=3	58.65	54.13	69.37[**]
(18)	#EX-k=5	57.88	54.54[**]	**70.41**[**]
(19)	#EX-k=10	58.26	53.97	69.15[**]
(20)	#EX-k=20	**58.84**	54.43	70.19[**]

Table 2: F1 scores for predicate sense and role labeling on the SR3de test set; *pd*: predicate sense labeling; *pd+ai+ac*: sense and role labeling (cf. official CoNLL scores); *ai+ac*: role labeling with oracle predicate sense. We report statistical significance of role labeling F1 with expanded data *#EX* to the respective *#BL* ([*]: $p < 0.05$; [**]: $p < 0.01$).

#FB: The full baselines #FB show that a larger training data set widely improves SRL performance compared to the small #BL training sets. One reason is the extended sense coverage in the #FB datasets, indicating the need for a larger training set. Still, FN scores are 6 pp. lower than PB (pd+ai+ac).

#EX: Automatically expanding the training set for PB leads to performance improvements of around 3 pp. to #BL for k=5 (pd+ai+ac and ai+ac), but the scores do not reach those of #FB. A similar gain is achieved for FN with k=1. Contrary to initial expectations, annotation projection tends to create similar instances to the seen ones, but at the same time, it also introduces noise. Thus, larger k (k>5) results in decreased role labeling performance compared to smaller k for all frameworks.

FN benefits most from training data expansion, with a performance increase of 5 pp. to #BL, reaching similar role labeling scores as VN for the oracle sense setting. For predicted senses, performance increase is distinctly smaller, highlighting that the sparse data problems for FN senses do not get solved by training data expansion. Performance improvements are significant for FN and PB for both role labeling settings. Against expectation, we do not observe improved role labeling performance for VN. We believe this is due to the more complex label set compared to PB and perform a analyses supporting this hypothesis below.

Analysis: complexity of the frameworks We estimate the role labeling complexity of the frameworks by computing $C(d)$, the average ambiguity of the role instances in the dataset d, $d \in \{$PB, VN, FN$\}$. $C(d)$ consists of the normalized sum s over the number n of role candidates licensed for each role instance in d by the predicate sense label; for role instances with unseen senses, n is the number of distinct roles in the framework. The sum s is then divided by all role instances in dataset d.

Results are $C(\text{PB})=4.3$, $C(\text{VN})=9.7$, $C(\text{FN})=60$. $C(d)$ is inversely correlated to the expected performance of each framework, and thus predicts the role labeling performance for #BL (pd+ai+ac).

When considering only seen training instances, complexity is 1.67 for both PB and VN, and 1.79 for FN. This indicates a larger difficulty for FN, but does not explain the difference between VN and PB. Yet, next to role ambiguity, the number of instances seen in training for individual role types is a decisive factor for role labeling performance, and thus, the coarser-grained PB inventory has a clear advantage over VN and FN.

The sense labeling performance is lower for VN systems compared to FN and PB. This correlates with the fact that GermaNet senses used with VN are more fine-grained than those in FN, but more abstract than the numbered PB senses. Still, we observe high role labeling performance independently of the predicate sense label for both VN and PB. This indicates high generalization capabilities of their respective role sets.[7]

The 5 pp. gap between the VN and PB systems is small, but not negligible. We expect that a suitable sense inventory for German VN, analogous to VerbNet's classes, will further enhance VN role la-

beling performance. Overall, we conclude that the higher complexity of the FrameNet role inventory causes data sparsity, thus FN benefits most from the training data expansion for seen predicates. For the other two frameworks, cross-predicate projection could be a promising way to increase the training data coverage to previously unseen predicates.

5 Discussion and Conclusion

We perform the first experimental comparison of all three major SRL frameworks on a small German dataset with parallel annotations. The experiment settings ensure comparability across frameworks.

Our baseline experiments prove that the generalization capabilities of the frameworks follow the hypothesized order of FrameNet < VerbNet < PropBank. Comparative analysis shows that PropBank and VerbNet roles generalize well, also beyond predicates. Taking into account the semantic expressiveness of VerbNet, these results showcase the potential of VerbNet as an alternative to PropBank. By contrast, FrameNet's role labeling performance suffers from data sparsity in the small-data setting, given that its role inventory does not easily generalize across predicates.

While VerbNet generalizes better than FrameNet, it does not benefit from our automatic training data generation setup. Currently, annotation projection only applies to lemmas seen in training. Thus, the generalization capacities of VerbNet – and PropBank – are not fully exploited. Relaxing constraints in annotation projection, e.g., projecting across predicates, could benefit both frameworks.

FrameNet suffers most from sparse-data problems and thus benefits most from automatic training data expansion for seen predicates, yet sense labeling persists as its performance bottleneck.

In future work we plan to a) further evaluate cross-predicate generalization capabilities of VerbNet and PropBank in cross-predicate annotation projection and role labeling, b) explore semi-supervised methods and constrained learning (Akbik and Li, 2016), and c) explore alternative sense inventories for the German VerbNet-style dataset.

We publish our benchmark dataset with strictly parallel annotations for the three frameworks to facilitate further research.[8]

---

[7]This is confirmed when replacing the predicate sense label with the lemma for training: the role labeling results are fairly close for PB (74.34%) and VN (68.90%), but much lower for FN (54.26%).

[8]`http://projects.cl.uni-heidelberg.de/SR3de`

Acknowledgements The present work was partially funded by a German BMBF grant to CLARIN-D and the DFG-funded Research Training School "Adaptive Preparation of Information from Heterogeneous Sources" (GRK 1994/1). We thank the anonymous reviewers for their valuable comments and suggestions.

References

Alan Akbik and Yunyao Li. 2016. K-SRL: Instance-based Learning for Semantic Role Labeling. In *Proceedings of COLING 2016, the 26th International Conference on Computational Linguistics: Technical Papers*, pages 599–608, Osaka, Japan, December.

Marco Baroni, Silvia Bernardini, Adriano Ferraresi, and Eros Zanchetta. 2009. The WaCky wide web: a collection of very large linguistically processed web-crawled corpora. *Language Resources and Evaluation*, 43(3):209–226.

Anders Björkelund, Love Hafdell, and Pierre Nugues. 2009. Multilingual semantic role labeling. In *Proceedings of the Thirteenth Conference on Computational Natural Language Learning (CoNLL 2009): Shared Task*, pages 43–48, Boulder, CO, USA.

Hans C. Boas. 2009. *Multilingual FrameNets in computational lexicography: methods and applications*, volume 200. Walter de Gruyter.

Bernd Bohnet. 2010. Top accuracy and fast dependency parsing is not a contradiction. In Chu-Ren Huang and Dan Jurafsky, editors, *Proceedings of Coling 2010*, pages 89–97.

Aljoscha Burchardt, Kathrin Erk, Anette Frank, Andrea Kowalski, Sebastian Padó, and Manfred Pinkal. 2006. The SALSA Corpus: a German Corpus Resource for Lexical Semantics. In *Proceedings of the 5th International Conference on Language Resources and Evaluation (LREC 2006)*, pages 969–974, Genoa, Italy.

David Dowty. 1991. Thematic Proto-Roles and Argument Selection. *Language*, 67(3):547–619.

Michael Ellsworth, Katrin Erk, Paul Kingsbury, and Sebastian Padó. 2004. PropBank, SALSA, and FrameNet: How design determines product. In *Proceedings of the Workshop on Building Lexical Resources From Semantically Annotated Corpora, LREC-2004*, Lisbon, Portugal.

Christiane Fellbaum. 1998. *WordNet: an eletronic lexical database*. The Mit Press, Cambridge, Massachusetts.

Charles J. Fillmore, Christopher R. Johnson, and Miriam R.L. Petruck. 2003. Background to FrameNet. *International Journal of Lexicography*, 16(3):235–250.

Hagen Fürstenau and Mirella Lapata. 2012. Semi-Supervised Semantic Role Labeling via Structural Alignment. *Computational Linguistics*, 38(1):135–171.

Jan Hajič, Massimiliano Ciaramita, Richard Johansson, Daisuke Kawahara, Maria Antònia Martí, Lluís Màrquez, Adam Meyers, Nivre Joakim, Sebastian Padó, Jan Štěpánek, Pavel Straňák, Mihai Surdenau, Nianwen Xue, and Yi Zhang. 2009. The CoNLL-2009 Shared Task: Syntactic and Semantic Dependencies in Multiple Languages. In *Proceedings of the Thirteenth Conference on Computational Natural Language Learning (CoNLL): Shared Task*, pages 1–18, Boulder, CO, USA.

Birgit Hamp and Helmut Feldweg. 1997. GermaNet - a Lexical-Semantic Net for German. In *Proceedings of the ACL workshop Automatic Information Extraction and Building of Lexical Semantic Resources for NLP Applications*, pages 9–15, Madrid, Spain.

Karin Kipper-Schuler. 2005. *VerbNet: A broad-coverage, comprehensive verb lexicon*. Ph.D. thesis, University of Pennsylvania, Pennsylvania, Philadelphia, PA.

Beth Levin. 1993. *English verb classes and alternations: A preliminary investigation*. University of Chicago press.

Paola Merlo and Lonneke van der Plas. 2009. Abstraction and Generalisation in Semantic Role Labels: PropBank, VerbNet or both? In *Proceedings of the 47th Annual Meeting of the ACL and the 4th IJCNLP of the AFNLP*, pages 288–296, Suntec, Singapore.

Tomas Mikolov, Ilya Sutskever, Kai Chen, Greg S. Corrado, and Jeff Dean. 2013. Distributed representations of words and phrases and their compositionality. In C. J. C. Burges, L. Bottou, M. Welling, Z. Ghahramani, and K. Q. Weinberger, editors, *Advances in Neural Information Processing Systems 26*, pages 3111–3119. Curran Associates, Inc.

Éva Mújdricza-Maydt, Silvana Hartmann, Iryna Gurevych, and Anette Frank. 2016. Combining Semantic Annotation of Word Sense & Semantic Roles: A Novel Annotation Scheme for VerbNet Roles on German Language Data. In *Proceedings of the Tenth International Conference on Language Resources and Evaluation (LREC 2016)*, pages 3031–3038, Portorož, Slovenia.

Sebastian Padó, 2006. *User's guide to* `sigf`: *Significance testing by approximate randomisation*.

Martha Palmer, Daniel Gildea, and Paul Kingsbury. 2005. The Proposition Bank: An annotated corpus of semantic roles. *Computational Linguistics*, 31(1):71–106.

Ellie Pavlick, Travis Wolfe, Pushpendre Rastogi, Chris Callison-Burch, Mark Dredze, and Benjamin

Van Durme. 2015. FrameNet+: Fast Paraphrastic Tripling of FrameNet. In *Proceedings of the 53rd Annual Meeting of the Association for Computational Linguistics and the 7th International Joint Conference on Natural Language Processing (Volume 2: Short Papers)*, pages 408–413, Beijing, China.

Ines Rehbein, Joseph Ruppenhofer, Caroline Sporleder, and Manfred Pinkal. 2012. Adding nominal spice to SALSA - Frame-semantic annotation of German nouns and verbs. In *Proceedings of the 11th Conference on Natural Language Processing (KONVENS'12)*, pages 89–97, Vienna, Austria.

Michael Roth and Mirella Lapata. 2015. Context-aware frame-semantic role labeling. *Transactions of the Association for Computational Linguistics (TACL)*, 3:449–460.

Michael Roth and Kristian Woodsend. 2014. Composition of word representations improves semantic role labelling. In *Proceedings of the 2014 Conference on Empirical Methods in Natural Language Processing (EMNLP)*, pages 407–413, Doha, Qatar.

Lin Sun, Thierry Poibeau, Anna Korhonen, and Cedric Messiant. 2010. Investigating the cross-linguistic potential of VerbNet-style classification. In *Proceedings of the 23rd International Conference on Computational Linguistics (Coling 2010)*, pages 1056–1064.

Kristian Woodsend and Mirella Lapata. 2014. Text rewriting improves semantic role labeling. *Journal of Artificial Intelligence Research*, 51:133–164.

Beñat Zapirain, Eneko Agirre, and Lluís Màrquez. 2008. Robustness and generalization of role sets: PropBank vs. VerbNet. In *Proceedings of ACL-08: HLT*, pages 550–558, Columbus, OH, USA.

Author Index